To my grandch.

Megan and Angus

Oscar and Charis

BY ANY OTHER NAME

Dr Frank Clifford Rose

An autobiography

Edited by Angela Rose

"What's in a name? that which we call a rose

By any other name would smell as sweet"

William Shakespeare

Romeo and Juliet: act 2, scene 2

BY ANY OTHER NAME

The Life Story of Dr F Clifford Rose

CONTENTS

LIST OF ILLUSTRATIONS

PREFACE

In 2008, the Marlborough College Summer School brochure included a course on "Writing one's Life-history". It had never been my intention to write an autobiography but, on retiring from the National Health Service in 1991, it was clear that my sons and extended family did not know much about me or my background. The whole family encouraged me to join this five-day Summer School course, with its signal statement that "your life story is the greatest gift you can give your family". This meant racking my brain to recall the happenings of past decades, covering such times as the 1930s Recession and World War II that followed the 1926 General Strike, which occurred a few months before my birth. This strike involved millions of workers who downed tools because coal-mine owners wanted to reduce the miners' pay by a penny; the strike was broken when middle-class people stepped in to drive buses and trains. There followed the rise of Hitler's Germany in 1933, with the onset of the Second World War in 1939, and then the Cold War between the Soviet Union and the democracies. These events all occurred from the time of my birth in an East End slum, through my school days in the English countryside and university in London to the climb up a professional ladder that led to a life of global lecturing and writing, a story of "rags to riches" that seemed worthy of putting down on paper.

Chapter 1

A COCKNEY CHILDHOOD

My parents were orthodox Jews, born in the Austro-Hungarian Empire. They emigrated to England in 1913 from Falticeni, a small town with a population of 5,000, between Bukovina and Moldova in the north-east of what is now Romania; this village had been founded as a Jewish settlement, originally called Faltishen. My father worked as a "roofer" making tin roofs for houses; tall and handsome with red hair, my mother fell for his good looks when she was only twenty and he was ten years older. Conscripted into the Austro-Hungarian army, he saw the Emperor Franz Josef at a military parade; he was physically very strong and could hold a rifle by its muzzle end with his arm extended, an exercise I attempted and failed. The reason for my parents' emigration was that, in spite of having served in the army, my father, being a Jew, was still regarded as a second-class citizen. They chose England because my mother's brother, Uncle Joe, and his wife, who were first cousins, had established a successful fish-and-chip shop in Shoreditch, London. My parents sailed from Bremen in 1913 with two children, Solomon (Solly) and Zigmund (Sid), two older children having died in early childhood. My mother claimed she was seasick all the way to England but as she was pregnant at the time with my eldest sister Mary, this could have been part of the cause. The family settled in Stepney in the East End of London in a one-roomed flat. With the declaration of the First World War in 1914, my father worked in a munitions factory for the duration, despite his surname of Rosenberg and the understandable anti-German sentiment of those times. My mother told me about the bombing of London by a German airship with people staring skywards in amazement and not taking shelter, as this was said to be the first occasion of bombing anywhere in the world.

In 1918, after the War, my father started a cycle repair shop, having experience of working with metal; being good with his hands, he used to make all sorts of metal toys for me and I particularly remember a train. Part of his business involved buying and selling second-hand bicycles, one of which he bought at a ridiculously cheap price and was promptly arrested for "receiving stolen property"; he pleaded with the magistrate that he had not known it was stolen but, perhaps partly because he spoke such poor English, or could not afford a lawyer to defend him, he was sent to prison for three months. From that time, he maintained that his life was ruined and complained of visions, suffered from paranoia, and local children would call after him in the street "Ginger, you're barmy", referring both to his hair colour and odd behaviour.

My mother had four more children before me, two sisters, Mary and Mathilda (Tilly) and two brothers, Israel (Izzy) and Pinchus (Percy), making me the youngest of her nine children, of whom only seven survived to adulthood. I was born on 29 August 1926 at home in 40 Raven Row, Whitechapel, a turning off Sydney Street famous for its "battle" in 1912, when Winston Churchill was Home Secretary and police officers and troops shot two Russian anarchists who were sheltering there. Although my Hebrew name was Ephraim, my sisters were sufficiently anglicised to persuade my mother that Frank would be more appropriate for my birth certificate. Our terraced house had only three bedrooms for the family of nine (two parents and seven children) so that five children slept in one bed. My father also slept at the back of the house during the summer months; there was only one lavatory which was also outside at the back of the house, but no bathroom so bathing meant filling a zinc bath with hot water. On one side of this terraced house was a public house whilst; on the other, was a much larger property owned by the manager of a brewery, Mann, Cross and Paulin, which was on the opposite side of the street. Here drays were drawn by large carthorses which would occasionally slip and fall on leaving the brewery; this always drew a large crowd, including me, to watch the animals being restored to their feet, occasions for learning the inevitable swear-words from the drivers.

As the British economy was in recession, there was widespread unemployment; so much so that in the 1930s, the first question local people asked each other on meeting was "are you working?" There was one man, a communist, who refused to work for anyone, asking "why should I make a profit for someone else?" A few years later, as a young child, I joined an unhappy crowd of workers outside a nearby clothes factory; the atmosphere was so tense and one striker attempted to hit another with a chair, after which I ran home crying to my mother.

As the last of seven siblings and my mother's favourite as the "baby" of the family, my childhood was very happy but I was terribly spoiled. At the age of two, measles left me with blindness in one eye due to corneal scarring, which meant regular check-ups at the nearby London Hospital, in the Whitechapel Road. On one such occasion, having been instructed how to bathe the damaged eye, after what seemed a long time with my arm tiring, I asked the nurse's permission to rest and she burst out laughing, possibly because she also thought this treatment was useless. The left eye was normal, although I needed spectacles for short-sightedness from the age of nine, but neither my schooling nor early adult life were affected. However, at the age of seventeen, on being examined when "called up" for military service, having vision in only one eye marked me as grade 4 and ineligible for military service; my objection to the eye specialist's decision was because all my friends were doing National Service, often in exciting places such as Malaya, but he quickly pointed out that if anything happened to the good eye, it would make me useless.

Solly, my eldest brother had rheumatic fever as a child resulting in severe heart disease; listening to his heart with my stethoscope as a medical student, revealed an irregular heartbeat as well as horrific murmurs. He married an attractive local girl, Gertie, and had two daughters (Maureen and Adele) and a son (Barry), the latter emigrated to Australia; the two girls married, each having two children. Although not very bright, Solly was an excellent mechanic and I well remember him replacing a lost toggle on my Scout's uniform by making a new one from the leather of a bicycle pedal strap. Once, on returning from hospital after having had my tonsils out, he was outside the shop repairing a bicycle and bending down,

8

which was perfect for a playful kick; he stood up with an angry face which quickly changed to a smile when he saw his baby brother was home again. Solly died at a young age of a stroke as a result of his heart condition.

My brother Sid was an upholsterer and a keen sportsman and once cycled to Bath, roughly a hundred miles from London. Outside our Raven Row house, he had a fight with a local lad and, although the loser, was nevertheless respected thereafter.

One day when about six years old, on returning home to Raven Street, my father, who was on his own repairing a bicycle, told me to go to my mother and the rest of the family, who were a few hundred yards away in Cambridge Heath Road. This was my first realisation that my parents had separated. From that time on, Sid was more like a father to me and remonstrated when my "gang" of a few boys built a fire in the basement of our house; on reaching the age of ten, he also stopped me sleeping in my mother's bed.

Solly outside cycle shop with me, aged 12 wearing school cap, and Izzy smoking

Sid married an attractive woman, Terry, moving to Leeds when the London Blitz started in 1940, where they remained for the rest of their lives; they never had children. With a friend, Sid established a successful upholstery business. Approaching retirement, he suffered a stroke and was admitted to the local St James' Hospital, where I visited him; he lived for several years with weakness of the right side and a speech impediment. After his death, Terry considered returning to London but, as all her friends were in Leeds, she remained there; she finally moved to a care home, being nearly blind and sadly died in June 2011, just weeks before her hundredth birthday.

My father at Sid's wedding 1935

Sid and Terry

My eldest sister Mary was very pretty; she went to a Central school which was more academic than an Elementary school but not up to the standard of a Secondary school. She worked as a secretary and had lots of male suitors; one was a taxi-driver who developed a neurological illness many years after his friendship with Mary and attended a hospital where I worked, but he did not recognise me. One of the benefits in having a pretty sister was that some of her boyfriends wished to curry favour by giving her little brother treats; on one such occasion an insurance agent took me to see Chinatown in Poplar, East London where there were many Chinese restaurants and, so he said, opium dens; he taught me never to walk over iron gratings, as a client had been injured falling through them. Mary eventually married a working man who was a keen Trades Unionist; they had one son, Alan, who emigrated to California where he married, had a daughter and then divorced. Mary's husband developed a brain tumour and died after surgery, again in the hospital where I worked. She remarried some years later very happily and was survived by her second husband.

Mary before the Second World War

Tilly also went to a Central school and became a secretary. During the Second World War she worked for the Royal Army Pay Corps in Leicester, which she enjoyed. She also had two husbands, the first drowned in the early part of World War II while working as a radio operator on a merchant ship off Iceland; her second husband, Maurice, was a Czech who had escaped the German occupation of his country by getting to the Far East and eventually joining the Czechoslovakian Forces in England; he had been in the Dunkirk evacuation and told me hair-raising stories of those times. Visiting him in Scarborough, Yorkshire, while he was serving in the army, he introduced me to another Czech soldier who was a dare-devil and looking forward to getting to grips with the enemy; my brother-in-law told me that this character pounced on enemy soldiers by starlight, but was eventually shot. When demobilised, Maurice became a commercial traveller; he and Tilly had four children, two sons and twin girls, one of the latter dying of multiple sclerosis at the age of 40, when there was no effective treatment for her illness. Maurice died relatively young and Tilly died at the age of 93 in 2010, and was my last living sibling; her funeral was the only time I have shed adult tears.

Mary and Tilly with me in a sailor suit in front of the cycle shop.

Izzy at his barmitzvah aged 13

Izzy worked in the family's cycle shop. On 29 December 1940, before being sent overseas, he married, and the brief honeymoon was at a West End hotel; this was a day of major blitzes and, seeing the fires from our home in the East End, my mother understandably refused to let me go and see them. They had one son, but his wife divorced him soon after his return to England and did not keep in touch with our family. He was called up and served in the Royal Engineering and Mechanical Corps (REME) working on armaments; sent to the Far East, he volunteered to become an officer but was rejected. Invalided out of the Army with schizophrenia, on receiving a telegram, my mother initially thought this was the name of the ship in which he was coming home, having not understood that was his diagnosis. He had been a heavy cigarette smoker, and spent the rest of his life in mental hospitals, dying at the age of 61.

The brother closest to me, and only four years my senior, was Percy, and we would enjoy mock fights, competing to see who was "quickest on the draw". He was not very bright and my mother encouraged me to teach him "fractions" so he could pass the test to get into the Royal Air Force rather than be drafted into the Army; this proved impossible and he fought with the Royal Lincolnshire Infantry and was killed near Nijmegen, Holland in 1944, during Operation "Market-Garden" – a battle that was enacted in the film "A Bridge Too Far."

Percy in army uniform with my mother

All the children got on well together and there was one game I enjoyed with my sisters when they would put a bowler hat over my eyes and push me from one to the other; another game of mine was lifting the backs of skirts of young working girls as they walked past our house, and then quickly running away – both games when under the age of seven, approximately the time my parents separated because of my father's womanising, playing dominoes and chatting in the pub next door and smoking cigarettes (he had a hacking cough), rather than working. Sid tried to get my parents back together after their separation, but his efforts ended in tears. My mother took all the children and moved to a larger house in Cambridge Heath Road, about half a mile from my birthplace, where she opened another cycle shop; my father remained at the old house in Raven Row; they divorced several years later. Only one or two of the seven children regularly visited my father in his cycle shop after the separation; myself, possibly because he gave me the occasional penny. The last time I saw him was in hospital when he was dying at the age of 82.

At the age of five my first primary LCC (London County Council) school was in Redmans Road, Stepney where my intelligence proved to be above average. Assessors tested my knowledge and were generally pleased with my answers except when asked, "If a white cow gives white milk, what colour milk would a black cow give?" Never having seen a cow, my reply of "black" was followed by general laughter, including my own. Another incident at this school was being punished for talking in class; the master beat my backside with a cricket stump, possibly because he did not have a cane. Although I do not remember much pain, the wheals on my bottom horrified my mother, who took me to complain to the headmaster, after which there were no further beatings.

On moving to our new home in Cambridge Heath Road, the new cycle shop opened, now called Soll Brothers; Solly and Izzy did the repairs and my mother sold sports clothes. The business prospered, one reason being that medical students at the nearby London Hospital often had bicycles in need of repair, and taxi-drivers needed bicycles to learn the London streets ("The Knowledge of London"). On one occasion, my mother challenged a young customer whom she noticed had put something in his pocket for which he had not paid; when he refused to empty his pocket, she simply took the object out herself, after which the guilty lad sloped off, duly humiliated.. Another customer aggressively told my mother he was a member of the British Union of Fascists (Bethnal Green was nearby), to which she replied that she was not afraid of him, and he beat a hasty retreat

My second primary school was in Cephas Street, only a few minutes walk away from our new house. The headmaster regarded me as one of his best pupils and each year on prize day gave me a poem to recite under his tuition, one was Sir Henry Newbolt's *Vitai Lampada,* "Play up and play the game", in which he told me to emphasise the words by raising my right arm in a theatrical gesture. He once tried to get me to sing a note, which he first played on a piano, in front of the whole class; unable to do this after many repeated attempts, he excused me from all further singing classes, and sent me to another room to do maths exercises instead; this inability to sing in tune has remained and may partly explain my facility for maths. Occasionally we went by bus to a delousing centre, where our heads were bathed in a foul-smelling solution which seemed effective for a time; head lice were a common problem and there was no shame attached to these visits.

At Cephas Street School there was a boy who was my wrestling friend; whenever we met, including in the street, we fought and the winner would be the one who could pin the arms of the other to the ground with his knees; although older and heavier than me, this friend occasionally let me win, but whoever won, my clothes always ended up dirty. One female teacher gave me a present of the book "Rob Roy", which surprised me at the time, and lead to the discovery many years later that my education had sadly missed out on the classics and particularly children's literature. My class did go on an educational outing to a Shakespeare play but my mother did not let me go, firstly because she could not afford the princely cost of sixpence and, secondly because she had never heard of Britain's greatest playwright.

Those early years in poverty did not prevent my regular and frequent attendance at the cinema, the reason being that our shop window advertised films showing at the three local cinemas. My family was given two tickets a week to "the flicks" for each advertisement posted in our shop window, so there were few films to which one of my brothers or sisters did not take me. As a result, I still have vivid memories of the films of the later 1930s, such as "San Francisco" in 1936, which showed the 1906 earthquake of that city, and played to packed houses – including standing room – with long queues to get in and some people actually fainting during the wait. One of the cinemas was the Paragon in Mile End Road, where Charlie Chaplin and Lord Delfont had performed.

A special treat was to go to Johnny Isaac's fish-and-chip shop in the Mile End Road where there was always a queue; the food was freshly deep-fried in oil and tasted particularly good, although it was expensive (sixpence a portion in the 1930s). Another special gastronomic treat was salt-beef or smoked salmon sandwiches bought from Bloom's in Brick Lane, once a Jewish enclave, but now mostly inhabited by Asians. One of my leisure activities was to play table-tennis (ping-pong) at the Oxford and St. George's Boys Club where the game was known as the "workers' tennis".

On 30 January 1933, Adolf Hitler became Chancellor of Germany and, the following April, there was a boycott of Jewish professionals and businessmen. In the East End signs went up reading "Boycott all German goods" but, being only seven years old, this did not mean anything to me, even after my brothers and sisters attempted an explanation; there was agreement with my mother, however, that Hitler was a "pig". By 1936, when the Germans marched into the Rhineland, it was clear that they were not going to continue to accept the Versailles Treaty, thought by some British as too harsh, for which they blamed the French. The first realisation of fascism for me was the Civil War in Spain (1936-1939) when one of our customers, much admired because he was tall and heavily built, volunteered for the International Brigade to fight in Spain against Franco. On his return, he was a shadow of his former self, having lost several stones in weight. Listening wide-eyed to his tales of "dum-dum" bullets, which exploded on impact, he taught me the songs of the International Brigade. Being anti-fascist, my regular walk to Petticoat Lane market on Sunday mornings allowed me to study the literature on a Communist Party stall. In 1936, Oswald Moseley led his British Union of Fascists to Cable Street, Stepney where many Jews lived and worked; being only ten years old, my mother would not allow me to go and help stop the march.

Before the Second World War a quarter of a million Jews lived in the East End, thought to be due to its proximity to the London Docks, where most immigrants landed. Known for cheap lodgings, it was where Stalin and his Jewish revolutionary friend, Maxim Litvinov, stayed when they attended the Russian Social Democratic Labour Party meeting in 1907, sharing a bed at Rowton House, Whitechapel for sixpence a night. Although Jews were expelled from Britain by Edward I in 1290, they were allowed back in 1556 under Cromwell; the largest influx of Jewish immigrants was in the early part of the twentieth century, mainly from Russia, because of its anti-Semitic pogroms. In 1939 the East End of London was full of Jewish street markets, Yiddish theatres and a hundred active synagogues. Before the Second World War, my mother once took me to a Yiddish theatre in Whitechapel, in spite of my not understanding it at all; she read local Yiddish newspapers, of which there used to be three published daily. This part of London is now almost entirely inhabited by Indian and Pakistani immigrants but, in the '30s, coloured people were so rarely seen that on one occasion my brothers called me into the shop to see and talk to a man with black skin.

On Saturdays, the Whitechapel Road was crowded with people and it was said that if you walked the mile from Aldgate to Mile End Gate you would meet everyone, meaning all the Jews you knew; Mile End Gate was so-called because it was a mile from Aldgate, one of the Gates of the old City of London. My father had a stall every Saturday in the Mile End Waste, the continuation of Whitechapel Road, where he sold old gramophone records and small objects related to the cycle trade; I occasionally helped, often changing the gramophone records.

Each Christmas, a wealthy local shoe manufacturer would give each pupil at Cephas Street School a bag containing such treats as an orange and a sixpenny piece. Nearly all the boys and girls were very poor, bearing in mind the area in which we lived, and these presents were a real treat. My mother initially had difficulty in making ends meet and my brother's school-teacher asked to see me as apparently my trousers and clothes were more acceptable than Percy's, whose "flies" were done up with a safety pin.

In 1902, Balfour's Education Act had created a state secondary education system where upper class children went to public schools as boarders, the middle class to fee-paying grammar schools and working class children to elementary schools. From 1907, grammar schools were given grants if they gave a quarter of their places to working class pupils, who could take an extra exam at the age of 11 and, if they passed, go on to the grammar, or secondary, school free of charge. Until the twentieth century, a quarter of children in London did not attend school, but free places in grammar schools were later given if pupils passed the necessary examinations in English and Arithmetic, such pupils often progressing later to university. Long regarded as a "scholarship boy", there was no surprise when, at the age of eleven, the Headmaster of Cephas Street School told me to run home and tell my mother of my success in the '11- plus' scholarship exam with an award of a grant. This meant the next educational step was to a secondary (grammar type) school and there was even a mention of my going to a public school, Christ's Hospital but, being the baby of the family, my mother would not consider my leaving home for a boarding school, nor did she like its name.

The two secondary schools considered for me were the "Davenant", which was in Whitechapel Road and nearest to my home, and the Central Foundation School, Cowper Street in the City of London. My Headmaster thought the address of the Davenant would weigh against me in the future, so Central Foundation School was duly chosen. This school was founded by the Reverend William Rogers, Rector of St Botolph's Church, Bishopsgate from 1863-1896 who was also Chaplain to HM Queen Victoria; he recognised the need for education of the children in the City of London and The Central Foundation buildings were opened in 1869, with the Great Hall finished in 1873; for a long time there were over 1,000 boys attending. The Prince and Princess of Wales (later King Edward VII and Queen Alexandra) visited the school in 1870, as did Prince George of Wales (later King George V) in 1874, when the school colours of Royal Blue and Gold were adopted. During my time at the school, Mr N M Gibbins M.A., was headmaster (1922-1946)); he had served in the First World War in the Royal Flying Corps, the precursor of the RAF.

Starting my new school at the age of 11, I had to travel each way by tram which passed our shop in Cambridge Heath Road. Although there was no formal uniform, we had to wear the school cap outside school; one morning on leaving home without it, my mother ran after me and threw the cap, hoping it would land in the tram, but without success. Coming late to school meant that you were not allowed into the Great Hall for morning prayers. There was an initiation ceremony at the school when new boys were taken to a basement area and water was poured over them but somehow I avoided this indignity. The school motto, *Spe, Labore, Fide* (Hope, Work, Faith), was printed on our exercise books.

The school sports ground was in Muswell Hill, North London and we travelled there by bus. Cricket was initially demonstrated by one of the masters standing on his desk in class showing us how to use a bat. When asked to bowl for the first time, I soon discovered that if the ball was held with a finger each side of the seam, it would curve after bouncing. Such a ball breaked markedly to the right and on my first bowl the batsman's wicket was shattered, and this was repeated with the second batsman. When the third batsman came to the crease, he had discussions with the previous two players who seemed to be warning him of my leg breaks. The sports master promised me that if a "hat-trick" followed with a third ball, he would give me tuppence – quite a prize in 1938. A change of tactics was required and the next ball delivered was straight and went to the middle stump, much to the master's dismay when reminded of his promise; the rest of my cricket career was far less successful, as the reader will later discover.

Before the Second World War, I joined the Boy Scouts; the 39th Stepney Troop met each week at Camperdown House in Half-moon Street, Aldgate. My group was called the Rabbit Patrol, whose Leader became a supporter of mine, possibly because of my rapid accumulation of "badges" given for passing such tests as First Aid. At the age of 12, I was given an autograph book and Mary's husband wrote in it, "Good luck in Scouting". At an election to become a "second" to the patrol leader, another boy was elected, with resultant tears from me and sympathy from my supportive Patrol Leader. He encouraged me to go in for the Scout's boxing competition and taught me how to avoid punches; to everyone's surprise my winning the first bout was awarded with a certificate but, with no further instruction, the second bout was lost and, to my embarrassment, had to be stopped.

Scout camp, Isle of Wight, 1938

In the summers of 1938 and 1939, the Scout Troop went on its annual camping trip to the Isle of Wight. The first trip was such fun, that on the second visit, my brother Izzy came as a guest. On returning by train to London, he thought his suitcase was very heavy and, on opening it, found several bricks had been put in as an unkind joke by some of my fellow-Scouts. My mother also took me to Southend for two extra summer holidays in 1938 and 1939, which she enjoyed very much as she loved listening to the brass bands. These seaside visits were scornfully laughed at by my Scouting friends.

On holiday in Southend with my mother

At the onset of the Second World War, my school was evacuated from London, first to Newmarket, Suffolk and, six weeks later, to Fakenham in Norfolk; although 450 boys went with the school in 1939, only 50 presented themselves for readmission when the War ended in 1945.

Chapter 2

THE SECOND WORLD WAR

On Sunday 3 September 1939, war against Germany was declared by Neville Chamberlain, the Prime Minister of Great Britain. Two days before the official start of hostilities, on 1 September, three-quarters of a million London schoolchildren were evacuated to the country and I was sent to a boys' school in Newmarket, Suffolk. Evacuation meant that my thirteenth birthday celebration of Barmitzvah, the Jewish religious recognition of a boy achieving "manhood", which had been due to be celebrated on Saturday 2 September 1939, was cancelled. Following the separation of my parents, when I was about six years old, any religious education was negligible, so that preparations for this occasion had taken months to learn from a religious teacher, which included "singing" a section of the Torah (Jewish Law) in Hebrew, particularly difficult for me as I could neither sing in tune nor understand the meaning of the words. This normally happy and important day when friends and relatives are invited to the festivities, which included throwing around bags of sweets, raisins and chocolates for which young boys would scramble to pick up. The 13-year old "man" receives presents, which nearly always included at least one fountain pen. At the reception following the religious ceremony, the celebrant gives a speech, the traditional start of which was "Today I am a man", but the joke often told was "Today I am a fountain pen". When complaining to my Hebrew teacher that I would be missing all of this, he replied, "A lot of worse things will happen during this war", a prophecy which proved only too true.

With a school friend, our first billet in Newmarket was with a family who, the day after our arrival on Saturday 2 September, were celebrating a family wedding; we were each given sixpence to go to the cinema to "get the two evacuees out of the way". The first night away from home, already missing my mother, I cried myself to sleep, but my friend seemed unaffected. . The first horse-race I ever saw was the Newmarket Handicap which, at the onset of war, was for women riders. After only six weeks, my school was moved to Fakenham in Norfolk, where there was a secondary (grammar) school which had facilities to accommodate us. Most of our teachers had been men and called up for military service, with the result that we were not taught Latin, Greek or German, leaving a considerable gap in my education.

My first Fakenham billet was with a woman whose husband was serving in the Royal Norfolk Regiment; she was surprised that her two evacuees did not "look like Jews", but was told by her neighbour that we would change as we got older. My mother took me back home during the "phoney" war when there were no air-raids on London, but soon returned me to Fakenham when the Luftwaffe blitz started and, on this occasion, my sister Mary came with me to avoid the London bombing.

At my second Fakenham billet, with another school friend, the husband was an elderly gardener who worked on his allotment. His wife showed us photographs of herself as a beautiful young girl but, at the beginning of the War, they were in their seventies and he had markedly shaking hands. As rather noisy thirteen year-old city boys, the two of us were soon moved to other families. My next foster-parents were quite stuffy and complained about my not talking at meal times; trying to make conversation by commenting on the Russian army's successes as it steadily pushed the Nazis out of their country, my efforts were met only with grunts. My hosts, who had never had children of their own, may have hoped that their London evacuee would be a substitute son, but were clearly disappointed. On one occasion they enquired what I wanted to do after leaving school; replying that I wanted to be a doctor, their only comment was "some hopes". One day the man of the house asked me to go with him on a partridge shoot which, not knowing how to shoot, surprised me, but discovering I was to be a beater, the topic was soon dropped. One of their friends was a farmer who told me dogmatically that those who live in cities only *exist* and that real life could only be experienced in the countryside.

About two years later, when in the sixth form, another billet was found for me where the husband was a highly respected solicitor who had an office in Holt, about eight miles from Fakenham; he would occasionally drive me there stopping on the way for a cigarette. His wife was a keen gardener who introduced me to the names of the flowers in their rather large garden. The home was considered to be very smart and, when my previous hostess heard where I had been moved to, made a point of visiting, perhaps worried that I may have complained about my stay with her. This last billet was very enjoyable and it was a pleasure to be there for two years whilst studying in the lower and upper sixth forms. These hosts took a great interest in my proposed career, particularly when presenting myself for admission interviews with the Deans of London Medical Schools, who required recommendations in addition to the school headmaster's report.

Me as a sixth-former with my Czech brother-in-law, Maurice Jackson

In order to progress to the sixth form, one had to matriculate, which could give exemption from the Higher School Certificate; before this we all took seven subjects and my results proved satisfactory in English and advanced maths, with distinctions in the other five subjects which included French, physics, chemistry and elementary maths. These subjects stood me in good stead for the sixth forms to study four subjects for the Higher Schools Certificate: Botany: Zoology, Chemistry and Physics. Passing the Higher Schools Examination in all four subjects gave me exemption from the Intermediate Bachelor of Science (B.Sc.) degree and was essential for admission to university.

Towards the end of the war during my visits to London for medical school interviews, Hitler was attacking with V1 bombers: these "doodlebugs" were unmanned aircraft travelling at 150 mph with the engine stopping a few seconds before plunging to the ground and exploding. One of these fell opposite my family home in London and killed several people. After one interview in London, on returning to Fakenham the headmaster called me to his office to request my not speaking of this new weapon to the other boys as it would make them worry about their own families in London.

Whilst in Fakenham, I was a stallholder three times for the Annual War Charities Week on the Rectory Lawn, sharing stalls with Sackovitch. With another school friend called Schneiderman, we sat together in class because our surnames followed each-other alphabetically and also variably came first, second and third in the end-of-term exams (these two friends also became doctors). On sports day in 1943, having come first in the high jump, one of the masters removed a handkerchief from my back pocket, pointing out that, without it, a higher jump would have been possible. The boys in the sixth forms, both lower and upper, joined the Ambulance Brigade as part of War Service, the alternative would have been the Home Guard.

Ambulance Brigade in Fakenham, 1943 (me centre)

I found a poem I had written at this time praising the Ambulance Brigade:

The Second Front has started!

And Rome was ours last week

Soon Hitler will be parted

So that will stop his cheek.

But if you have to worry

And feel a little nervous

Don't hesitate to call on me

p.p. The Ambulance Service

During my time in Norfolk, several form prizes came my way with a
chemistry prize in the Lower VI in 1943, whilst my reward for being First
Boy was a French dictionary, which I still have – albeit in a very battered
condition. In 1944, as well as the Wm.Rogers Senior Science Prize, I was
also awarded the Alleyn Exhibition Scholarship, this being worth £40.00

per annum, a considerable sum of money in those days. At the Central Foundation (Cowper Street) School, I belonged to Wormells House, being Captain in 1943 and a Prefect for my final year in 1944.

Returning home to London after evacuation, there were bugs in my bed and, at my mother's suggestion, it was stripped and successfully treated with pesticide. My first interview for admission to medical school was at the London Hospital, just a few minutes walk from my home in Cambridge Heath Road, but nervousness prevented me from articulating any decent response and it was no surprise when I was not offered a place. The second interview was at St Bartholomew's Hospital, where they asked about my hobbies; on replying "reading chemistry books", the Chairman of the interviewing committee muttered, "mugging up your chemistry"; he was a urological surgeon and would not accept my denial. There were two further interviews, University College Hospital and Westminster Hospital. With the former, one of the interviewers took out his cigarette lighter and asked me to explain how it worked; this lateral thinking took me completely off-guard and my later suspicion was that he was after a comment on hydrocarbons but, in spite of this failure, my name was put on their reserve list, which meant a provisional acceptance depending on exam results. The Dean at Westminster Medical School was a Scotsman and we obviously got on well as his willingness to admit me was unequivocal.

There were many British military deaths between October and November 1944 whilst fighting to clear Germans from the region South and West of the River Maas before a final attack on the Rhineland; so fierce was the battle that the British dubbed it "A Second Caen". The Divisional Commander concentrated on the village of Overloon, where the Germans had "a heavily reinforced stronghold…" The British eventually occupied the ruins on 12 October 1944 and of the 279 in the Overloon cemetery, where my brother Percy is buried, 261 are from the British Army. He had been conscripted in 1943 and was very proud of his soldier's uniform; he had several photographs of himself with his rifle, giving me the assurance that he knew how to look after himself. After preliminary training at Catterick camp, he was enlisted into the Lincolnshire Infantry and was killed in action in Operation Market-Garden, trying to relieve British paratroops in Nijmegen. I twice visited his grave in the Overloon Cemetery where he lies next to four other Lincolnshire infantrymen and their commanding major. On my first visit soon after the War, the Commonwealth Graves Commission arranged and paid for the whole trip. On my second visit many years later, Angela came with me. During the whole war period, my brother-in-law, Tilly's husband, served with the Czech Forces in the British Army.

My first day at Kings College, University of London was devoted to the Freshers' party, where new students reveal their weaknesses by joining various clubs; the three that attracted me were the Chess Club, Table Tennis Club and Socialist Society. Although winning both chess and ping-pong at King's for two consecutive years, my activities at the Socialist Society were limited to being elected in charge of its publicity. The Second World War continued during my second year at King's College; a V2 rocket, against which there was no defence, landed in our quadrangle leaving a large hole, terrifying us as there had been no warning; fortunately there were no casualties. Because of a better than average performance at the end of term exams, some students proposed my name as Secretary of the King's College Medical Society but the successful candidate was a friend who much later became a consultant anaesthetist. Later, meeting at a Savage Club dinner, we became close friends and fellow-Freemasons

It was the Women's Common Room of Kings College who decided a mascot was needed and found a lion of beaten copper in Euston Road Brewery, which seemed suitable because of its King's crest, so it was bought for seven pounds; in spite of its obvious male gender, it was initially christened Lucy. When officially adopted as the King's College mascot and renamed Reggie, it was displayed in the main entrance of the college in the Strand. . In 1929, the three year old Princess Elizabeth (our present Queen) was given a small furry Reggie on wheels and apparently refused to play with anything else. In 1950, Reggie was kidnapped by students from Queen Mary College, London and taken to Inverness, so that King's students had to travel to Scotland to "rescue" him; he was stolen again in 1960, this time by University College, London (UCL) students, and had to be rescued from Newcastle. On the evening of 8 May 1945, VE (Victory in Europe) Day, Reggie was "borrowed" by students of Guy's Hospital, who painted him in their colours of blue and gold before returning him by marching over London Bridge and up the Strand with a police escort.   A thousand students, including myself, were involved in Reggie's rescue and two students, both sons of clergymen, were arrested. The antipathy between the medical faculties of King's College and Guy's Hospital further increased when the latter was "invaded" by medical students of the former, with much throwing of flour bags and water squirted from siphons, which flooded the Guy's mortuary. On his return to King's College, there was a milling crowd around Reggie with assembled medical students tearing off bits of metal from his body, at the same time blocking traffic in the Strand, much to the annoyance of the police. Little permanent damage was done at these rags except one student did lose vision in one eye from a torrent of water. Reggie still reigns in the Student's Union of Kings College, watching over generations of students. During the "invasion" of Guy's, a red-haired Guy's student in shorts, tee-shirt and plimsolls confronted me in a boxing position, but when told firmly "no boxing, only wrestling", he stalked away, much to my relief. Years later we worked together at Atkinson Morley's Hospital and he went on to become a successful neurosurgeon. I recounted this story of our VE Day confrontation many years later when introducing him as my successor as President of the Section of Neurology of the Royal Society of Medicine.

Being keen to travel before starting clinical studies at Westminster Hospital, my first trip abroad was to France in 1946; I arrived in Paris one year after the end of the Second World War. Enquiring of a middle-aged woman in the street if she knew of a cheap, clean hotel, she obligingly took me to one which proved satisfactory; flattering my schoolboy French by taking me for a Belgian, she wanted to see me again, but accepted my polite refusal. This Parisian sojourn ended by staying very cheaply in rented accommodation on a bomb-site managed by a White Russian couple who spoke perfect English and attempted to correct my poor

French. As a result of trying to see as many tourist sites as possible in just a few days, sleep overtook me in the Tuileries gardens opposite the Louvre; when awakened by a ticket-collector to pay for my deck-chair, she took my 100 franc note with a surprised expression, obviously having thought this young boy in student's clothes must be a tramp.

Being only nineteen years old, my mother thought that travelling alone to a foreign country so soon after the War might be dangerous, but my sisters persuaded her to allow me to go on condition that I visited my aunt and family who lived in Perigueux, not far from Bordeaux. The aunt in question, my father's sister, had emigrated from Romania to France before the War where she married a man who sold clothes in the markets of South-west France; they and had two grown-up children. My uncle, meeting me for the first time, told me how he had fought with the Maquis, the French resistance movement, against German forces. Although managing to communicate with my School Certificate distinction French, my uncle was astonished when his children approved of my usage of the imperfect tense, which he, as an immigrant, did not know. These relations had lived in unoccupied France until Germany had taken over the whole Vichy-governed area when fearing invasion by Allied forces. My eldest cousin was hoping to study medicine at the University of Bordeaux, but failed the entrance examination and eventually became a teacher in the French colonies of North Africa. Meeting him many years later in Lyons, where he and his wife had settled, he was very keen on compiling our family tree. His sister, my only other French relative, had contracted poliomyelitis as a child and had a resulting limp; she, too, stayed in France, marrying and settling in Paris.

My cousin, Michel Rencus in Bordeaux 1946

My interest in wine dated from this time, on first visiting the wine growing area of Bordeaux; even then it was surprising to see my relatives drink their wine diluted with water. They very kindly took me on a tour of Périgueux and the surrounding countryside, including the Lascaux caves, with its primitive wall paintings; such visits are no longer possible after the discovery that visitors' breath was damaging the colours of the paintings, but a replica of the caves was constructed so that tourists could get a concept of what they looked like.

After Périgueux, my ambition was to see the Riviera, called *Côte d'Azure* by my French relatives. At the train station, asking for a ticket to Cannes, the official was about to give me a ticket to *Cagnes,* presumably because he had not understood my English accent and because it was soon after the Second World War when Cagnes had been a centre of fighting for the British. In the South of France, I stayed at a youth hostel which cost only sixpence a night, but meant sharing the mattress with bugs; nevertheless, the beaches and holiday-makers were an eye opener. Chatting to a young Frenchman, he could not answer my query as to why such a great country as France had toilets that were holes in the ground and without proper seats. On returning to England by train, the French ticket inspector asked me how much money I was carrying; when the reply was "nothing" (having spent everything buying last-minute presents), he asked to see my wallet. His search for money resulted in the expected negative findings but he found a contraceptive and, returned the wallet rapidly, saluted, calling me "Monsieur" and very nearly clicking his heels. Looking back, it was amusing that a nineteen year-old virgin was equipped for all eventualities.

In the early 1940s, an international body of university students was founded and a medical student, who was one year older than me, asked me to succeed him as Secretary to this International Union of Students for Westminster Hospital Medical School; the organisation was not popular with Westminster medical students, who voted after a debate to withdraw, the only branch to do so, mainly because of its Left-wing reputation. Its first international meeting in 1947 was held in Prague, Czechoslovakia. My visit there included skiing in the Tatra Mountains to the east of the country, where the facilities were at that time very basic. During this trip I became lost in the beautiful countryside, but was able to ask the way from a local peasant with the help of pidgin Czech taught me by my newly-acquired brother-in-law. On my return to Prague, as my hair needed cutting , I went to a barber in the railway station (named after President Woodrow Wilson, who promoted the country's independence after the First World War) and asked if he could exchange English pounds for Czech crowns. He was unable to oblige, but another customer overheard my request and said he could if we went to his flat on the outskirts of Prague. On arrival, we found another member of the British student group who was from Oxford University where one of his lecturers had asked him to find out about the Czech secret police. A Left-wing government had been democratically elected to the Czech parliament with 40% Marxists and 20% socialists, and it was thought that the country would be the bridge between the Communist East and the Democratic West. However, there was a coup in April 1947 with the country joining the communist countries of Eastern Europe; it was clear that the Czechs' experience of German suzerainty had made them hate their masters so much that they swung to the political left. Another threat to Czechoslovakia being a "bridge" was the machinations against the government, as evidenced by the Oxford student in our own group.

Chapter 3

MEDICAL SCHOOL

After the monastic St Bartholomew's and St Thomas' Hospitals which were founded centuries ago, Westminster Hospital was one of the earliest teaching hospitals in London. In the 1930s, the original hospital was in Broadway, opposite the Houses of Parliament but, in 1938, the new Medical School and the Nurses' Home opened in nearby St John's Gardens, followed in May 1939 by the hospital, which was opened by its Patron, King George VI. This was just before the start of the Second World War when two bombs landed on the hospital in 1940 followed by a land mine in 1941.

Students accepted by the Dean of Westminster Hospital Medical School would have preclinical training at King's College, London in the Strand adjoining Somerset House, before seeing patients, "walking the wards", it was necessary to learn anatomy, physiology (bodily functions) and pharmacology (drugs), the whole course being for five terms of three months each. Anatomy was learned by dissection of dead human bodies, donated before death either by patients or relatives; we were asked by the professor of anatomy to treat the human body with respect, which we usually did but, being teenagers, there was considerable humorous discussion in the dissection room. In spite of this, we became familiar with all the organs of the human body and most students passed end of term exams. The same interest was displayed in lectures on the functions of the body accompanied by experiments to demonstrate human physiology; one particular test involved each student swallowing a tube which went down through the gullet to the stomach where gastric juices were then sucked out and analysed to show the chemical nature of hydrochloric acid. Being a serious and ambitious student, my examination marks proved high enough to be proposed as Secretary of the Medical Faculty, but the voting went to another candidate who was possibly not as dedicated to swotting as me. Other medical schools that sent their students to the Strand for preclinical studies included the Charing Cross and Kings College Hospitals.

Dannie Abse, the well-known poet, was studying at medical school at the same time as me. On the short side and not a very good student, he was already writing poetry in those days more than sixty years ago. His importance to me was that, as Captain of the football team at Westminster Hospital Medical School, he selected me to play right inside forward, although he thought of my football much the same as I did of his poetry – not highly. My football did not improve, in spite of later playing with my three sons, but my interest in poetry did gather strength. Now retired, Dannie Abse spent his medical career in the specialty of thoracic medicine; decades later his brother Leo, a Welsh MP, often lunched with me at our London Club.

Going to Westminster Hospital for three years clinical training was exciting because this was learning about being a doctor was all about. The medical school was one of the smallest and there were only eighteen students in my intake, admissions being every six months. Those who were already at Westminster Hospital "threw their hands in the air" asking "where are we going to put them all?" Having done all the preliminary training in science, we were now allocated actual patients whose complaints and history we could write down and then physically examine. Taking an individual history could be prolonged because of determining all possible factors in a person's life that might influence the presenting illness; we were taught to ask first the patient's chief complaints and what troubled them the most, and next when the present illness started and its subsequent development; we would then ascertain all the previous illnesses and finally take a full family history, which could be very relevant, but "bedside manners" were not taught in those days. With our physical examination, we followed a strict pattern, starting with an assessment of the mental state; after these preliminaries, some concept of what was wrong was determined and followed by necessary special investigations needed, which were left to qualified doctors, who explained the diagnoses to us.

Since Westminster was such a small medical school, the "firms" in which we were divided consisted of only six students, an advantage because teaching was more individual and we came to know our teachers, whether recently qualified junior doctors or senior, well-known, consultants. There was one instance where a senior surgical registrar asked me to look at the leg of a patient; about to approach the suspect's lump with my hands, the registrar rapidly *slapped* my hand and a further attempt produced the same result, much to my embarrassment. Following this, the leg was examined by another student, who approached the patient and bent down to study the leg for the best part of a minute, *looking* at the limb; he was congratulated by the teacher on the correct way to examine an abnormal part of the body – namely Inspection (looking) had to come before Palpation (touching). The teaching of medical students was thus a slow, but necessary, process. On one ward, while being taught by the consultant, there was a blonde staff-nurse helping an attractive brunette ward-sister to change a bed – quite a distraction for the medical students and although I do not remember, I am sure it was not the only such occasion.

Following a three month introductory period, which included the Accident and Emergency rooms, we had lectures on medicines, public health and many other subdivisions, including dentistry. We were then allocated to different clinical firms, some medical and others surgical, each usually consisting of two consultants and several junior doctors. After two, three-month terms of general medicine and general surgery, we moved to firms that taught us something of all the different specialties: for example, gynaecology and obstetrics. One of the latter consultants, who became President of the Royal College of Obstetricians and Gynaecologists, had not heard of a rheumatological disease affecting one of his patients; after my telling him about it, he wrote a paper on the case which was published in his specialist's journal. On the obstetrics firm, we had to attend the delivery of twenty babies in the surrounding homes, "on the district". This meant we stayed at a students' hostel in Pimlico and could be called out for any delivery taking place in the locality; fortunately, there was always a midwife present who supervised the whole procedure. There were some surprises for me such as once, immediately after the birth of one baby, the mother promptly lit a cigarette, and another recently delivered mother asked how soon she could have sexual intercourse.

More time was spent in the various branches of pathology, even though the Head of the department himself did little teaching. Bacteriology, the science of germs, was well-served, as was chemistry of the human body. Although coming to know my fellow-students well, spare time was also spent in the excellent medical library with its up-to-date journals and renowned classical texts. My peers regarded me as a swot, which went to one extreme when mentioning a diagnosis in the specialty of one particular teacher, who had not heard of it.

One teacher, whose statements could not be gainsaid, was Dr Swithin Meadows, the consultant neurologist. Very down-to-earth and unpretentious, he asked me to look at the back of the eye of one of his patients with an ophthalmoscope, and to report what was seen. My reply was, "Optic atrophy, Sir", meaning that the visible head of the optic nerve at the back of the eye was dead-white, rather than pink. Asking me further whether the atrophy was primary or secondary, meaning was the circular margin of the disc sharply delineated due to trouble with the nerve itself, my unequivocal reply was "Primary, sir". My correct diagnosis was so pleasing that my mother was persuaded to provide an ophthalmoscope, an expensive instrument, because it would come in useful for the rest of my professional life, which it did. Much later, another student on this firm was given the same test; he used the ophthalmoscope but faced it the wrong way! He became a distinguished surgeon.

My closest friend at medical school was Chris Hoyte and we spent a lot of leisure time together; his parents had been medical missionaries in Rhodesia where he was born. He knew of my fell-walking and youth-hostelling holidays in the Lake District in the long vacation between college and medical school and persuaded me to go rope-climbing in Snowdonia; my initiation with him had taken place in the Harrison Rocks between Tunbridge Wells and Tonbridge. The scenery in North Wales was superb, but each morning I felt ill, and thought this light-headedness was due to the high altitude but soon realised that the stress of our climbs made me drink more than my usual fare of beer at the pub in the evenings; my illness was no more than a "hangover". The exposure on our climbs scared me, particularly walking along a high ridge, when Chris suggested we took off the rope that connected us; at the end of this walk, with dense mist on both sides so that we could not see the ground below, I asked the reason for our uncoupling; his reply was simple – if one of us had fallen, there was no point in dragging the other down. I never went rope-climbing again but he did, going on a course in the Alpes Maritimes and getting stuck on an exposed cliff, a position described by his French guide as "*intéressante*". Years later he climbed in the Himalayas with an experienced group which nearly reached their target peak, but the clouds suddenly came down; he never returned, dying in his early thirties. Many years later, a Tibetan guide found his snow pike on the mountain and brought it to London, where the Eighteen Club (eighteen students who qualified as doctors together) had a memorial meeting for him which his sisters, who had been nurses at Westminster Hospital, attended. I had met them years before when Chris invited me for lunch at his family home in Birmingham, where his father practised as a GP on returning from Rhodesia. As medical missionaries, they were very religious and on my visit they said a prayer for me, somewhat to my embarrassment. After Chris's death his father asked me whether Chris had any life insurance, but I had no knowledge of this.

For some time my surname had worried me, largely because it was German and a senior Nazi minister had the same name; discussing this with Chris a few months before qualification, he agreed with my concerns and suggested that if it were to be changed, it should be before qualification. This was done by Deed Poll and the name changed from Frank Rosenberg to Frank Clifford Rose; the only disapproving comment made was by a class-mate who thought both the name and my origin were Scandinavian; the choice of the surname Rose was because my elder brother Sid had already chosen this name when starting his business in Leeds.

I was the first to qualify in March 1949. There were three main ways of becoming a medical doctor; the most popular route, taken in the summer, was by a degree of the University in London, the MB BS (Bachelor of Medicine and Bachelor of Surgery). The second was not a university examination, but a diploma, taken in the spring, and called the Conjoint Examination, because it was awarded jointly by the Royal College of Physicians as a Licentiate (LRCP) and the Royal College of Surgeons as a Member (MRCS). All those students who qualified with me took the MB BS later in the year but, because of my keenness to become a doctor, my qualification was earlier at the age of 22 with the LRCP, MRCS diploma, considered to be an easier examination. The third way, mainly for those trained from abroad, was the Licentiate in Medicine and Surgery, Society of Apothecaries and considered the easiest of the three routes, chiefly because the separate parts of medicine, surgery, obstetrics etc, could be taken at different times.

One of our lecturers, a GP teaching us Public Health, asked the class their preference for the future; only one student put up his hand to opt for a GP career, but he was the eldest of us all with a wife and children to support, and needed to start earning straight away. As the other younger doctors married, they had to give up their ambitious hope of specialising and the eventual split between consultants and GPs was 50:50, a ratio that existed nationally at the time.

The nurses' library was named after the late Edwina, Lady Mountbatten, who had served as a volunteer nurse at the hospital during the war. After her husband, Lord Mountbatten, was assassinated by an Irish terrorist bomb, she had a period of coma, which she spoke about to a meeting of the Medical Society of London. This was how I met her after she became President of the British Red Cross Association.

It was at medical school that I learned to play squash and bridge, both taught me by more senior students. The squash courts were underground and games were always followed by a shower. The Dean, a tall, well-built Scot, always positioned himself towards the centre of the court so that he did not need to move far in any direction if his opponent's ball went either side of the court; watching him play was a lesson in itself. I continued to play occasionally throughout my early career but less as my workload increased. On one occasion, the tendon of my right heel tore and I decided that in middle age I should really play more regularly or not at all, so gave up completely. I was taught bridge by a senior student who was an expert and played for a London club but never qualified as a doctor; he was disappointed with my not taking the game more seriously, at least until one of our opponents cheated and I threw down my hand of cards in disgust. I took up the game much more seriously decades later after my retirement from the NHS, when I played regularly at the Savile Club.

Chapter 4

BECOMING A DOCTOR

After qualifying as a doctor, successful candidates try to get their first job at the hospital where they trained and passed their final exams, either as house physician (HP) or house surgeon (HS). In 1949, doctors could practise immediately on passing these tests although a year or two of medical experience is now required before being registered with the General Medical Council (GMC). The future of a doctor was partly determined by whether he (then nearly always men) wished to be a general practitioner (GP) or a specialist; the latter being more difficult because of the need to pass higher degrees or diplomas, depending on the specialty chosen. A houseman was paid poorly (my first monthly cheque in 1949 was £11.00) and would not be able to support a wife, let alone a family; this meant that those doctors who became engaged to be married had to give up their wishes of becoming consultants. At Westminster Hospital, my application for the post of HP to Dr Swithin Meadows, the consultant neurologist, failed; the successful candidate later became a GP. The fact that my first post was not at my own teaching hospital was definitely a mark against becoming a specialist. Although perhaps brighter than the average student, my not getting this job seemed likely, not least because of changing my surname just a few months before qualification.

New End Hospital, Hampstead

The National Health Service (NHS) began in 1948 and it was in the following year that my first medical appointment was as house physician to New End Hospital, Hampstead, originally founded in 1800 by the Hampstead Board of Guardians as part workhouse, part casual ward and part infirmary. Rebuilt in 1845, its patients until the First World War included the unemployed, unmarried mothers, children, the homeless, destitute, returning wounded soldiers, and psychiatric patients. The Guardians modernised the institution, taking it over in 1930 from the London County Council (LCC) and naming it New End Hospital, after its location. Gradually becoming recognised as a hospital for acutely sick patients, it gained a reputation as a centre for ductless glands, famous because the first removal of the thymus gland in Britain was performed there for an uncommon condition of variable weakness (myasthenia), by no less a surgeon than Sir Geoffrey Keynes, who was on the consultant staff of St Bartholomew's Hospital; a famous bibliophile who was also brother of Maynard Keynes, the pioneer economist.

Hampstead was considered an up-market residential area so that it was inevitable that occasional celebrities would be treated at New End Hospital. One was the painter, Francis Bacon, born in Ireland in 1909, who was 41 when we met to talk about his close relative who was a patient being looked after in one of my "Chief's" beds. Bacon had come to London in 1920 and, although already well-known, I did not realise the significance of his paintings. Bacon gave one of his paintings as a present to his GP, who sold it at Sothebys in November 2010 for 14 million dollars (*Daily Telegraph* 4.1.2010 p.22). Another famous painter I met whilst working at New End was Stanley Spencer, when he came to visit his first wife, Hilda, who was under our care.

New End Hospital was known as a "good" hospital because, although not a teaching hospital, nearly all its consultant staff had only just missed achieving the accepted apex of becoming a teaching hospital consultant. For me, its advantage was my mother's home at that time was in Finchley, adjoining Hampstead. Every LCC hospital had a Medical Superintendent who at New End was a Canadian surgeon, Jack Piercy who, with his one secretary, satisfactorily ran the whole hospital from 1932 to 1965, without other managers or administrators. On beginning my job, Piercy was concerned that my name was not on the Medical Register, legally kept by the GMC but, having just qualified, it would not yet have been inscribed; it did not stop him from ringing the GMC who assured him my name had full registration from 1 June 1949, when still aged 22.

The working conditions of a houseman in the late 1940s varied with the hospital but, at a London teaching hospital, it was not unusual to work *full-time* for six months, full-time meaning without setting foot outside the place of work. At the end of his six months stint as a House Surgeon at Westminster Hospital, my close friend Chris Hoyte telephoned me to say he had been given some money for his assistance at operations on private patients; he had decided to spend it all on a holiday weekend in a south coast resort and invited me to join him. We booked the best hotel and, with every meal, drank good wines including champagne, claret and port.

Chris and me at a south coast resort

At New End Hospital, one was on duty for thirty-six hours at a stretch because, in addition to the usual ward duties, the houseman had to be on call for the Accident and Emergency (A&E) clinic when the appointed doctor for this was off duty. In 1949, there was only one HP (me) in the whole hospital who, each morning, did his ward round with the nursing sister, and once or twice weekly with his chief, the consultant physician. The management of A&E patients was not considered my real job, which was looking after in-patients on the medical ward, but it gave valuable lessons: for example, a young Irish girl had been stabbed in the chest in an attempted murder. Examination confirmed the injury to her chest but the accompanying two detectives pointedly asked my familiarity with these types of wounds; although every doctor is taught and examined in Forensic Medicine, my reply was understandably in the negative (being only 22 years old). We learned that she was the daughter of a politician in the Dail (the Irish parliament) and did not wish to return to her home country; the wound, according to the policemen, had been self-inflicted, but it was never clear to me why this should have favoured her desire to remain in England. On another occasion when called to A&E, there was a man who had multiple wounds caused by crushing a wine glass in his right hand; examination revealed he smelled of alcohol and it became clear that there had been an argument with his wife, but again it was not easy to understand how this self-inflicted condition could settle their problem. My extra duty was because the doctor in charge of A&E had gone on his skiing honeymoon, during which he sustained a fracture so that his leave had to be extended, as was my A&E experience. Another case was a drunken young man who had a deep wound through his scalp several inches long; it required stitching under local anaesthesia but, because of his alcoholic condition, he would not keep his head still so that I had to give an intravenous anaesthetic; on the ward round next morning, he came to thank me for sewing up his scalp and sheepishly apologised for the problems he had caused.

My chief was a likeable youngish physician who had trained in Ireland and achieved the rank of Lieutenant-Colonel in the Royal Army Medical Corps (RAMC) during the Second World War, which had ended four years previously. Early in a houseman's post, all new doctors were physically examined and, although passing me, my chief warned me of becoming round-shouldered, a vice borne in mind all my life. He was still ambitious enough to continue research work on drugs that thinned the blood and measuring the bleeding times; another of his achievements was to write a textbook of medicine for nurses but he never left New End Hospital and died before retirement.

When a patient was admitted in coma, it was sometimes necessary for feeding purposes to start an intravenous drip by inserting a needle into a vein of a limb; if this were not possible, the skin had to be cut and the needle inserted directly into the vein. Never having done this minor operation as a medical student, this "cut-down" intravenous drip had to be undertaken on a young, attractive Indian actress, admitted after attempting suicide with an overdose of pain-killers. Following her stomach wash-out, a needle was inserted into the vein of her lower ankle but, on full recovery from her unconscious state three days later, she complained about the one inch long scar in her lower ankle, but it was pointed out this seemed a small price to pay for her escape from death. Another attempted suicide, not an uncommon reason for admission, made a total recovery and her grateful father, a self-made wealthy property man, invited me to dinner at a nearby restaurant; being newly qualified, this invitation was accepted but proved to be a mistake, and taught me to maintain space between my work as a doctor and any related social activity. Another admitted case was where the bone marrow produces too few red blood cells; instructed by my chief to give a blood transfusion of so many pints (now called units), my question was whether this was not too much; my chief reconfirmed the amount but, as a result, the patient's heart was overloaded and he died, an event which made me always recheck instructions as to dosage. Having been intrigued as a student by rare eponymous diseases, where the condition is named after its discoverer, my local reputation gradually developed as someone familiar with such illnesses.

While it was uncommon for a newly qualified doctor to have only one superior, it had the advantage of frequent contact with the Chief. Most "firms", as the groups caring for patients were called, had an intermediary between the houseman and consultant called the registrar, who could advise when the Chief was not available; this happened to me with a registrar who had not yet achieved the higher diploma of Member of the Royal College of Physicians (MRCP), a necessary step in becoming a consultant physician. During one weekend, a four-year old child was admitted with a raised temperature, loss of appetite and neck stiffness, the latter feature being indicative of irritation of the covering of the brain. As this might indicate meningitis, it seemed appropriate for the registrar to see the child, who pointed out that neck stiffness in a child did not have the same significance as in an adult, and reassured me. On the following morning the child was worse and, being a Sunday when the registrar was absent, the next step for suspected meningitis was to perform a spinal tap where the cerebrospinal fluid (CSF) surrounding the brain and spinal cord is removed for examination in the laboratory. The child's CSF had all the hallmarks of inflammation indicating meningitis and the need for penicillin, which led to rapid recovery. When the registrar returned after the weekend, he apologised for his error and we became the best of friends. Other cases did not put me in such a good light – a comatose disabled adolescent was brought in by relatives; on examination he showed no signs of life, the first case of Dead on Arrival (DOA) seen by me; frustrated and upset, this made me ask the assembled relatives why the patient had not been brought to hospital earlier, with the reply from the distraught relatives that he had been born with several congenital defects.

These junior years with lack of experience produced several problems: an elderly woman was admitted having woken from sleep with severe shortness of breath; examination revealed that she had high blood pressure indicating the diagnosis was heart failure, which would be rapidly relieved by an injection of morphine. On leaving the ward her son, who was much older than me, asked for her to be seen by a consultant and, when told he was not available, verbally abused me. There was a consultant in the hospital at the time but he was a surgeon and not my Chief; explaining to him the situation, he came to see the patient, who by that time had fully recovered and, when she left the ward her son apologised and thanked me profusely. This surgeon was in fact a South African locum who was "standing in" while the consultant was away; he was learning surgery and was so keen on anatomy that he used to dissect dead bodies at night in the mortuary and asked me to join him; this was in 1949 before such activity became impossible. He also asked me to assist at an operation for a rupture at the navel, which had produced a huge abdominal protuberance; his incision had to be so large that he had difficulty in stitching the skin together again. We both perspired profusely during the latter part of this operation, but the happy result was a middle-aged patient delighted and grateful with the result.

Another surgical registrar working at the hospital came from Rhodesia hoping to pass the higher examination in surgery of the Fellowship of the Royal College of Surgeons (FRCS). He asked me to take a blood specimen from one of his patients and some minutes later asked for it but, when told of my delay by telephone calls, chastised me with the phrase "Get on with it", which taught me that, in the medical profession, speed is all-important; we became good friends and used to go to the local pub for Sunday lunch. At the same time there was a woman hospital resident training for anaesthesia; she was interested in men – especially the Rhodesian surgical registrar. Once we were playing chess together and he completely ignored her, so she suddenly knocked the chess pieces off the table to end our game; although we were upset by the untimely end to our game, the female resident anaesthetist was even more so. A senior surgical registrar, also originally a South African, came to see a patient diagnosed by me as appendicitis because of tenderness in the right lower half of the abdomen, as well as all the other signs of this condition carefully noted. After examining the patient, the surgical registrar thought my diagnosis wrong but agreed to obtain the opinion of the Superintendent, who explained to the senior registrar that a good theoretical case had been made for inflammation of the appendix in the case notes; the registrar operated and removed the appendix but later pointed out that the offending organ was only mildly infected and would have resolved with bed rest alone. We remained on speaking terms, but only just.

Another admission was a young woman with rheumatoid arthritis, for which the then recommended treatment was gold injections; the dose in the medical books was much less than the chief ordered which, being young and ignorant, I pointed out. The chief stuck to his original dose but, some time later, the patient developed exudates at the back of her eye with signs of kidney failure, recognised signs of gold over-dosage; the correct dose was later given and the patient improved. On discharge the husband thanked me effusively and presented me of a box of cigars.

On the morning ward rounds, it was customary to ask each patient how they were and, with any ongoing symptoms, there was a daily examination. There were two attractive young, women in neighbouring beds who both had air around the lungs, a common condition requiring aspiration of any accumulated fluid, easily detected by tapping the chest; they both made a complete recovery but it is doubtful whether the assiduous attention they received was entirely responsible. A much sadder case was a man dying from cancer, where no more could be done; one morning he called me over during my daily ward round to say "you never stop to ask me how I am"; he was a Catholic and completely at ease with dying but, in those days, doctors were never taught counselling. At the end of six months, the time a house job lasted, my chief asked me to serve another such period, an invitation accepted with alacrity, because of the wide experience and responsibility gained at this hospital. There was also the attraction of the nearby Hampstead Heath and, at that time, I was also taking German lessons, which I had missed out on at school during wartime.

Hillingdon Hospital

My next appointment was at a more peripheral London hospital, recognised for its good consultant staff who had just failed to obtain appointments at teaching hospitals. Hillingdon Hospital was opened in 1930 as the Middlesex County Hospital, and still had some wards in Nissen Huts dating from the Second World War. With the intention of taking the postgraduate Diploma of Child Health (DCH), which I hoped would help me to pass the examination for the MRCP, essential for becoming a consultant physician, my appointment was to the children's ward. The paediatric firm consisted of a consultant, senior registrar and I was the senior house physician; to fulfil DCH requirements, besides being taught by my superiors, there was an external course in childhood disorders to attend. Although not obligatory, this included acquiring knowledge of feeding babies, such as the advantages of breast over bottle feeding, and learning the average weight of a child from birth (7lb) to the time the infant was five months old, when the birth weight was nearly doubled. We also learned about children's teeth; primary dentition with the first teeth being the lower central incisors starting at 6 months and completed by the age of two years, and their loss from the age of six years. The work on the ward, although interesting, was quite different from dealing with adults. At the initial interview my new chiefs had asked about my experience of spinal taps in children, perhaps wondering if having only one good eye, this could be a problem, but their question was confidently answered. When filling in the form for the laboratory examination of CSF *before* completing the lumbar puncture, both seniors were surprised, since this manoeuvre was considered so difficult that most of their juniors completed the form only *after* the spinal tap had been successful. The excellent features of this hospital included very good postgraduate rounds in the adult wards, where attendance would help with the MRCP. The best teacher was Dr Cyril Barnes, who at that time was in his early forties; he had been a candidate for the post of consultant physician at his own teaching hospital (St Mary's), but was beaten to this post by an applicant who had been Captain of Rugby for England – which meant no one else had a chance. Respect and preferment were given to all sportsmen by London teaching hospitals, particularly St Mary's, where Dr (later Sir) Charles Wilson (later Lord Moran) was the Dean. Cyril Barnes published a book entitled "Medical Disorders in Obstetric Practice" which went to five editions and was translated into several languages. Always immaculately dressed, he spoke precisely and remained at Hillingdon Hospital until he retired in 1971, earlier than usual because he disliked "the increasing powers of non-medical administrators". This hospital had a good medical library and a recently added book was on X-ray advances which, while idly leafing through it, revealed an article on a child with an angled lower leg; this interested me because there was an almost identical case in the children's ward which had puzzled us. Showing the volume to my superiors, they agreed on the similarity of the cases and, when another child appeared in out-patients a few months later, we decided to report these two personal cases and review some of the previous papers on the subject. The finished article was sent to the *Archives of Diseases of Childhood* and was the first time my name appeared in a published paper. Experience of childhood illnesses was an advantage in later professional life but a very sad memory of those days was a child with tuberculous meningitis which, at that time before the advent of streptomycin, was invariably fatal. This particular child had persistent high-pitched crying, having developed water on the brain, upsetting the other children and nursing staff. It seemed that if the child did not die soon, it would require an injection of insulin to end its agony; mercifully the child did die soon afterwards and no such action was required. Since then, with the discovery of streptomycin, recovery from this condition is now the usual result.

Whether working harder during this period was the cause, I developed a throat infection and my chief ordered me to bed with antibiotics which produced a rapid recovery. It would be wrong to suggest that this house-job was all hard work. Christmas in hospital is always celebrated with parties and nurses singing carols around the wards. Being in a children's department, they thought it was a good idea for me to dress up as Father Christmas and enter the ward by the fire escape; not realising there was only a thin board for the ceiling and, getting ready to climb down the ladder of the fire escape, this event ended with my crash-landing through the plywood into the ward, a spectacular entrance remembered no doubt by the children and their carers. The other memory of that Christmas Day was attending three parties given by the nurses, an occurrence which was to be repeated every Christmas during my hospital residencies; the result was that 26 December was always a day of feeling unwell, so much so that consideration was given to my founding a "Society for the Abolition of Christmas".

Besides the excitement of learning, there was a great camaraderie amongst the junior medical staff. One pleasant character was an anaesthetics registrar who taught me snooker and played almost as well as a professional; he was also a great performer at mess parties where his standard recital was: **A hippopoem …**

A lady hippopotamus

Thought life was too monotonous,

Her mother hadn't told her what was what.

She was young and quite attractive

And her glands were very active

But her love-life simply went to hippopot.

She saw with awful clarity

Her hippopularity

Did not extend to gentlemen she knew,

And the hippopportunity

For loving with impunity

Was not the hippoproper thing to do.

She was sad and she was lonely, and she had the hippopip,

Then one night she took the fatal step to drink.

And though it seems irrelevant,

That night she met an elephant,

Though of course she saw him then as hippopink.

Quite what happened I am sure

Is just a little hippobscure,

Hippapparently she didn't think to stop.

.Now the wages of her sin is

Several Hippopicanninies,

Who have never even met their hippopop.

St Stephen's Hospital, Chelsea

My next appointment as Senior House Physician was again at an LCC
hospital, but with close connections to Westminster Hospital. A map of

1884 showed a site known as "The hospital in Little Chelsea" which was followed by an infirmary, and then a workhouse until St Stephen's Hospital was founded in the late 1800s. One of my chiefs there, Dr Dudley Hart, was in addition to being a consultant physician at St Stephen's, also a consultant at Westminster Hospital. Although a general physician, he did research in rheumatology and was one of the first in 1951 to work on a new anti-rheumatic drug, butazolidine. Because it had side-effects such as retention of water, it is no longer used, but it was my first introduction to the value of clinical trials of drugs. Dudley Hart had a benign personality and was supportive of those junior doctors who worked for him, to the extent that he suggested my reading a paper to the Heberden Society and joining the Society; it was meant for rheumatologists and, by that time, my ambition was to specialise in neurology.

The staff of St Stephen's Hospital included other well-known physicians, one of whom was a member of the Communist Party so that, on ward rounds, if a patient was reading the *Daily Worker*, they would embrace each other. Outspoken and direct, this consultant, although having passed the MRCP, was not elected a Fellow of the College (FRCP). He boasted of going to medical school in running shoes, since his family could not afford proper footwear; in spite of his political allegiance, his son went to public school and later became a consultant and FRCP. Another physician specialised in chest diseases and consumption (pulmonary tuberculosis, TB of the lung), which resulted in my looking after a whole ward of 28 young women, whom he would visit each week. In 1951, the first effective drug for this previously fatal condition, streptomycin, had just been introduced, so that these patients did not share the fate of those operatic Prima Donnas who died young, singing beautiful arias. My chief duty was to take blood samples from these patients each week to check that their inflammation was subsiding. In my early twenties, it was only towards the end of this six months appointment that I noticed all the patients were freshly made up for my weekly ward rounds. In more chronic cases, when fibrosis or cavitation of the lung had occurred, another treatment was to inject air around the collapsed lung; on one occasion a staff nurse assisting me in this procedure left suddenly, leaving me the difficult task of continuing alone; severely reprimanded by the ward sister, the reason for her sudden departure was never discovered.

About this time, I was woken up at night by pain in my abdomen, which tended to occur whenever the stomach was empty but would be rapidly relieved by food. Diagnosed as a peptic ulcer, the pain was provoked by spicy foods, and particularly garlic. Following this diagnosis, it was with great regret that Indian food was removed from my diet, with only an occasional very mild curry. Interestingly enough, proof of this diagnosis was delayed because several barium meals at St Stephen's Hospital failed to reveal any ulcer, which is usually in the duodenum, the part of gut that succeeds the stomach. It was only by putting a fibre-optic tube down my gullet much later that the ulcer was revealed, in the more unusual site of the upper part of the stomach; thankfully this problem has never bothered me sufficiently to require surgery.

One in-patient in the general medical ward was a teenage girl suffering from inflammation of the lower gut; steroids had just been introduced but were not readily available and she deteriorated and died. The cause of this condition was uncertain but one explanation was psychological and, for this reason, her mother was asked not to visit as it seemed her daughter deteriorated following those occasions. After the girl died, her mother asked why she had not been allowed to visit her daughter; my feelings of guilt over this case remained for the rest of my life.

At this hospital, a brilliant senior registrar, Dr David Weitzman gave a weekly postgraduate round and later became cardiologist at his own teaching hospital. Among other lessons, he taught me how to bet on racehorses at the King George VI Stakes on Boxing Day; he studied the form of horses every week and reported his average winnings over a year to be £400.00 (in the early 1950s). When asked why he spoke fluent Italian, his explanation was that when stationed in Italy during the Second World War, he went to the opera frequently, and it was to understand the libretti that he learned the language. Overweight, with a slight hunchback, he was humble in spite of his brilliance. Occasionally, a retired Westminster Hospital consultant, Sir Adolphe Abrahams, who had been one of my teachers, would visit St Stephen's, when he and David Weitzman would discuss horses and athleticism; Sir Adolphe's younger brother Harold, was the 1924 Olympic sprint winner featured in the film *Chariots of Fire*. Because of the links with Westminster Hospital, medical students would come to St Stephen's for tuition, one of whom became a successful plastic surgeon in Canada and, when visiting London, acknowledged his appreciation of my teaching by treating me to an expensive meal. As St Stephen's Hospital was in Chelsea, it was easy to visit a local night club where there was a pianist and drummer with drinks sufficiently cheap for young doctors, although the only visit I actually remember is when I played the drums in the two-piece band and being chastised for not keeping time.

Fees for my secondary (grammar) school and medical school had been paid by the London County Council on passing the necessary exams. Confident of obtaining the MRCP, as examination failure up to that time had never occurred to me, my first attempt was a rude awakening, even though first time failure was not unusual for this test, with only about 10% passing. The examination used to consist of two parts, the first being theoretical questions on paper, and the second to make clinical examinations of patients and answer questions on diagnosis and treatment. In spite of having read the standard textbooks and memorising as many medical conditions as possible, a second failure followed six months later. It was about this time that a registrar helping his chief with the examinations told me that his chief had commented that the jersey worn for the clinical examination was hardly suitable for a future consultant.

National Heart Hospital
Teaching courses for the MRCP were rare and, having read the then standard, extremely large, textbooks of general medicine, practical experience was necessary to get through the clinical part of the exam. My next appointment was for twelve months as a Senior House Physician to the National Heart Hospital, the main building of which was in Marylebone in the West End of London. During the Second World War, the hospital had been evacuated to a large country house in the village of

Maids Moreton, a mile or two from Buckingham. After the War, when the hospital re-opened in London, the country house was retained as a convalescent home, particularly as heart operations were increasingly being performed and needing longer convalescence. This branch of the hospital was in the house that had belonged to Samuel Pepys, the famous diarist, but was known for its large garden with a huge variety of trees.

National Heart Hospital, Maids Moreton, Bucks

The hospital housed thirty-five patients and the ward Sister would accompany me on the morning ward rounds; this was an opportunity to appreciate heart disorders with abnormal murmurs heard using a stethoscope and there was also plenty of time to read and study for my next attempt at the MRCP. In addition, a different consultant cardiologist came down from the main hospital each month giving me additional teaching from world-famous heart specialists as, after the ward round, we would have further discussions during lunch. A letter written home during the early part of this training gives a flavour of what my concerns were at that time:

> *Dear Mum and Folks,*
>
> *Am settling down nicely and am liking it very much.*
>
> *My country mansion is in good repair, the gardeners are keeping the lawns and hothouses in fine shape and the various servants*

are all efficient and hard working. My chief trouble at the moment is trying to return some of the turkey, bacon, eggs etc without offending the cook! My "corporation" has been delimited.

All being well, I shall take my weekend on the 18th/19th/20th January. There is a dance at Westmoreland St. on the 18th so that I shan't be home until late. As it's in evening dress, perhaps you would give my suit to Maurice (my brother in law) *as I'm hoping he will visit me next week. Enclosed is list of other things I'd like him to bring.*

The weather has been wonderful and there is excellent opportunity here for studying wild life. Today I saw a robin for the first time in my life. And yesterday I saw a wood-hatch (whatever that may be!).

I'm already getting tired of reading but there are lots of good cases here.

Hoping to hear from you soon and don't forget to send on my correspondence and journals. Frank.

Having been at school in Norfolk for five years and loving the country, I took riding lessons and learned to hunt and shoot; otter hunting turned out to be country walks along small rivers but I only once spotted an otter. I learned to ride at stables adjacent to Stowe, a public school (private boarding school) where horse-riding over their grounds was allowed. My riding lessons took place once or twice a week during the winter of 1952 but progress was such that my teacher suggested an early morning ride "cubbing", which meant chasing young fox cubs; if one was caught, the youngest rider was "blooded" by having the blood of the young fox cub smeared on her (usually) face. My graduating to fox-hunting near Buckingham was because my mount "knew the ropes" and all that was necessary was for me to hang on to the reins, but foxes were rarely seen on these occasions. Shooting experience consisted of one crow and one partridge, the latter just flying out from a hedge, pointed out to me by the hospital gardener, who taught me how to use a gun. A local farmer would regularly ask me to tea and country life gradually became more familiar; his weekly invitation may have been because he had an unmarried daughter, who asked me to local functions and hunt balls. One of these was held at a country mansion which had a squash court and swimming pool, belonging to a local dignitary, one of whose relatives had been a fellow medical student.

One of the visiting cardiologists, Dr William Evans, lunching with me after his ward round, asked "Did I tell you the story of how I changed the history of England?" He explained that, as a senior medical registrar at the London Hospital, he was one of the first to train in the USA in the electrical examination of the heart, (electrocardiography [ECG]), eventually writing a book on the subject. Willie Evans was asked by his chief, who in 1936 was the Royal Physician, whether he still had this "new-fangled" machine in London; replying in the affirmative, he was asked to bring his apparatus as they were going to see an important patient. Thinking they were going to Buckingham Palace to see King Edward VIII, who had succeeded his father, King George V, but was not yet crowned, Willie met his chief but had also brought the ECG technician, whereupon he was told in no uncertain terms by his chief that she must travel in a separate car because he was going to give Willie the clinical history. Their destination turned out to be, not Buckingham Palace but Chequers, the traditional country house of the Prime Minister, who was then Stanley Baldwin. Willie's chief concluded his briefing by indicating that Baldwin was getting old and tired and should retire. Having taken the ECG recording, which in those days had only three channels, and developed it under the stairway, Willie noted only a reversed wave in the third channel (an inverted T3 wave) which experts in those early days were not certain of its meaning. Willie asked himself what his opinion would be in Whitechapel at the London Hospital, where he saw National Health Service patients, and so reported to his chief that the record was within normal limits. Asking whether he or his boss should explain the results of this investigation, his chief, who had been pacing up and down, replied that the Prime Minister was Willie's patient. Going into the bedroom, where Mrs Baldwin was also present, he explained what an ECG was and that Baldwin's was normal; the patient jumped out of bed saying "I knew I was OK, it's all this intrigue that has upset me". The truth later emerged that King Edward VIII said he would go through with his coronation only if he could marry his mistress, Mrs Wallis Simpson. Baldwin found this unacceptable, to the extent that he consulted the Heads of the Commonwealth countries, who agreed with Baldwin that the King should abdicate, but the Royal Physician was a "King's man" and hoped that, if Baldwin retired, there was a possibility of Mrs Simpson becoming Queen of England. The King's mother, Queen Mary, was reputed to call this "a fine kettle of fish". History records that the King abdicated, Baldwin had his way and lived for many years after this consultation.

Until that time, Willie had been his chief's "blue-eyed boy", being given papers to write and other advantages of patronage, but these ended after their joint consultation, although Willie made little of this change of attitude in his autobiography. Willie Evans was a great charmer and conservative, even decrying warfarin, the commonly used anti-clotting agent, as a "rat poison", which had previously been one of its uses. For those patients who had cardiac surgery and were convalescing at Maids Moreton, Willie would ask not the expected "are you feeling better?" but "are you feeling worse?"

Visiting the National Heart Hospital in London once weekly gave me the opportunity to attend teaching outpatient clinics. Willie Evans was surprised how little cardiology had been taught me, but another consultant was impressed when he learned from me that the sex of a new baby could be guessed by the foetal heart rate. The most eminent cardiologist at the hospital was Dr Paul Wood, an antipodean who was sometimes called the "Father of British Cardiology"; he had forceful views and disconcerted me when he criticised (or more accurately "told off") those below him, one of whom, already respected, was seen blushing under this invective. Paul Wood had been RMO at this hospital and was later appointed full physician in 1937; he died at the age of 55 but the "junior" he told off was "going strong" many years later. On one occasion, returning from London with the House Governor of the hospital, who lived in Maids Moreton, one of the patients, a young girl with congenital heart disease, had in my absence "gone bad", developing a swollen abdomen due to accumulating fluid; she could have died if the pressure from this had not been relieved by simply draining the abdominal fluid, which was done immediately upon my arrival. She fully recovered but my explanations for late arrival were brushed aside and not forgiven for some time. Much later, one patient asked to be discharged but after explaining that she needed daily examination for a further period and refusing her request, she replied "I was only trying to see how tough you were".

General Practice

Having twice failed the exam for the MRCP, it was important to take time off hospital work in order to study daily for a third, and possibly final, attempt. Signing on at the local labour exchange, clearly not a common practice for a member of the medical profession, the interviewer questioned why I was not in employment. The quite truthful answer was that close examination of the advertisement columns in the weekly *British Medical Journal* was necessary while awaiting a suitable appointment to further my ambition of specialising. This answer was accepted but left me with a feeling of guilt at not having gainful employment, and persuaded me to take three temporary locum appointments in general practice, with the added excuse that it is wise for a specialist to have experience in this field, since nearly all his future work would be based on referrals from family doctors.

My first GP experience was in the charming village of Thaxted, Essex where the doctor had fallen ill and needed a *locum* until his recovery. One necessity for this job was the ability to drive the doctor's car for visits to patients in outlying villages. The GP's wife taught me the essentials on their "old banger" and my driving test was in Colchester in 1953, where the examiner passed me, perhaps on discovering my job and the importance of driving to visit sick patients. Staying in the doctor's house as he steadily improved, and looked after by his attentive wife for only a few weeks, we all remained good friends for many years. In a nearby village, another GP was fatally ill and his wife was keen for me to take over her husband's practice; she had come to know about me from a patient with gonorrhoea, the only such case I ever treated, who was rapidly cured by penicillin injections and was so grateful he thrust a ten-pound note into my pocket, in spite of my insistence that his treatment was all part of the National Health Service.

My next locum was in Great Yarmouth, Norfolk where the GP was going on honeymoon for two weeks. Sleeping and eating in the local hotel, chiefly used by travelling salesmen, the one exception was a pretty young woman selling beauty products; my suggestion to the waiter to ask her to join me for coffee and brandy after dinner was accepted and she immediately asked me what sort of doctor I was; on receiving the answer a "Doctor of Divinity", she gasped exclaiming "Oh, my God", to which my reply was that this was not the usual thing to say to a Doctor of Divinity; we both had a good laugh on her learning the truth.

The third and final GP locum was in Dover, where the Royal Cinque Ports Yacht Club granted me honorary membership for the short period of my stay. It was the time of the Calais-Dover Yacht race and, while at the bar, a lady, obviously English, asked me if I spoke her language, to which my reply was *"Je ne parle pas anglais"*; the rest of the conversation was conducted in Pidgin English but, on later hearing the reason for my being in Dover, she forgave me. Another young woman was not impressed with my being a locum GP but, when she later learned I had become a registrar at a London teaching hospital, repeatedly telephoned my place of work, but I was never available. These experiences, as well as being enjoyable, stood me in good stead and a GP's expertise to know something about everything never ceased to surprise me, as opposed to a specialist's knowledge of knowing everything about something.

Royal Free Hospital, 1953-54
My next appointment was as Senior House Officer to the Department of Rheumatology at the Royal Free Hospital, clearly a step-up as it was my first at a London teaching hospital. My previous experience with Dr

Dudley Hart at St Stephen's Hospital, one of whose interests was rheumatology, may well have helped my being accepted for this post. The Royal Free Hospital included the London School of Medicine for Women so that all the students, and many of my colleagues there, were women. At that time, the majority of London medical schools did not take women students but this changed about 1950 and by 2011 there were more women doctors qualifying in the UK than men. My duties in this department were to "clerk" (take histories and examine) patients admitted to the rheumatology wards. Rounds for those taking the Membership were often a regular feature in teaching hospitals and, although preparing for the MRCP, for some unknown reason, my senior registrar was not keen on my attending these teaching rounds. The rheumatology wards were housed in Lawn Road, Hampstead although the main hospital was in Chancery Lane, Holborn necessitating driving between the two. This was the cause of my first traffic violation of not stopping at a zebra crossing where a mother and child had not yet reached the central island. Asked by the magistrate my distance from the island when seeing this couple: "Was it the length of this courtroom?", my careful study of the courtroom and reply that it was about the same, resulted in a fine of ten shillings, the magistrate clearly taking a benign view, possibly because of my profession and relative youth.

One of the common disorders in this department was when the spine was inflamed and could become stiff and fixed. Having seen a family with three sisters, a brother and an uncle all with the same symptoms it seemed that this could be a familial condition, so we published a paper in the *British Medical Journal;* although known before, it was still a matter of controversy, but the causative gene is now recognised. During my first six months as Senior House Physician, it initially seemed that rheumatology concerned only a limited number of diseases, the diagnosis and treatment of which were soon learned, but this was far from the case. After six months, my consultant chief asked me to stay for a further year as Research Registrar to his Department of Rheumatology. This job entailed examining fluid from knee joints with a technique known as paper electrophoresis (soaking strips in fluids removed from joints, through which an electric current was then passed), a technique soon outmoded when no progress was made. Another project was to measure the temperature of arthritic knees before and after injection of local anaesthetic. Osteo-arthritis, although ending in "itis" and therefore suggesting inflammation, was not considered as such, since it differs from rheumatoid arthritis by affecting weight-bearing joints such as knees and hips, rather than small joints of the hands and feet; we found that giving an injection around the joint did lower its temperature, a finding later published. My predecessor as rheumatological research registrar gave up clinical medicine and eventually became a director of the Wellcome Institute for the History of Medicine.

The Royal Free Hospital gave travelling awards to young doctors to visit specialist centres abroad and I was given one to attend rheumatological centres in Spain (my non-supportive senior registrar wondered why I had not chosen the Balearic Islands) as I had met the senior Spanish rheumatologist, Professor Barcelo Batalla of Barcelona, when working with Dr Dudley Hart. Travelling to Spain in my first new car, a Ford Anglia, my driving companion was Dr Gerry Keen, a member of the Eighteen Club (the eighteen graduates who had qualified with me). Travelling through France we explored northern Spain, where we found lobsters just as expensive as elsewhere. On the way to Andalusia, he was driving westwards with the sun in his eyes and crashed into a lorry; we asked a local for the "Policia" and were told that *he* was the police; we immediately realised our best plan was to go to the local garage and remain in this out-of-the way village until repairs were completed. After this, Gerry returned home while I drove on to Barcelona.

The commonest disorder seen in the rheumatology department was rheumatoid arthritis which is three times commoner in women, who have inflammation of mostly the small joints of the hands and feet. Although various medications like gold injections had been tried, the first effective therapy was corticosterone (steroids) which were anti-inflammatory and became available in the early 1950s. Like most drugs, they could have side effects which, in this case, were increase of weight due partly to fluid retention, a moon-shaped face, diabetes and high blood pressure. During my work at the Royal Free, there were three deaths of patients on steroid treatment, where post-mortem examination revealed that all had died from unrecognised pneumonia, the symptoms and signs of which had been masked by the steroid therapy. This resulted in my lecture at the "Third International Congress of Chest Disorders" in Barcelona speaking on unrecognised pneumonia with steroid treatment, and led to publication. This was my first time speaking at an international conference and, when the American chairman of my session congratulated me, his praise proved to be an excuse for a later propensity to give many further papers at meetings round the world. In Barcelona, the unmarried Professor Batalla invited me to dinner at his home where his only other guest was an elderly mother who, on hearing me speak English, could only declaim that it was always foggy in England (she spoke no other English).

The combination of rheumatoid arthritis with a skin condition was known as *Psoriasis arthropathica* but, having seen a combination of this skin condition with spinal arthritis, I gave this condition a new name, calling it *Psoriasis Spondylitica.* Accepted by the *Lancet*, the prestigious medical journal, it was difficult for me to resist the subheading of *"Occam's razor"* which meant that "entities should not be gratuitously multiplied"; *William of Occam, (d.c1349)* wrote this in Latin: *Essentia non sunt multiplicunda praetor necessitatum*, a language not taught to me at school (as this subject had been dropped during evacuation in the Second World War). Occam's razor taught students the principle of a single cause for putting as many symptoms and signs of a patient together in just one diagnosis. William of Occam (also spelt Ockham) was a Franciscan monk who had studied theology at Oxford and Paris; his Latin phrase has also been given as *"Numquam ponenda est pluralities sine necessitatax"* which has been translated as "Plurality ought never be posed without necessity".

At this time there was an appeal for translations into English of French medical journals, which helped my knowledge of the French language, but one of these was a long article from Lyons on "viper wine". Although the translation pay was very poor, a slight reward came years later when the occasion arose for me to write a letter to the *Lancet* about "viper wine", giving a reference to the *Journal Lyonnais de Medicine.* One colleague was so impressed he congratulated me, perhaps thinking this journal was part of my regular reading.

Teaching hospitals are often used for higher examinations such as the MRCP and the Royal Free was no exception. Medical registrars had the privilege of helping visiting examiners choose suitable patients, and then could listen to the examiners' questions; this gave me insight as to why the majority of candidates failed – it was their own fault. Since these candidates were people who could one day be consultant physicians, for which the Membership was the first hurdle, they had to *look* like future specialists: for example, one examiner took exception to a candidate wearing a jumper for his "clinicals", that part where the candidate examines the patients. Another mistake was to blurt out a simple "yes" or "no" rather than to say, "if such and such were present then such and such should be considered"; these considerations, after all, are what happens in later consultations. Whether or not these points, learned assisting at the examinations, were the reason, my next attempt at the Membership was successful, even though my knowledge of medicine may not have been more than on the previous two occasions.

On achieving the Membership, an Australian colleague accused me of being "a dark horse". As a bachelor, it was almost inevitable that all my girlfriends worked in hospitals, either as doctors, nurses or students so that it was not surprising that a relationship developed with a female registrar, who was successful at the MRCP at the same time as me. When she invited me to meet her family, I took fright, particularly as I had no intention of "settling down", being intent on furthering my career, the end point of which was uncertain, and the relationship ended in tears.

Chapter 5

BECOMING A SPECIALIST

Having worked in general medicine for several years, including teaching students and doing research, the appointment I wanted most was at my own teaching hospital, where Dr Swithin Meadows was the neurologist. Having succeeded in this ambition, I regarded him as my mentor and paid less attention to the other chief on this firm, who was a gastro-enterologist. As his registrar, Meadows once asked me to repeatedly examine the visual fields of a patient whose eyesight was difficult to understand; doing this with great interest, at each ward round I demonstrated to him how the vision had changed, which challenged us both since we could not find any satisfactory explanation. With Meadows as consultant, Walter van t'Hoff as senior registrar, and myself as registrar, the firm was a very friendly group. After outpatient clinics, the three of us would lunch together in the Medical School refectory, usually later than other colleagues because our work took longer. At the end of the meal I, as the junior, would buy the coffee; occasionally the chief would take all three of us to the pub behind the hospital for lunch.

The chief would investigate new patients whilst the registrars would observe the follow-up appointments. One patient I saw had been diagnosed as a stroke affecting the brain-stem, which particularly bothered me as the defect in eye movements fitted more with the rare condition of myasthenia. Bringing this to the attention of Walter, the senior registrar, he agreed that we should ask Meadows for his opinion; he accepted my diagnosis and a test cured the squint, and proving our view to be correct. It was not long after this that the chief asked me to be his clinical assistant at the National Hospital in Queen Square (NHQS), where he was also one of the consultant neurologists. Readily accepting this invitation meant going every Wednesday to clerk a new patient in a separate room at the National Hospital, after which he would hear my history and findings on examination leading to the differential diagnosis (this was before modern diagnostic machines were invented).

One of Meadows' clinical interests was in tumours of the pituitary gland and a patient with this diagnosis occupying one of his beds at Westminster Hospital was Percy Wyndham Lewis (1882-1957), a British artist born in Canada and a co-founder of the Vorticist movement of art – the name given by Ezra Pound, the American poet, and intended to show it as the vortex of modernity. After Wyndham Lewis died, I attended his post-mortem examination which revealed that his tumour was not the typical pituitary one, but was derived from congenital tissue. Becoming interested in this rare manifestation, I collected a large number of these cases from London teaching hospitals; I worked out that the only institute with a larger number was in Moscow.

After a year, the senior registrar, Walter, went to the United States for a twelve month period and the chief asked me to do his job as locum senior registrar whilst he was studying abroad. Explaining to our new junior registrar the tradition of the youngest on our firm paying for the coffee after lunch, he refused to accept this arrangement so we shared the cost – not a significant sum in the early 1950s, but he was married and I was not. As senior registrar, even in a locum capacity, one privilege was to sit at the consultants' table in the refectory; there was excitement when a new Consultant in Obstetrics, Roger de Vere, took his place in 1954; fifty years later we were to be neighbours in our retirement in Wiltshire. During Walter's absence, my chief asked whether I would like to be "on the House" at the National Hospital, which meant being a full-time registrar rotating service to all the eminent consultants on the staff. This had been my ambition but when the first vacancy was advertised, my chief advised me not to apply as this position had already been earmarked for a New Zealand candidate.

At the National Hospital there were five members of the House Staff who mostly came from abroad, namely Dick Hornabrook from New Zealand, Dick Rischbeith from Melbourne and, also from Australia, Peter Ebling, who was the RMO; originally from Wales was P K Thomas. They all became successful neurologists. When the next post was advertised, the chief told me to apply; although called a house physician, it was more highly paid as a registrar. Only one of the consultants wanted to interview me; he was 47 years of age, unmarried and we were not happy working together, not least because he always came to the hospital in the late evening and spent an exhausting time with his patients

.

My time at NHQS was very happy, not least because at the time it was a mecca for training neurologists from all over the world; in the years between the first and second World Wars, many American trainees came for further study. At the end of the nineteenth century (the hospital was founded in 1860) and the early twentieth century it acquired its superb and longstanding reputation. After two years "on the house" rotating with all the "firms", it was my turn to become the RMO (Resident Medical Officer) which meant being paid as a senior registrar. The RMO was a significant person since it used to be traditional for a consultant to ask permission if he wished to dine in the residents' mess.

House Staff.   Queen Square
~ October 1957 ~

Resident House Physicians, National Hospital Queen Square 1957

Every Christmas the RMO would dress up as Santa Claus and tour the hospital with the nurses, singing carols. During this time only the very seriously ill patients were kept in hospital and anyone well enough was allowed to spend the holiday at home with their families.

During this period, my cousin, who was the ballet correspondent of a national newspaper, invited me to the world première of a new ballet and, as it was a weekend, a fellow registrar agreed to stand in for me; it so happened that he became worried about one of the patients and rang my chief; on telephoning him the following morning to apologise for not having told him of my absence, he replied, "I do not expect my house physician to apologise; I expect him to ask my permission"; we were not the best of friends after that.

During my time as RMO, I proposed a wine club where diners could help themselves to wine, being on their honour to record this in the provided book; unfortunately, not everyone remembered so the club did not last long. Another of my ideas was to invite eminent neurologists to dine with us; the first was Sir Gordon Holmes, whom I went to meet at the train station in my small car as, by then, he had retired to the country. The next day I boasted to my fellow residents on the House Staff that I would not clean my car ever again. On another occasion, we had invited a well-known personality from the north of England, who told several splendid stories; known for his fondness for alcohol, he tended to "nod off" between tales.

At Christmas, the RMO would invite all members of the consultant staff with their spouses to a festive dinner. One consultant lived with his wife in the south of England where he would spend each weekend but, during the week he lived in a London flat with his mistress. Embarrassed about which one to invite, in the end all went well. Another well-known consultant, known for his acting ability when giving lectures, had a wife living in a nearby flat and an accommodating secretary in the hospital, but on this particular occasion his wife was unwell and not able to come.

After Queen Square, Dr Dennis Williams asked me to be his First Assistant (senior registrar) at St George's Hospital, where he was the senior neurologist; the junior consultant neurologist was Dr Patterson. Delighted to accept this invitation, particularly as the job was not advertised, a letter arrived from the Deputy Secretary of St George's Hospital confirming my duties as part-time First Assistant to the Department of Neurology at Atkinson Morley's Hospital, Wimbledon from 1 February 1960. The neuroscience departments of neurology, neurosurgery and psychiatry of St George's Hospital were located in Wimbledon, although out-patients were seen at the main hospital at Hyde Park Corner. At that time, about one fifth of all the acute neurosurgery in the UK was performed at Atkinson Morley's Hospital so, for example, patients who had a bleed in their brain were admitted on most days of every week, occasionally landing by helicopter from all over England. McKissock (later Sir Wylie) and his neurosurgical team performed trials to ascertain the best type of operation because, without surgery, approximately 50% of these patients died - a mortality rate substantially reduced by surgery; he asked me to be his research assistant to examine the survivors, comparing those with and without surgery. As my position lasted for about four years, this unique experience resulted in the publication of several scientific papers.

The junior consultant neurologist at St George's Hospital, Dr Hamilton Patterson, was also a consultant at NHQS. Born in China, he was the son of two medical missionaries and qualified as a doctor just before the Second World War, working with McKissock for eighteen months before being attached to the Military Hospital for Head Injuries at St Hugh's College, Oxford. After demobilisation in 1946 he went to UCH for one year with Dr (later Sir) Francis Walshe, and then to the NHQS as a consultant. He became assistant neurological physician at St George's in 1951 and, in his last five years of active work, was subdean at the National Hospital. Examining his in-patients thoroughly, his ward rounds lasted much longer than average; in 1962, at the age of 47, he developed cancer and died following a major operation. As senior registrar to the neurological department, it was thought that a possible candidate to succeed him would be me, especially because of support by some consultant members of the St George's Hospital staff. It was a great disappointment not to be chosen, and the successful candidate, a friend of mine whose father was a consultant anaesthetist, later proved to be more interested in writing novels than neurology, publishing many, but under a pseudonym.

University Of California, San Francisco, 1960
My Westminster Hospital mentor, Swithin Meadows, lived in Highgate, North London and when Robert Aird, Professor of Neurology at the University of California, San Francisco (UCSF) visited England, Meadows hosted a party for him at his home. Introduced to the honoured guest, we had a brief chat during which Professor Aird invited me to join his department as Visiting Assistant Professor for three months. Never having been to the United States, a visit to California, particularly San Francisco, was appealing to a young English doctor, giving me the BTA, spurious initials meaning "Been to America", which any young British doctor aspiring to specialise wanted to achieve, especially at a postgraduate research centre. In 1960, an Englishman could fly to America with an immigrant's visa for only £10.00, an opportunity not to be missed. Until World War II, neurosciences in San Francisco were relatively isolated, until California was "discovered" by many Easterners, including physicians. This "isolation" of the West Coast was not overcome until dependable transcontinental airline service became available in the early 1950's. Prior to this, an excellent train service was available, but the trip from coast to coast took 3½ days, so that, aside from any time spent on the West Coast, the round trip required a week. Relatively few neurologists came to the West Coast and, except for a handful of dedicated physicians, the journey east to attend meetings was not common. This isolation was not attractive for recruitment of the better, well-trained young men, who preferred the established, more populous centres of the East Coast, a situation that gradually changed, especially with the recruiting enthusiasm of Professor Aird, but it was not until the advent of jet aeroplanes during the 1960's that the medical isolation problem in the western States was fully overcome

.

On arriving for the first time at Professor Aird's office in San Francisco, he put his hand into his jacket pocket, which I thought was to extract a list of lectures for me to give to undergraduate medical students but, instead, he took out a map of southern California, informing me that on the following weekend we were going with his wife and son on a lecture tour in Southern California, ending at Yosemite Park. I was thrilled to have a preliminary grand tour and, unlike his wife and son, it would also be beneficial to attend his lectures, which were mainly concerned with epilepsy. "Bob" Aird told me that he was originally an American Easterner who had migrated to the West as one of its first neurosurgeons, but changed to neurology to become head of the department at UCSF. One of the reforms Aird instituted in San Francisco was to invite European, but particularly British, neurologists to work in his department; many were consultants from the NHQS which is how Aird knew Swithin Meadows. When I arrived in San Francisco there was already a British trained neurologist on Aird's team, Dr Macrae; he also took me with his family on a tour of other parts of California, telling me how he had made his name in San Francisco by achieving local newspaper headlines, because he had restored a long-term paralysed woman to health by prescribing a drug that benefited her rare condition of muscle weakness (myasthenia). During this sojourn in San Francisco, my mother, who was already terminally ill, died; my family did not immediately inform me as they did not think it necessary for me to return for the funeral.

Another member of UCSF's staff who befriended me was Franklin Keville, the Resident Neurosurgical Officer, who was in the training programme to become a fully qualified neurosurgeon. He told me that if a man had a "clean white shirt" in 1960 San Francisco was an open city and, as bachelors, we went to various social gatherings together; looking back, there was no better place for a first visit to the USA than San Francisco. What made matters even more interesting was that my accommodation was in the nurses' home on Mount Parnassus. Franklin liked a rather nice nurse (whose surname was Hollister, the same as a small town in the south of California, which had been "discovered" by one of her forebears) and he eventually married her. To fast-forward a year or two, when this couple started on a honeymoon tour of the world, their first port of call was London, where they stayed with me at my home in Finchley. As Franklin's surname was so unusual, he looked through the London telephone directory to see if any Keville's was listed; to his delight there was and, most conveniently, this person lived near Finchley, so that he went visiting. On his way back he must have been excited, with the result that he was involved in a nasty accident while driving his rental car and fractured his ribs resulting in a punctured lung around which air was accumulating. We admitted him to St George's Hospital at Hyde Park Corner, where I was currently working; he recovered well and stayed convalescing at my home for some time, but it was the end of their honeymoon world-tour.

Franklin was a high ranking officer in the US Naval Reserve and, for my leaving party from UCSF, he booked Treasure Island, the name given to the naval base in the Bay of San Francisco. Having bought a 1946 Chrysler for 35 dollars, my intention on departure was to drive and lecture across the United States but, when taking the car to a local garage and emphasising that it would not matter how far it went, the garage refused even to check it, pointing out that the car would not get over the Rockies nor cross the Salt Lake Desert. At the Treasure Island party, a map of my proposed route to the East was put on the wall and guests took bets on how far the car would go before breaking down. Suffice to say it had no handbrake except for a block of wood to put under the front wheel (very quickly) and it also used more oil than gas (petrol). Although I did not realize it at the time, the car was really a present from two UCSF ophthalmological colleagues and the 35 dollars I paid was for the licence. The car went like a "bomb" across the whole country; on arrival at each destination on my route, a postcard was sent to the relevant doomster who had bet that this particular site would be the end of my trip.

The drive took three weeks, lectures being given at neurological centres along my route, one of which was Salt Lake City, where Professor Leonard Jarcho was head of neurology. We first met when he was a postgraduate student at the National Hospital in London; he introduced me to his wife who was a lapsed Mormon. Leonard had asked one of his juniors to accommodate me; the thought of having to look after a "typical Englishman" appalled him, imagining the sort of character portrayed in Hollywood films. Reassured when we met, he was relieved his imposed guest was not at all what he had expected. Whilst staying in Salt Lake City, besides tourist visits to hear the famous Male Voice Choir and visit Smith's "This is the place" where the Mormons ended their travels, I visited Las Vegas and then the Grand Canyon on a 'milk-float' plane that landed in every small town on this triangular trip; fortunately, lectures were not required. When buying a stamp in one small town, my British accent resulted in an invitation to talk to the locals, an example of the typical friendliness of the average American. One relative of an American doctor colleague could not understand why a young Englishman would want to travel by himself across the States, but my only time of concern was driving across the Salt Lake Desert, when I gave a lift to a hitch-hiker, a soldier in uniform, on the grounds that in the event of a break-down any passing vehicle would be more likely to stop to rescue him than me. Suffice to say the soldier slept the whole way across the desert and the extra water bag tied to the front bumper was superfluous to needs.

Returning to England on a transatlantic Cunarder from Montreal, after lecturing at the Montreal Neurological Institute, necessitated crossing the border from the USA to Canada. Explaining my position to the American border guard, he told me that Canadians did not like second-hand American cars being dumped in their country and suggested that, since the car had been driven all across the States and cost me only $35, he would buy it from me for $25. Going to the nearest village, I sold the car for $60, after which a bus took me to Montreal. The Atlantic crossing was uneventful except that a man asked me to partner him in the ship's bridge competition. We were playing two Americans, one of whom asked my partner, whose surname was Montgomery "Mr Montgomery, are you named after Field-Marshal Viscount Montgomery?" to which he replied "No sir, he was named after me; I am his elder brother", which was true – he was a farmer in Canada. The point of this story is that we won the competition so that, in those days, my bridge play could not have been too bad.

Perhaps as a result of a game we played making speeches, whilst on a motoring holiday in France, Spain and Portugal, Harold Ellis asked me to be his best man at his wedding in 1958. On the back of a wedding photo I still have, his wife, Wendy, wrote "... we particularly liked this express picture" but I am not sure what she meant by this.

Best Man at wedding of Harold and Wendy Ellis, 1958

Hôpital de la Salpêtrière, Paris, 1961

In 1961 Anglo-French Exchange Bursaries were supported by the Ciba Foundation and funded by the pharmaceutical company of the same name. The only requirement for a university graduate was a working knowledge of French; in applying to study at the Hôpital de la Salpêtrière in Paris, my thought was of Charcot who had worked there as the first professor of neurology in the world. The hospital's name, meaning saltpeter, was derived from originally being an arms factory but, by the time Charcot was appointed in the nineteenth century, it housed literally thousands of people, mainly beggars, prostitutes, ex-soldiers and sick people. He classified many of their disorders and set up laboratories and photographers to found, at that time, the best scientific establishment for neurology in the world. Sigmund Freud had been a pupil of his, starting his career as a neurologist by writing an excellent book on speech disorders, before switching to hypnosis and hysteria and founding the subject of psycho-analysis. While working there, I attended lectures by the Head of the department of neurology, Professor Garcin. My knowledge of the French language also improved by attending classes at the Alliance Française, so that I could take a patient's history in French. This was just after the Algerian conflict when French nationalists planted plastic bombs in Paris, a truly challenging time. Having taken my own car to Paris, it gave me the opportunity to visit the local tourist sites, spoiled on one occasion by a car accident near the Madeleine cathedral; the other (French) driver eventually forgave me.

The teaching hospitals in Paris have their own traditions, one of which I was honoured to attend; this was lunch for junior doctors in *La Salle de Garde,* a tradition that started in the 1850s and was in the style of *la Belle Epoque*. When I attended, it was male-oriented with pornographic murals. Resident doctors, mainly housemen and registrars, arrived after 12.30 p.m, greeting those present with a tap on the shoulder and lunch started at 1 p.m; white coats were worn and discussions encouraged but not on medical topics. Much alcohol was consumed and the sacred lunchtime of France preserved with coffee being served well after 2.00 p.m.

Although fortunate to have had post-graduate training in both San Francisco and Paris, at least one of my London chiefs was none too pleased with my absences abroad. In 1960, because my job at St George's Hospital included reporting on patients' brain-waves, my joining the Electroencephalography (EEG) Society and the International League Against Epilepsy was inevitable. From 28 August to 2 September 1961, going to the first Advanced Course in Electroencephalography (the study of electrical brain-waves) held in Marseilles, France, I received a certificate signed by Professor Henri Gastaut, an expert in epilepsy. This meeting preceded my car drive to the 1961 World Congress of Neurology in Rome; driving from Marseilles, I was flattered to give a lift to the Professor of Neurology from Glasgow, Iain Simpson. There had been an advertisement in the *Sunday Times* of a 'bed-and-breakfast' in the outskirts of Rome and, on arrival there, the owner turned out to be an

Englishwoman in her late thirties who had come to Italy to convalesce following an illness and operation. She later confided that she was uncertain about providing me with 'bed and breakfast' until, during our initial conversation, I said "not to worry", which familiar phrase reassured her. She had inherited money from her family and we became friendly to the extent that one evening on my return from Congress activities, she called me after I had going to bed, but I pretended to be asleep. The next day I moved to a smart hotel near the Spanish Steps to meet my regular girlfriend, a clergyman's daughter, who was a therapist at St George's Hospital.

For a neurological specialist, there are two main pathways to follow, either to become a full-time academic ending as a professor and to work in laboratories, or to maintain contact with patients and become a clinical neurologist; the second choice is financially advantageous if one also does private practice. I took the first option when one of my chiefs suggested I apply for a Rockefeller Fellowship. If successful, this would mean a year or longer in an American postgraduate centre, possibly becoming a full-time academic on my return to the UK. Before the interview, going on a skiing holiday, my return flight was unable to land at Heathrow Airport due to fog which meant spending the night in Paris, missing the interview for the Rockefeller Fellowship. To my surprise the two distinguished interviewers came to NHQS to conduct this all-important meeting. The outcome was unsuccessful, possibly because the Centre my chief recommended was where one of his students was the Director and did not meet with the approval of my interviewers.

After San Francisco, a second invitation to the USA came in 1963, from the University of Rochester in New York State, which was looking for someone to head their department of neurology. Although said at that time to be one of the top ten universities in the United States, my short visit of two weeks did not encourage me to emigrate to Rochester. As on my previous visit to California, my travels to the States had been on an immigrant's visa, with its financial advantage. The town of Rochester was recognised for the Eastman Kodak company which had been generous in its support of the university and to a centre for music; the town was near the Canadian border so a visit to the Niagara Falls was obligatory, but without passport, the visit was restricted to the southern (American) side of the Falls.   I was surprised not to be met on my arrival, at Rochester airport, since a potential head of the neurological department would customarily have been met by the assistant professor. However, during the course of my stay, it emerged that the assistant professor, Dr Forbes Norris, was himself a candidate hoping to get this top appointment and was not keen on an English neurologist being invited to look at the centre. During my stay, we came to know each other well, so that he learned of my lack of interest in Rochester and that, if successful, it would be only temporary as my eventual aim would be to live and work on the West Coast. The final result was that I did not apply for the position, neither did Forbes Norris, who settled in San Francisco, where he worked for the rest of his life. Rochester's search for a head to its neurology department was not successful until some years later, when it appointed an excellent American neurologist.

Royal Eye Medical Ophthalmology Unit, 1963

Not all eye disorders are treated with surgery and the Professor of Ophthalmology at the Royal College of Surgeons wished to create a Royal Eye Medical Ophthalmology Unit at the Royal Eye Hospital; this meant appointing physicians to deal with medical disorders and teach ophthalmic postgraduate students who wished to learn about non-surgical conditions of the eye. The beds for patients admitted to the Unit in 1963 were at Lambeth Hospital and, although my application was successful, this was for only two sessions a week, a session being a morning or afternoon, so that most of my work was still at St George's Hospital. The brainchild of Professor Arnold Sorsby, these consultant appointments were for three part-time physicians in different disciplines: one for immunology (Dr Geraint James), another for vascular diseases and the third for neurological diseases. At the Appointments Committee for this latter post, one of the interviewers was very keen to promote another candidate, who had worked for him at Maida Vale Hospital and he questioned me aggressively on my neurological experience. Possibly because of my four years' work as Meadows' clinical assistant at Moorfields Eye Hospital, the job as consultant neurologist went to me; the three physicians met regularly each week to discuss various medical problems of the eye.

There was no lack of problematic cases at the Medical Ophthalmology Unit, and on one occasion reading a paper on visual problems of diabetes at the RSM, one "eye man" was overheard complaining that my talk was too difficult, but it was nevertheless published. There was also a need for a locum consultant neurologist for one session per week at the Royal Eye Hospital, enabling me to observe many referrals of inflammation of the optic nerve. As steroids were claimed to be effective for its amelioration, we undertook an early clinical trial using one of these substances, which showed that, although they helped initially, there was little difference in the final result. We undertook a deeper study of diabetes and optic atrophy in juveniles; to obtain a wide coverage of this study, my ophthalmological colleague came with me to the National College of the Blind in Hereford to obtain further experience but our series of patients, which again was published, were limited to seven cases. This college later became the Royal National College and for many years Angela attended a week's summer course for piano players there, occasionally with me as an observer.

The Founder of British Neurology, Hughlings Jackson, was one of the first to use an ophthalmoscope, the instrument to view the back of the eye where, besides the retina, arteries, veins and the head of the optic nerve (which is part of the nervous system) could be seen, so much so that my students were taught that more diagnoses could be made with an ophthalmoscope than a stethoscope. Hughlings Jackson always used this instrument when examining patients, which became routine until rendered no longer necessary with the advent of modern techniques. About this time I was a founder member of the Eye Physic Club, where medical, as opposed to surgical, disorders of the eye were discussed informally. Working as a consultant neurologist to the Royal Eye Hospital,

I joined the Ophthalmological Society of the United Kingdom in 1964, serving on its Council, and remained a member until 1985.

In May 1962, I met David Cohen at a dry-skiing class in Chelsea Town Hall. Following one class, we went to the New Assam restaurant opposite the Chelsea Town Hall, and my new-found friend was impressed when we ended up dining with two young ladies who, unbeknown to him, were nurses at the hospital where I was currently working. Being bachelors, we went on skiing holidays together; on one train journey, he told me he wanted to be a doctor; at the time he was working in property development and, although financially very successful, this did not satisfy him. Pointing out he was 27 years of age and that it would take the best part of seven years before he could practice medicine, in spite of my discouragement, it was clear he had made up his mind. There was some opposition by one or two Deans of the London medical schools where he applied for admission because they objected to the fact that he already had a university degree from Oxford, albeit in languages; he was eventually accepted by Westminster Hospital Medical School where he qualified and then enjoyed many years in general practice.

Although years younger than me, David was married to Veronica, and knew that, at the age of 35, I was ready to "settle down". They had told me all about Veronica's cousin, Angela, who was away on a year's trip to Australia and New Zealand. Several months later, in May 1963, they invited me to a party – just one day after my return from Rochester, New York. In spite of my jet lag, I went to the party, where I met the mystery cousin who had recently returned from her travels; we chatted at the party and David gave me her telephone number! Telephoning her the next day, she was not sure who was calling but accepted my invitation to dinner that evening at the Pheasantry in Chelsea. Having been friendly with several girls at that time, the following week was spent in "extricating" myself. Two weeks later, on our way to a Hampstead pub to meet my friends, Mike and Brenda a'Brook, he being a handsome psychiatrist-to-be who had been engaged seven times, Angela told me she was planning a holiday with her best friend, Val. I said she did not know what might happen by the summer – she says my comment was "we may be on honeymoon then". To cut a longer story, we became engaged within two weeks of meeting and married within four months.

Our wedding on 16 Sept 1963

We did our courting (from May on meeting, to the September wedding) around Rivermead Court, where she lived, and Hurlingham Club where her father took me to watch the cricket. Because my parents were dead, my older brother, Sid and his wife, Terry stood in at my wedding. Val Besser, who later became a Judge, was our Maid of Honour and Angela was dressed in the traditional bride's white with me in morning dress; Angela remembers me walking down the aisle very quickly after the ceremony – almost running, she says! The two little bridesmaids were her god-daughter, Emma, who was the daughter of her close friend Sheila Gampell, and Caroline Moss, the daughter of a close family friend, and the small pageboy was the son of Seymour Robinson, a dentist who was a member, like me, of the Westminster Hospital Masonic Lodge (he said I was the best after-dinner speaker he had heard). The wedding reception was held at the Cumberland Hotel, owned by J Lyons and Co , the family business of the Salmons and Glucksteins; Angela's mother, being a daughter of a Gluckstein; "Uncle Norman" did the catering for Buckingham Palace garden parties, and he organized the whole wedding reception. He also arranged our wedding night at the Ariel Hotel at Heathrow airport, also owned by J Lyons, where they insisted we had dinner *à deux* in our suite; Angela remembers forgetting to bring her suitcase which had to be brought post-haste to the hotel.

The plane journey to our honeymoon hotel in Tenerife was very bumpy; arriving late at night and we did not realize we had to adjust our watches. The next day or two we could not understand why we were the first in the dining room for dinner, until finally told of the time change. From Tenerife, we went to Gran Canaria. At our hotel, Angela was using her travel iron in our bedroom when all the lights went out; they came back on again after a couple of minutes and she resumed ironing – and the lights went again: after that we discarded the iron! On the way home we had a stop-over in Madrid where Angela had a stomach upset and was advised to eat only yoghurt.

My niece, Maureen, had a baby in the autumn of 1963, having married some time previously; this news upset Angela who was in tears on my arrival home, because she now had a niece with a baby and yet no children of her own. On telling this story, it was completed by my saying "She demanded instant impregnation", which may not be quite true but she was delivered of her first baby – Sebastian – on 29 August 1964 on my birthday (we were married in September 1963). She had the baby at St George's Hospital which, at that time, had its obstetric unit at Hyde Park Corner (now the Lansdowne Hotel) but without me, as the practice of having the father present at birth only became popular some years later. Angela was pregnant for the second time a year later but this did not stop us having a skiing holiday in St Moritz; although pregnancy prevented her from skiing, as well as having a 16 month-old baby in tow, and she was never really keen having fractured a leg at this sport years before we met. Jolyon was born two months later in March 1966, this time at the new St George's Hospital in Tooting, and Fabian completed our family in March 1968, also born at St. George's Tooting.

At the time of our marriage, Angela was living with her parents in West London, overlooking the River Thames. Born in London, her family moved to various places during the war, the family finally settling in Roehampton, "South of the River", where she grew up. The River Thames divides Londoners, to the extent that if one comes from either north or south of the river, the former regard the latter as "barbarians" and vice-versa. After marrying in 1963, for the first two years we lived in the house in Finchley, North London left to me by my mother; my work was mostly south of the river, so there was a good deal of driving six days a week. We therefore decided to move south of the Thames and bought a house in New Malden, Surrey where we stayed for four years until Angela discovered a new development of spacious, modern houses being built nearby. After viewing the show house, we bought a plot and then watched the house taking shape from the very first hole in the ground. As the garden was on two levels, my ambition to have a wine cellar was realised when it was built under the upper level with the entrance just opposite my study, which seemed appropriate. We later added a swimming pool, which my bank manager advised could be used for rehabilitation in my medical practice, apparently an advantage from the point of view of a bank loan.   The house cost £27,000 when we bought it in 1969, most of which was borrowed on a twenty-year loan; a colleague in the insurance industry having secured a fixed interest rate of 8%, which proved fortunate as rates more than doubled during subsequent years. After living in this house for over twenty years, where our three sons grew up, we sold it for nearly twenty times the price we paid; it was not far from Charing Cross Hospital, my place of work before retiring from the NHS in 1991. While working there, I also practiced privately at the New Victoria Hospital, a small private hospital nearby, having succeeded Lord Brain as its neurologist.

Moor House and John Horniman Schools
 In 1965, there were two residential schools in the UK for children with speech disorders, the larger being Moor House School at Oxted, Surrey. Its consulting neurologist, Worster-Drought, was above retirement age and the Chairman of the Board of Governors was keen to replace him. On

the recommendation of Dr Denis Williams, my chief at St George's, I was appointed in spite of the opposition of another honorary member of the Moor House staff, a plastic surgeon whose wife was a film actress I met when he invited me to his Harley Street consulting rooms to dissuade me from taking the job, which my previous acceptance made difficult. The appointment entailed going to Oxted every Friday afternoon after applicants for admission to the school had been tested during the preceding week by speech therapists, a psychologist and teachers; my work was to review their reports, examine the child and to report on the suitability for residential treatment. There were several classes in the school, which took children from the age of nine years to sixteen, but the class which interested me most was for those with a language disorder (*dysphasia*) where there was a failure of comprehension and execution of words. In studying these cases, it seemed they fell into two groups, those who were born with the disorder and those who developed it during life following an illness, often associated with epileptic attacks. These results were presented to a congress in New York in a session where the French chairman introduced me in his mother tongue; I started my talk with the sentence "*Je regrette je ne parle pas francais*" to general laughter, and continued in English. The junior residential school for speech disorders was John Horniman, in Worthing, Surrey which accepted younger children from the age of six to nine years and which I visited every three months; the teachers there were equally dedicated and some of their children went on to Moor House School.

Chapter 6

CONSULTANCIES

Charing Cross Hospital, which had been a familiar landmark opposite Charing Cross Railway Station in the Strand, started as an idealistic dream of a medical student, who conceived the idea during the famous Hundred Days between Napoleon's flight from Elba and his defeat at Waterloo. In 1815, this young student, Benjamin Golding opened a surgery at his house off Leicester Square, and for five hours a day gave free treatment to all in the surrounding slums. For 150 years, the area of Charing Cross had been the market place between the cities of Westminster and London, with consequent quarrels and fights which led Samuel Johnson to write "… the full tide of existence is at Charing Cross". Golding persuaded two doctors to join him in his house, which was next to the stage door of the Haymarket Theatre, where they formed what was originally called the West London Infirmary and Dispensary. In 1818 its name was changed to Charing Cross Hospital, with the medical school being recognised by London University. As the number of patients increased, a new Charing Cross Hospital was built in 1831 and its medical school taught T H Huxley and David Livingstone, the famous explorer, amongst many others; it was at this hospital that the first operation for appendicitis was performed.

After completing my neurological training in the early 60's, the only job that would satisfy my ambition was to become a consultant neurologist at a London teaching hospital, which was finally realised in 1965 when I was appointed to Charing Cross Hospital and its Group, which included the West London and Fulham Hospitals. This position was not considered ideal because there was no department of neurology with adequate facilities for neurosciences such as neurosurgery or neuroradiology. Previous holders of the post had usually been on the consultant staff of neurological hospitals like the National Hospital, Maida Vale or the West End Hospital for Nervous Diseases, where specialist investigations could be done; the last holder of the Charing Cross post had emigrated to Philadelphia, where excellent facilities were provided, to become professor of neurology. Short-listing for a consultant post involved being interviewed by those members of the hospital staff interested in seeing candidates in order to decide and vote for their preferred choice. The favoured candidate for this 1965 consultant appointment was supported by the professor of neurology at the National Hospital, who was reputed to have previously taken the senior Charing Cross neurologist out to dinner. The final Appointments Committee consisted, as always, of seven specialists, who were well aware of the wishes of the hospital's consultant staff; the two most concerned were on the staff of Charing Cross Hospital, namely the senior neurologist, Dr Gerald Parsons-Smith, and the neurosurgeon, Mr Leslie Oliver, the latter having been appointed to advise on relevant neurosurgical cases but *not* to operate at the hospital, or so he had been told by the senior physician. By sheer coincidence, Leslie had come to know me because he was also the consultant neurosurgeon at the Royal Northern Hospital, which had a large private (St David's) wing where patients were seen by me at the request of a colleague, Dr Geraint (Gerry) James, who was also the Dean at the Royal Northern Hospital and ran post-graduate courses; Gerry had become my colleague when we were both appointed at the same time, in 1963, to the Royal Eye Medical Ophthalmology Unit. Since that time, he would ask me to see those private patients at the Royal Northern needing a neurological opinion, any of whom might require neurosurgery, which I then referred to Leslie Oliver.   As one of the seven assessors on the Appointments Committee, Leslie proved to be an important supporter because, wanting an active experienced neurologist, he put a good case for my appointment. The happy result of my success was published on page 54 of the *Lancet* of 11 September 1965 under *Appointments*, where it was announced that "Doctor F C Rose was consultant neurological physician to the Charing Cross Hospital group".

Leslie became a great friend and we regularly lunched out together. When he died at the age of 82 years, I was asked to write his obituary for one of the national daily newspapers. Although it is customary to conclude obituaries with a short reference to close relatives of the deceased, this latter proved difficult: Leslie had first married an Irish nurse by whom he had a son. Divorced from her, his second wife was French and they had a daughter and a son, but he had been separated from her for some years and was living with a woman whom he first met at the West End Hospital for Nervous Diseases, where he held the post of consultant neurosurgeon and she was a laboratory assistant. Since I omitted to comment on his family, the editor of the obituary column telephoned to ask the reason; having briefly explained my concerns, the editor agreed with my decision and the obituary was published without amendment. My arrangement for a memorial service to Leslie in the chapel of the new Charing Cross Hospital was followed by lunch at the Hurlingham Club, where Leslie had been a member; several of his family and friends were in the party, including the son of his first marriage, his second wife and the ex-laboratory assistant; although they all spoke to each other, the conversation was, understandably, somewhat reserved.

Following my Charing Cross appointment, the senior neurologist suggested that we divide the neurological services in the three main hospitals of the group, so that he would work at Charing Cross Hospital itself (300+ beds), whereas my work would be at West London Hospital (300 beds) and Fulham Hospital (600 beds), a division of duties which was readily agreed. The result of this arrangement was that my consultancies for the NHS would be seven sessions at West London and Fulham Hospitals and two sessions at the Royal Eye Medical Ophthalmology Unit, giving me a maximum part-time NHS contract; the two remaining sessions could be spent seeing private patients at 10 Harley Street, where the rent for a consulting room was one pound ten shillings per session (in 1965). One of my chiefs had told me it took him five years to pay his private expenses; the situation had changed dramatically since then, and it took me only five weeks..

Although there were twelve teaching hospitals in the University of London, the West London Hospital, founded in 1856, used to be a thirteenth and also admitted female medical students, as did only one other London teaching institution, the Royal Free Hospital. For this reason, the West London had a distinguished consultant staff who did not feel inferior to their colleagues at Charing Cross Hospital, although this opinion was not reciprocated. In fact, these two groups of consultants were hardly on speaking terms, an antipathy that lasted until the last member of the West London consultant staff retired; this form of relationship was not unknown among other hospital groups where there had been compulsory "mergers". For a time, I was asked to act as locum consultant neurologist at St Mary Abbots Hospital which had been a Kensington workhouse and was founded in the late nineteenth century; the general physician there did not think much of neurologists and never referred any patients to me, but this did not prevent him from consulting me for his own illness.

The West London Medico-Chirurgical Society

Soon after being my Consultant appointment in 1965, I joined the West London Medico-Chirurgical Society and was its Secretary in 1969 and 1970 and its President in 1976 and 1977, when my Presidential Address was on "Medicine and Art", since the audience included many non-medical people. This Society was founded in 1882 and it was claimed that it made "the most important attempts at postgraduate education in the nineteenth century"; publishing its first proceedings in 1884, these became The West London Medical Journal in 1896. Louis Pasteur was elected the first honorary member of the Society, but it is doubtful that he ever attended, although Lord Lister used to come from Scotland for its meetings. In 1883, Dr Thudichum, the founder of neurochemistry, gave his Presidential Address on "The Life and Labours of Henry Cavendish", the great physician who lived nearby; later that year the Cavendish Lecture was inaugurated to be given annually, on one occasion by (later Sir) William Osler. In its prime, the Society had 600 members and was, for twenty years, the largest medical society in London; in 1906, the Society decided not to be incorporated into the Royal Society of Medicine.

The situation at Fulham Hospital could hardly have been more different from the West London Hospital as it had started as a workhouse and was an LCC hospital until taken over by Charing Cross; as with many LCC hospitals, there was an adjoining cemetery. Fulham Hospital was the chosen site for the new 17-storey Charing Cross Hospital, which was cross-shaped, the longer arm housing laboratories, whilst the other three arms were wards. It opened in 1972, but the planned underground car park for 500 vehicles was abandoned for financial reasons and the Henry Moore sculpture, generously presented by the artist, and displayed at the front of the hospital, was not as well appreciated as had been hoped.

Being a member of the New Hospital Building Committee gave me the opportunity to discuss the needs of a modern neurological department. Besides neurosurgery, this included EEG, EMG, neuropathology and neuropsychology. Although the need for neurosurgery was understood, the members of the Governors' Committee were all laymen and clearly unaware of the other services required. With regard to EEG, the old Charing Cross did have a designated room, as did the West London, the latter being one of the first hospitals in London to use such a machine, but, by 1965, these workhorses were completely outdated, much to the dissatisfaction of the EEG recordist. On my appeal to the House Governor, we were rewarded with a new machine, a new department and, whereas previous EEGs were reported by the neurologists, we were able to obtain funding for a specialist clinical neurophysiologist to supervise the department; there was only one applicant, who was duly appointed.

A more difficult post to get recognised was for neuropsychology, because the governing lay body had to be persuaded that this appointment could be a life-saving measure. The Governors confused psychological testing with occupational psychology (testing for business acumen), psychotherapy or psychoanalysis but eventually we were able to appoint an excellent clinical neuropsychologist, albeit for only four sessions a week. Even more difficult was persuading medical colleagues the need for a well-trained neuroradiologist; indeed, one senior consultant (an anaesthetist) asked me "What's so special about neuroradiology?" Because the senior radiologist was also the Dean of the medical school, he felt that nothing more was necessary than sending a radiological registrar to a neurological hospital for a few months training; this meant that it was several years before we were able to appoint a dedicated and well-trained neuroradiologist.

The first research grant obtained after my appointment was in 1965 from Harris' sausage factory in Calne, Wiltshire. This came about because the husband of one of Angela's best friends was a solicitor who had been asked by a client to find a suitable project for a research grant. No neurological research until then had been undertaken at Charing Cross Hospital but John Sloper, professor of histopathology, had a strong interest in neuropathology, especially of muscle, so the money was given to his department. Another financial reward came to me after lecturing to the Harrogate Medical Society in Yorkshire at the invitation of a friend who was the Secretary of the Society. Here, my talk was on "Advances in Neurology". In the audience there was someone who, unfortunately, I did not recognise but he was the local neurologist, to whom I should have paid more attention. He had been chosen to give the vote of thanks, which was the most hostile I had ever received. One of the general practitioners at this meeting referred a patient with motor neurone disease, a fatal condition for which there was no specific treatment at that time. After her consultation with me, she sent an additional cheque for research which again was passed to John Sloper's department.

Another large gap in neurosciences was neuropathology so when Professor William Blackwood retired from his post at the National Hospital, I asked him if he would visit Charing Cross Hospital once a week to help establish work in this area. Delighted that he accepted, we were even more pleased when he continued to come weekly for several years. A consultant recruited in this field was Dr Ellen Grant, who had been a co-author with me; she was given an honorary contract in Professor Sloper's department in spring 1985. These successes gave me courage to ask another of my old chiefs from the National Hospital, Dr Carmichael, whether after his retirement, he would be willing to help teach Charing Cross students; he accepted and continued for many years.

When Dr Gerald Parsons-Smith, my senior neurologist colleague, reached the age of 65 years, he was obliged by NHS rules to retire. A notice appeared in one of the national daily newspapers:

"... Charing Cross Hospital

The Department of Neurology gave a dinner last night in honour of Dr Gerald Parsons-Smith on the occasion of his sixty-fifth birthday. Dr F Clifford Rose presided. Mr Derek Mullis, Director of the Migraine Trust, attended, as did colleagues, past registrars and house physicians. At this dinner Dr Parsons-Smith was presented with three bottles of fine wine, each a vintage from the years of his birth, qualification and retirement". He was delighted with these gifts, which came from my own cellar. Our relationship had always been friendly and at a dinner he gave for Angela and me he presented me a silver salver, engraved in Latin, which had been a tradition for centuries; I continued this with my successor but the practice has now died out.

On my return journey from a meeting of the Academy of Aphasia in Victoria, British Colombia, I took the opportunity to visit the First International Congress of Paediatric Neurology in Toronto, for just one day, when aphasia and handedness were discussed. Having obtained the Diploma in Child Health did not make me a paediatric neurologist but Per Saugman, the Director of Blackwoods Books of Oxford, persuaded me to take on the task of editing a book on this subject, as he had published my first book (with Vincent Marks) in 1965 on *"Hypoglycaemia"* which had been well reviewed and translated into Spanish in 1967. The reason Saugman's attempts in paediatric neurology had foundered was that there were only about eight child neurologists at that time in the UK, meaning these specialists were too occupied with clinical work to take on volume editorship. He accepted my view that only a quarter of the chapters would be written by child neurologists, a quarter by paediatricians with an interest in neurology, a quarter by neurologists with an interest in children, and the rest by such specialists as ENT or eye surgeons. When Saugman showed the finished manuscript to the local Oxford specialists, they rejected it; as there was little in the UK on this subject at that time, my attitude was to go ahead and publish, a view he accepted. It was also the first time a publisher invited me to a champagne dinner to celebrate the sell-out of a first edition. Four years later, I took a preliminary copy to the Second International Congress of Paediatric

Neurology in Sydney, Australia, where a German attendee told me that it contained "nothing new"; however, it was the only edited book of mine that earned significant royalties, reaching a second edition, with two additional contributors in 1981, and published in Japanese in 1989

The year of my appointment to Charing Cross, 1965, was also the year of the third World Congress of Neurology, to be held in Vienna. Although international meetings of neurology had been held before the Second World War, the first Congress of the World Federation of Neurology (WFN) was not until 1957 in Brussels, which I attended while still a resident house physician at the National Hospital. This International Congress is organised every four years by the WFN, which links all the national societies in this field; each national society sends a delegate to a planning meeting two years before the World Congress to vote on the venue, programme, main speakers and the Officers of the WFN. There is strong competition between countries to host this event because the profits of the World Congresses, mainly from pharmaceutical company sponsorship and attendees' registration fees, are shared equally between the successful national society and the WFN. Having attended every World Congress of Neurology from the first in 1957 in Brussels (until 2007, when it was held in Sydney Australia), I was not too upset to miss Vienna in 1965 since my recent appointment to Charing Cross Hospital meant that the time could not be spared.

In 1967, I became a Recognised teacher of Medicine (neurology) in the University of London and, from 1968-1976, taught medical ophthalmology at the City University. In 1969, my appointment to the Academic Board of Charing Cross Hospital Medical School for four years proved its proceedings to be a waste of time, even though I repeated the exercise in 1985, but fortunately for only three years. It was natural to join the Association of British Neurologists (ABN) in 1967, becoming a Member of its Council from 1983 to 1985. Being the UK Delegate to the World Federation of Neurology (WFN) from 1977 to 1989 my loyalties and work were predominantly concentrated on international neurology rather than just British. My later teaching included Training in the Pharmaceutical

(TPI) from 1986-88 and courses for the Pharmaceutical Industry .υm 1988 to 1991.

Having taught at the Aldrey-Fleming School of Speech Therapy in the NHQS from 1960-63 and at the Central School of Speech and Drama in 1962 and 1963, I was appointed in 1966 to the Examinations Board of the College of Speech Therapy. Years later in 1982 and 1983 I was the Course Organiser and Lecturer in Neurology at the Blackfriars (Kingdom-Ward) School of Speech Therapy: activities here culminated in an invitation to its jubilee celebration when the Queen-mother attended and briefly chatted to me.

During 1968 I had several television interviews, e.g. on Horizon and Frontiers of Science; at that time there was also a special medical programme on TV entitled Medicine Today. The episode on stroke was watched by my father-in-law who apparently shed tears because, having read a modern languages degree at Oxford, felt he had wasted his life ending up as the proprietor of a tailoring a shop in the Strand, which he had inherited from his father-in-law.

Life Assurance
In 1965, an ophthalmologist colleague, who was born and trained in South Africa, asked me to visit one of his patients who was the wife of a director of a new life assurance company, Abbey Life. There was no doubt about the diagnosis, not least because my research in her condition had culminated in a monograph being written by me with my senior house physician. After this domiciliary consultation, the patient's husband asked me to undertake the underwriting of life-assurance clients who had medical disorders likely to limit life expectancy. Although a neurologist, the fact that reports would deal with the whole range of general medicine was no problem for me, having worked in general medicine for eight years before concentrating on neurology.

When Life Assurance first began in the UK, a Select Committee of the House of Commons wrote: "Whenever there is a contingency, the cheapest way of providing against it is by uniting with others so that each man may subject himself to a small deprivation, in order that no man may be subjected to a great loss". Although the first known life policy was in 1583, a century later an effort was made to institute life insurance (assurance). Since the 1603 plague in the City of London, records were kept of christenings and burials, and these "Bills of Mortality" were published first in 1662. Since my only experience of life assurance had been examining the occasional client of a cousin who sold insurance policies, my hesitation before accepting this invitation was because my recent appointment to Charing Cross Hospital kept me fully occupied. When asking how much time was needed for the job, the reply was "not more than studying one or two forms a week without the need to examine the applicants but simply to give a considered opinion from the medical notes as to life expectancy". Finally accepted the invitation, within a relatively short space of time the work increased until it involved three visits each week to the company's offices in the City of London. At that time my weekly visits to nine different hospitals and schools etc meant spending 3½ hours a day in a car so my increasing workload was helped when the insurance company provided me with a chauffeur to enable me to work in the back of a car (with a reading light, telephone and Dictaphone). The success of the directors of this new company was the idea to link insurance premiums to the stock market, which proved hugely successful, so much so that they wished to fund a medical research project. Although the majority of life assurance applicants belonged to younger age groups, my recommendation was to fund stroke epidemiology, this word no longer meaning the study of epidemics but the analysis of groups. My reason for this was that stroke, which is still the third commonest cause of death (after cancer and heart attack), had not received sufficient attention. Underwriting impaired lives uses the techniques of epidemiology to give a statistical basis for longevity which makes this work rewarding.

Matters dealing with medical insurance were catered for by a society for doctors called The Assurance Medical Society, Assurance meaning life insurance. This group met three times a year at the Medical Society of London in Chandos Street just off Cavendish Square. Having served for five years as principal Medical Officer (PMO) of Abbey Life, I was asked in

1970 to be the PMO of Hambro Life. As the Principal Medical Officer of two insurance companies, the members of the Assurance Medical Society elected me as their President. At this time the Society was relatively inactive so I suggested joint meetings with Professor Benjamin's group of actuaries at City University, with whom we had published joint articles. This was followed by joint meetings with the Institute of Actuaries, highly trained individuals advising on life expectancy. A joint meeting was arranged in Edinburgh, which was the base for several British insurance companies. The lectures were held at the venerable Royal College of Physicians of Edinburgh and the symposium ended in a black-tie dinner at Hopetoun House which was flood-lit for the occasion and guests greeted on arrival to the music of bagpipes with the piper in traditional dress. Our host was the Marquis of Linlithgow, who gave an after-dinner talk on the history of Hopetoun House, his family home. The guests included the Presidents of the Royal College of Physicians of Edinburgh and the British Medical Association, who that year was a Scot. Whether it was a coincidence, the Assurance Medical Society prospered after this to become a wealthy Society which invited me to special events twenty years later. One of these was held at the House of Lords; when asking the reason for this venue, the convener, another ex-president of the Assurance Medical Society, replied the idea came from me at the Edinburgh meeting, because a peer was required to host a function at the House of Lords, and he had a patient in the Lords. I had to explain that the Marquis of Linlithgow had not been my patient but was a fellow-trustee of the Migraine Trust, a charity of which I was then Chairman.

A PMO of another company, Dr Walwyn-Jones, encouraged me to join the City of London Medical Book Society which was founded in 1821. There was no annual subscription, merely an entrance fee of One Guinea and the only condition for members, besides being a registered medical practitioner, was to reside or practice in the City of London. The proposal for my joining gave my insurance company's address which was just opposite St Paul's Cathedral in the City of London. At each dinner there was a display of non-medical books which members could buy. The dinners were held in a hotel near Liverpool Street Station and, because of this extra travelling, my membership did not last long, much to the surprise of my fellow-members.

Although the years 1965 to 1970 were highly successful financially for Abbey Life Insurance Company, the top executives had no share of the equity. There were two owners of the company; ATT, one of the largest companies in the United States (whose chief executive was a Mr Geneen), owned 50%, whilst the other 50% was owned by Georgia International Insurance Company, whose headquarters were in Atlanta, Georgia. I was asked to go to Atlanta to be vetted by the PMO of Georgia International as a suitable PMO to Abbey Life. Other than my seeing Atlanta, this turned out to be a non-event because, not only had the professor of neurology at the local university invited me to lecture there, but the Georgia International PMO knew of me and became a friend. When he came to London, I took him to dinner at a well-known restaurant in Jermyn Street, which he enjoyed very much, especially the cheese course of camembert, so that I bought him one as a present as he was returning immediately by 'plane to Atlanta. About two weeks later, there was a funny smell in the boot of my car – he had forgotten to take his cheese.

The deal between ATT and Georgia International was that either could buy the other's 50% share of the company but, if the offer was refused, the opposite half would pay the same price for the 50% of the company. Several years later, Georgia International offered ATT £15,000,000 (fifteen million pounds) for Abbey Life but the CEO of ATT, Geneen, refused in spite of being told by Abbey Life's executives that they would resign and form another company, a threat Geneen dismissed, reportedly saying he knew all the senior people in the City of London and none would invest in a new rival. Apparently, Geneen had forgotten that Abbey Life's property investments had been managed by Hambro Bank who offered one million pounds to support a new assurance company which was to be called Hambro Life (*Daily Telegraph*, 5 May 2008). Invited to be Hambro Life's PMO, for some time I was PMO to two rival insurance companies; this was no problem except when invited to each company's annual overseas jaunt for their top insurance agents; whether it was Istanbul in Turkey, Bermuda or a Greek island, we had to remember which company had invited my wife and me. Hambro Life eventually moved their head office to Swindon, Wiltshire and Abbey Life moved to Southampton. As this meant travelling every month to each of these headquarters, I eventually gave up Abbey Life and Hambro Life.

At Swindon, the Secretary of Hambro Life asked me to give him £40, but did not give me the reason, although I now presume it was used to buy shares in the company. Some years later, my bank manager rang to tell me "Christmas had come early" and there was a deposit of a six-figure sum in my account. Somehow my shares had been sold, I think to the disappointment of the Company Secretary, who became a very successful man and was awarded a peerage. From 1970 to 1996, as Principal Medical Officer of Allied Dunbar Assurance Company, my monthly visits to Swindon were to confer with the underwriting department, and usually followed by lunch at a local pub, *The Bleeding Horse*, in Ramsbury, which sadly no longer exists, but has become a private house.

Chapter 7

CHARITIES

Although migraine has been known since the time of the Ancient Greeks, the term being derived from *hemicrania* – one-sided headache - our knowledge of its causes and treatment is much more recent; the main basis for its long neglect was a failure to consider it a serious disorder, since "everyone has headaches". Even neurologists, specialists in disorders of the nervous system, gave it scant attention because of the need to deal with more serious and sometimes fatal conditions; this was in spite of the fact that a quarter of all out-patients to a neurological department came because of headache. Such neglect by the medical profession meant that, as a student, both undergraduate and post-graduate, including neurological training, there was not *one* single lecture on headache.

Patients were generally dissatisfied, so it was not surprising when one such sufferer, Peter Wilson, whose migraine started at the age of 12 and continued to his seventh decade, contacted others with the same complaint. In March 1958, he advertised in his local newspaper, the *Bournemouth Evening Echo*, that a meeting would be held for headache sufferers in the flat of one of the ten people attending; each contributed £10 so that a group was started with Wilson, a local government officer, as Honorary Secretary. Following the announcement in a national daily paper – the *Daily Telegraph* - of its formation, another two hundred people became involved, including well known writers, scientists, doctors and a Nobel Prize Winner; by the end of the following year there were over 1,000 members. In 1964, this group formed the British Migraine Association, its purpose being "to encourage the creation of headache clinics and to raise money for headache research". Although the Association was essentially a patients' organisation set up as a charitable trust, the need for more medical input was soon recognised. In the mid-1960s, Wilson on behalf of the British Migraine Association approached the Wellcome Foundation for support and a meeting on migraine for general practitioners (GPs) was organised. This was chaired by Dr Macdonald Critchley and concluded that "an organisation of sufficient weight" was needed to "gain the attention and support of the medico-scientific establishment". Her Royal Highness (HRH) Princess Margaret was asked to become the Patron of the Migraine Trust which she graciously accepted, Critchley agreed to be the founding Chairman; one of its most important functions was to organise meetings where clinical scientists could regularly review what was known about this complex disorder, stimulate research and report their results. .

In the UK, headache clinics had been started by Critchley at both the hospitals where he worked, namely King's College Hospital and the National Hospital, Queen Square. It was in the late 1960s that a pharmaceutical company, Sandoz, approached me to undertake a clinical trial on their new migraine preventative drug, known then only as CB 105. Having been appointed in 1965 as the new consultant neurologist to the Charing Cross Group of Hospitals, it was easy for me to start a weekly migraine clinic at one of its constituent institutes, the West London Hospital in Hammersmith, with a clinical assistant, Dr Felicity Harris, chosen to help and funded by Sandoz. The trial of CB105 as a migraine prophylactic proved successful but, marketed by the company as Sanomigran (with the generic name of pizotifen), it proved to have side effects of drowsiness and weight increase, which were particularly unwelcome in migraine patients, many of whom were younger women. In 1972, Derek Mullis as Director and Critchley as Chairman of the Migraine Trust, invited me to start a clinic for patients with acute migraine attacks who would be admitted to hospital for rest, treatment and observation. They were prepared to buy a house in Fulham for this purpose but, as the New Charing Cross Hospital was opening that year, ample accommodation would be available on-site; the Hammersmith Area Health Authority accepted "responsibility for the increased number of patients with migraine who would be attending", so that the only cost to the Migraine Trust was in providing a Research Registrar. I became a Trustee of the Migraine Trust in 1980 and was Chairman from 1987 to 1995. The Clinic at Charing Cross Hospital was given the title of The

Princess Margaret Migraine Clinic and she attended for the official opening.

Her Royal Highness Princess Margaret opening the Princess Margaret Migraine Clinic at Charing Cross Hospital)

In the 1970s Macdonald Critchley asked me to join the Research Group on Headache and Migraine of the World Federation of Neurology; I would later be its Secretary and finally succeed him as Chairman. This Research Group was limited to thirty international experts and met at the quadrennial meetings of the World Congress of Neurology. As one of twelve doctors responsible for the Classification of Headache and Migraine of the International Headache Society (1988), they elected me a life member and I still receive their monthly journal, *Cephalalgia*.

In 1976, on the occasion of the centenary of the birth of Sir Gordon Holmes, the famous British neurologist, Macdonald Critchley was keen to celebrate Holmes' achievements with a Symposium. He had first approached the National Hospital, Queen Square on whose consultant staff Holmes had also worked, but they did not seem keen, apparently because of their wish not to be recognized for historical contributions rather than recent research. Critchley therefore approached me because Gordon Holmes had been one of my predecessors at Charing Cross Hospital. Critchley's idea was to have a sessional meeting of a morning or afternoon and invite some of his more famous "clerks" (those who had studied under Holmes) to contribute a scientific paper. In the event, celebrations lasted nearly four days and the speakers included two former "clerks" who had become Nobel Prize winners (Sir John Eccles from Australia and Professor Ragnar Granit from Sweden); others included Professor Gunter Baumgartner of Zurich, Professor Paul Bucy of Chicago and Professor William Feindel of Montreal, the latter two being neurosurgeons. The medical aspects of this symposium were published in 1977 by Blackwells of Oxford entitled "Physiological Aspects of Clinical Neurology" and edited by me.

In the *Financial Times*, I read about a sculptor who could produce a bust from a photograph, which allowed us to invite one of Holmes' surviving daughters to unveil her father's bust at this conference. The Symposium dinner was held at Apothecaries Hall, the home of the Worshipful Society of Apothecaries, where a doctor joins as a Yeoman and, after three years, can become a fully-fledged Liveryman, in between which he can become a Freeman of the City of London. Seeking an appropriate Guest of Honour for the Gordon Holmes Symposium Dinner, I approached Derek Mullis, the Director of the Migraine Trust, who suggested its Patron, Princess Margaret, particularly as Apothecaries Hall was such a magnificent venue, having survived the Great Fire of London of 1666. Her Royal Highness, via her personal secretary, accepted but with two conditions; the first that there was to be no photography during the dinner, and the second that, on meeting the speakers, she did not wish their wives to be included. There was a third condition explained to me privately by the Lady-in-Waiting, namely that her drink should be Famous Grouse whisky, to be served, not in a wine glass, but in a silver goblet. There should have been no problem with these conditions, except that a German contributor brought out his camera and approached the top table before the dinner, whereupon Princess Margaret's Lady-in-Waiting and I hastily stopped him.

All the elderly male "clerks" were placed in a separate room to shake hands with our Guest of Honour. Paul Bucy, a distinguished and retired neurosurgeon, gave the speech of the Royal Toast which went down well except for his reference to "a young girl" but, being American, he was of course forgiven. The next occasion I was to meet HRH was a charitable function in aid of the Migraine Trust at St James' Palace where there was to be a concert, followed by dinner; as Princess Margaret was late for the concert, we sat together just outside the hall and listened to the music. At dinner, Angela sat with HRH and me as well as several celebrities, including Timothy West, his wife Prunella Scales, and David Jacobs, the radio compère. My wife's organ-playing at the harvest festival in the church next to our country home came up in conversation which led to HRH conducting the table in singing "We plough the fields and scatter". The Lady-in-Waiting, seated at the next table, turned round disapprovingly but, on discovering who was making the noise and leading the hymn, her facial expression changed rapidly. In 2010 at the bicentenary of the Kennet and Avon Canal, which is opposite my home, Prunella Scales and her husband Timothy West attended and, reminding them of this incident, we all had a good laugh.

In 1980, although serving on the Research Advisory Committee of the Migraine Trust, a more unusual request was to become a member of the National Health and MRC Panel of Assessors of Australia which fortunately meant vetting only one or two research applications

In 1990 the Migraine Trust held its 25th Anniversary meeting in Leeds Castle in Kent, where the foremost international experts in the migraine field were invited to stay at the Castle over 3 nights and deliver papers on their recent researches, after which the proceedings were published. The Symposium dinner, at what is said to be the most beautiful Castle in England, was attended by HRH Princess Margaret in her capacity as the Royal Patron of the Migraine Trust, as well as the then current Head of the Leeds Castle Trust, Lord Kingsdown, who was a previous Governor of the Bank of England. At the dinner HRH sat between the latter and me. Having previously checked the menu, as always, with the secretary to HRH, the first course of soup arrived, but HRH declined, saying that she *never* had soup; this meant that none of the diners could take soup. As twenty minutes had been allocated by the kitchen for this course, the plates for the main course, which had been warmed, cooled down and this caused a further complaint, quickly abated when Lord Kingsdown provided his plate which was still warm. After this the meal went well but, during the dinner conversation, the story of someone who had recognised but not placed HRH and was trying to find out tactfully who she was, asked about her father to which she replied he was dead; not yet giving up on his enquiries, she was further asked "And is your sister doing the same work?", "Yes" was her reply, "She is still on the Throne". Lord Kingsdown told me an anecdote of entertaining Princess Margaret, who when presented with a bowl of ice-cream, was unable to dent it with a spoon as it was frozen solid; she and the butler eventually agreed it was best she gave up and so all the other guests quickly decided they did not want ice-cream either.

The Migraine Trust again invited Princess Margaret to be a Guest of Honour at a charitable luncheon at the Mansion House, the traditional home of the Lord Mayor of the City of London during his year of office.

Angela, the Lord Mayor, the author and Lady Mayoress
with Princess Margaret at the Mansion House)

Looking for a speaker on this occasion, Julian Critchley, a Member of Parliament and the son of Macdonald Critchley, my predecessor as Chairman of the Migraine Trust, seemed eminently suitable. Julian accepted my invitation, remembering me from a previous occasion when we met at the Polish Embassy for his father to receive an award from that country. As Julian was a restaurant critic for a national newspaper, it struck me that a good place to meet and discuss details concerning his talk would be the Connaught Hotel, one of his father's favourite restaurants (and mine). Arriving early to order three half-bottles of wine, the first chosen as an aperitif was champagne, the second a claret and the third a sauterne to be drunk with the dessert. Upon his arrival, to my surprise, he informed me he was on a diet and had given up drinking wine for the present. When asked whether he would mind my drinking, he replied "By all means", which meant that all three half-bottles were consumed with my meal. At the actual charity lunch, after introducing Julian, he spoke for a long time, but very little on migraine and the speech was mostly a philippic against Mrs Thatcher, who was then Prime Minister but gave Julian no preferment in spite of his being one of her well-known conservative MPs; it was clear that she was not going to promote him to a knighthood, which Julian was given only after she was no longer Prime Minister. His talk, instead of promoting the Trust, was mainly criticizing Thatcher and was an embarrassing disappointment, particularly in Princess Margaret's presence. We were able to hold this charitable event at the Mansion House because the Lady Mayoress had come to me for an opinion before her husband took office, as she suffered from migraine and realised she would have to accompany him on official dinners every week; we were both satisfied when my advice enabled her to carry out her necessary gastronomic duties.

Motor neurone disease (MND) is an almost invariably fatal condition with an average life span of only a few years, depending on the time of diagnosis. Having taken an interest as a medical student, since it is a condition with a multiplicity of physical signs which can be elicited by doctors, as well as during my neurological training at the National Hospital, my main research project was using a new technique to study the junction of the nerves and muscles. Sent by the National Hospital to study the technique with a Belgian neurologist, my visit also occurred on the occasion of the First World Congress of Neurology held after the

Second World War in Brussels in 1957. Learning the technique initially on rabbits, I then used the technique on nearly thirty patients with MND, but the results were insufficient to merit publication, although it gave me a life-long interest in the disease. It was always difficult to tell a patient that they have an untreatable condition and that his or her life span was limited and medical students did not try to do so. In the USA, this fatal condition was called Lou Gehrig's disease since it was named after a highly successful top-hitter baseball player who rapidly failed in 1938 and died in 1941 at the age of 37. Better known in the UK as *Motor Neurone Disease*, knowledge of an American patients' group made me determined to start a similar organisation for patients in Britain. When sufferers and their relatives were told of my suggestion of the need for research and meeting others with this rare condition, they were full of enthusiasm, but this soon waned after the sufferer had succumbed to its universal progression and eventual fatality.

One Easter, while attending the annual meeting of the American Academy of Neurology in Washington DC, the sun was shining, obliging me as a sun-starved Englishman, to enjoy the warmth outside the lecture theatres, when a youngish woman came out of one of the surrounding meeting rooms where she had been attending the Research Committee of the National ALS Society, whose headquarters were in New York and was opposed to its rival organisation, the Californian-based ALSSOA (ALS Society of America). On discovering my interest, this group invited me to sit in on their proceedings, even though unsuitably dressed in shorts and T-shirt, and bearing in mind there was only one member of the Committee (Leonard Kurland) known to me. My disbelief that the USA had *two* national groups for a rare condition made me wonder why they did not join forces; eventually the two groups did come together, but it was a liaison that failed, and resulted in the present situation of several disparate groups across the US serving local communities. In 1981, ALSSOA asked me to be the UK representative which I continued to be until 1987.

Disappointed by my failure to get a patient group started in Britain, it was a special pleasure to be invited in 1978 to a private house in West London, the home of Mr and Mrs Prince, where there was to be a meeting of those interested in this disease; the original letter from Mrs J C Prince was published in the *Evening Standard*, a newspaper for the London area and stated: "May I ask any of your readers who suffer from motor neurone disease, or who are related to a sufferer from this condition, to write to me with a view to forming a patients' association". On 3 June 1978 twenty-five people attended a meeting at the home of the Princes in Ealing, which was "… a get together of patients, relatives, medics and professionals meeting with a common cause to form a self-help society". Those present included my registrar, Dr Marek Gawel, who gave the medical background of MND and Paul Walker, Director of the Muscular Dystrophy Group of Great Britain, claiming his Group included MND in the diseases they covered. We pointed out that muscular dystrophy was entirely different from motor neurone disease in terms of the age of onset (older for MND) and their progress (more rapid in MND). The Motor Neurone Disease Association (MNDA) was born, but by a strange quirk of fate, John Prince (not one of my patients) who was thought to have had MND was later diagnosed as having MS (Multiple Sclerosis), " … how strange its birth should have happened this way" later wrote Mrs Prince to me. Meetings were later held between the motor neurone organisation and the Muscular Dystrophy Group. The former agreed to "go it alone" and in June 1979 a draft constitution was accepted and the Motor Neurone Disease Association (MNDA) registered as a charity. John Prince wrote to the Cambridge astrophysicist, Professor Stephen Hawking to become the Patients' Patron, as he had survived over 40 years with a neurological disease diagnosed as MND and his name has often been used as an example to encourage sufferers. The Princes also suggested I should become the Medical Patron, a post held by me from its foundation in 1978 until 1990 after which my duty as Scientific Advisor continued for a further year until my retirement from the NHS. Lady McNeil, whose industrialist husband had died from MND, became the Honorary President, whilst HRH the Duchess of York became the Royal Patron, proving to be a great help both in fund raising and taking significant interest in patients. After her divorce from the Duke of York, she lost the honour of being called "Her Royal Highness" and with it the title of Royal

Patron to the MNDA. One of the most famous British sufferers who died from this condition was David Niven, who gave, during his illness, the "thumbs-up" sign which became the logo of the MNDA, whose headquarters were in Northampton, its offices being called Niven House. A patient in Nottingham, Roger Carus, also wished to set up a national charity for sufferers so that, in January 1979, an article appeared in the *Nottingham Evening Post* and a meeting arranged locally which was attended by 23 people.

Every Christmas, two senior on the *Daily Mirror*, a national newspaper, journalists known as the "Old Codgers", had a regular Christmas charity appeal and, in February 1980, sent £11,000 to the MNDA for research – its first really large donation. In May 1980 the membership of the MNDA was 400 and by 1988 it was over 3,000; the Motor Neurone Disease Association later proved to have more research funding than the Muscular Dystrophy Group. The first full-time research fellow of the Association was appointed to the Department of Neurology at Charing Cross Hospital.

In July 1986 I gave a lecture on the "Management of Amyotrophic Lateral Sclerosis" to the Sixth International Congress on Neuromuscular Diseases in Los Angeles; the Congress was sponsored by the Muscular Dystrophy Association and hosted by the University of Southern California School of Medicine (USC). Because of my interest in this disease, the International Amyotrophic Lateral Sclerosis/Motor Neurone Disease Research Foundation asked me to be its chairman from 1987 to1990; this new body held international research symposia every six months with their proceedings occasionally published under my editorship. One such meeting in June 1990 was to agree an international classification; this was held near Madrid and its diagnostic criteria came to be known by its place of discussion, the El Escorial classification. San Lorenzo de el Escorial is a palace-monastery complex constructed by Phillip II after winning a battle against the French on St Lawrence's Day in 1557; it is above the village of El Escorial and, besides the royal palace and monastery, there is a mausoleum for King Phillip's parents. It has been claimed that the WFN's El Escorial criteria have been confusing to GPs and lay people and there should be further international meetings (*World Neurology, October 2010 p.6*).

Another international meeting on MND was held in San Servolo, an island in the Venetian bay, which had been used as a psychiatric home for aristocratic Italians; as it no longer served this purpose, the Regional Council of Venice converted it to an International School for Neurological Studies, with me as the UK representative on its Council. My first effort there was to invite global experts on MND to exchange and report their views on this tragic disease. One of the funding-supporters of the MNDA was to be the American business tycoon, James Sherwood, who controlled Sea Containers, a company he founded in 1965, where the assets included the Venice-Simplon Orient Express train and the Hotel Cipriani in Venice. Having met Sherwood at Hammersmith Hospital in London, it was my suggestion that the Royal Patron of the MNDA, the Duchess of York, could travel on the Orient-Express to Venice and then stay in the Cipriani Hotel in order to open the symposium on MND at San Servolo. Although the Symposium went ahead, the plans for HRH fell through.

Following a research meeting by the MNDA at Cumberland Lodge in Windsor Great Park, HRH the Duchess of York invited me to fly in her helicopter to a charity lunch in Aylesbury; her private detective indicated the rear seat to me on this private flight, but HRH insisted on my sitting next to her at the front.

In 1921, Dr Lloyd Roberts had funded a Lecture to be given annually, rotating between the Medical Society of London, the Royal College of Physicians and the Royal Society of Medicine. Since this Lecture occurred during my Presidential year of the Medical Society of London, I had the idea of a talk on motor neurone disease. At the charity lunch of the MNDA, my neighbour was the secretary to the Royal Patron; to my question as to whether HRH the Duchess of York might be willing to address a medical audience (with the help of a script), she suggested that I ask the Duchess directly, which I did and she accepted. This talk entitled "All of one company", was given in December 1990, and the Duchess of

York was the first member of the British Royal Family to give the Lloyd Roberts Lecture, which was at the Royal College of Physicians where the theatre could accommodate more people. She was beautifully dressed and gave a word-perfect talk (which I had helped prepare). Following the talk there was a small dinner party at the Medical Society of London where my wife was introduced to her. The Duchess seemed surprised and asked how long we had been married; when Angela's reply was "over 30 years", a more surprising query was "But do you still love him?" It was only a short time after this incident that it became generally known that her marriage was going through a difficult time, eventually resulting in divorce. The Duchess of York's former right-hand woman, Jane Andrews, was jailed for the murder of her boyfriend, Tom Crossman, in 2001 and considered for parole in 2008 (*Daily Telegraph*, 02 June 2008). The previous Lloyd Roberts lecture hosted by the Medical Society of London three years previously was given by the King of Jordan; the then President asked my wife whether we would like to meet the King or the Queen of Jordan, my wife replied "The King" but my unhesitating reply was "The Queen" (Noor), with the result that we met both.

In August 1990, the MNDA asked me to give the Patrick Hamilton Lecture to its Annual Meeting at the Birmingham Congress Centre. The title I chose was "Incurable optimism – 33 years of Motor Neurone Disease Research", which reflected the time from my first research in 1957 when working at the National Hospital and being sent to Belgium to learn the technique of "in-vivo methylene staining of the junction between nerve and muscle." In one of our appeals, the Duchess of York wrote: "It is so sad that the only time that Motor Neurone Disease comes to most people's attention is when someone famous dies from it. I, too, came into this category as it wasn't until my friend Sir Robert Cooke died of MND that I learned about this dreadful disease which claims the lives of three people every single day. I am determined to improve public awareness in order that we can work towards finding a cure and, in the meantime, provide real help for all the patients who suffer and for their families who have to live through a loved one's decline. (The) team at the MNDA are tireless in their work; they cannot be praised enough for their achievements and dedication in the ten short years since the MNDA was formed. They can count on my continuing support. I hope that you will feel able to give yours too". In summer, the annual meetings of the MNDA were again held at the Birmingham Centre, the numbers who attended increasing every year. In January 1991, I received a letter from Mrs Joyce Prince at whose house the first meeting on MNDA was held, thanking me for my part in starting the society stating that: "The Association would have taken much longer to get on its feet – and perhaps would have foundered altogether. I hope you are finding time to do everything you want now you are 'retired'.

One day at about this time the doorbell at my home rang and on answering it, there was a man delivering a huge bunch of flowers. Somewhat surprised, my question was "Who has been sending my wife flowers?" to which he replied "They are not for your wife, sir, they are for you, from a VIP". Never having received flowers in my life, on opening the card, it said "with love from Sarah".

After the 1989 WCN, we had arranged a Memorial Symposium to "Ted" Norris, an American neurologist who had confined his work solely to motor neurone disease. (I first met him in 1963, when considering emigrating to Rochester New York.) Having spoken to his wife the previous year about my intention of organising a meeting in his honour, she had revealed he had inoperable cancer. As she was a nurse, we agreed that, if he did not survive, we would have a Memorial Symposium to celebrate his life and publish the proceedings, my contribution being on the French professor, Charcot, who had delineated the condition which he named amyotrophic lateral sclerosis. As the WCN, held every four years, was going to be in Vancouver, Canada it was agreed to have the Symposium immediately after this, but in San Francisco, where he had worked. Forbes H Norris died in 1993, before the Symposium was held, but printed proceedings were produced in his memory. At his memorial service, the following was written: "'Ted', as he was known to his friends, was born in Virginia, the son of school teachers, whose families had arrived in America in the 1600's. After sustaining a major hip injury in childhood, he spent long periods in body casts confined to bed, where he discovered his love for music, an abiding lifelong passion. This injury also introduced him to swimming as a therapy, with the ultimate discovery that it would become a serious athletic pursuit; at Harvard, he was five times All-America, twice winner of Gold Medals in the National Championships (4 miles), Silver Medallist two other years, and also Silver Medallist two years in the World Championships (10 miles). He reached the finals of the 1,500 meters in the 1948 Olympics.

His interest in medicine also began as a result of his hip injury. His orthopaedic surgeon, the renowned specialist Dr Smith-Peterson, rented a boat to row alongside the bright young swimmer, as he prepared for his swimming trials. The camaraderie between the two men inspired Ted's interest in medicine and in swimmers' muscle cramps, ultimately leading to his studies of amyotrophic lateral sclerosis (ALS) in his early fifties at the National Institutes of Health in Washington. This interest in neuromuscular problems became his life's devotion and lead to his pioneering work in ALS research and its clinical management as well as his advocacy of patient's rights, and his work in developing aggressive clinical treatment of ALS may prove to be his greatest legacy. "His compassionate concern gave direction for care and offered hope and dignity in a seemingly hopeless disease, and it endeared him forever in the hearts and minds of ALS patients, their families, and clinicians around the world".

The Duchess of York, when she was the Royal Patron of the British MNDA, wrote to me: "I was very pleased to receive the preliminary draft on "Charcot and Motor Neurone Disease" and the programme for The First International Congress on the History of the Neurosciences. I would like to thank you for your kind invitation to open and attend the congress. I would have been delighted to accept, but unfortunately I have previous commitments on these dates. I would however like to reiterate my interest in all that you are doing, therefore please do not hesitate to inform me of any similar meetings. I wish you a very successful congress". She did, indeed, attend a later meeting of the MNDA.

Although involved in MND research for nearly forty years, I was first aware of a patients' association for MND when visiting the United States in the mid-70s. At an American Academy of Neurology meeting, the Amyotrophic Lateral Sclerosis Society of America (ALSSOA) had a stand where I met Eames Bishop, the Director whose wife had the disease, and later visited their Head Office at Sherman Oaks in Southern California. On my return to the UK, I would explain to patients with MND and their relatives why such an Association would be worthwhile in the UK: not only would patients and their carers appreciate that they were not the only people involved with this condition but they could exchange information and encourage research. My attempts met with failure because, when the patients died, their family tended to lose interest in the project.

Dr Gawel, my erstwhile research registrar, is now a consultant in Toronto with his own neuromuscular unit and is closely involved with the Canadian MNDA. Professor Adrian Williams succeeded me as Medical Patron of the MNDA and later my period as Chairman of its Scientific Advisory Committee. The early days were not entirely smooth as the Muscular Dystrophy Group (MDG) felt that this disease should be under their aegis and many attempts were made by their officers to get our Executive Committee to be fully associated with that organisation. Indeed, their Director attended our first meeting and offered their administrative services. It was felt, however, that the disease was entirely different from muscular dystrophy since it affected a different age group, had a different prognosis and the cause was clearly distinct; further, the research monies raised are designated specifically for disorders of the motor neurons rather than primary muscle disease. It is interesting that the income of the MNDA has grown enormously and is now greater than that of the MDG.

Brunel, The University of West London, Uxbridge
On 17 December 1990 the Department of Human Science within the Faculty of Social Sciences invited me to be Professor Associate at Brunel University, which post I held from 1991 until 1998. This was for assistance in the collaborative research on multiple sclerosis and motor neurone disease, where a database was kept. Little attendance was required but on one occasion a candidate for the PhD had to be examined. This honorary appointment also resulted in a collaborative book with a co-

author on epidemiology, whose name was Stuart Neilson; he was successful in obtaining his doctorate and we published in 2003 a book together for the lay on motor neurone disease. In 1989, I became Chairman of the John Bevan MND Research Unit at Brunel University and, later in the same year, in the same position for the Institute of Brain Chemistry, which was associated with the London Zoo and held its meetings nearby. In March 1989, the European Aspirin Foundation held a two-day international meeting in Brussels under the title of "Aspirin – towards 2000". They asked me to be the Chairman of the session on "Pain" at which my registrar gave our presentation on "Aspirin and Migraine". It is to be feared that my attendance at the two days of the meeting was not whole-time, as the art galleries and Michelin-starred restaurants of Brussels were a decided distraction.

In 1987, I gave the T B Bharucha Annual Oration to the University of Bombay, India, but suspect this was partly due to my having looked after a senior Barucha as a patient many years previously. In May of that year, we started at Charing Cross Hospital a charity called "The Way Ahead", the leading celebrity involved was Joan Collins, the actress, who participated because her daughter had been involved in a road traffic accident sustaining a head injury which required hospital admission. She recovered well and it was her caring neurosurgeon who persuaded Joan Collins to front this charity where the funds raised would support research into her daughter's condition. A photograph was taken at the official opening ceremony by one of a large number of media workers, journalists as well as photographers, but when asked to attend this function, she laid down two conditions: the first was that the media should not sit in the front row of the hall and secondly, when asked what she would have for lunch, she replied caviar, a request perhaps not ideal for a voluntary organisation.

Although this occasion passed without mishap, Joan Collins attended no further meetings, which, in any case, were limited, nor did she contribute further in spite of being asked by a journalist whether she would, and the charity folded within a relatively short time.

Joan Collins and FCR, 1987

In spite of arranging fund-raising events such as a formal dance and a less formal choral concert at a church, our results were poor, collecting about £40,000 over four years which, after my retirement, were used to fund the chair in neurosurgery at Charing Cross Hospital.

The Royal Hospital for Neuro-disability, Putney

It was Andrew Reed, a philanthropist, who in 1854 helped found the Hospital for Incurables following a plea from Charles Dickens to "give permanent relief to such persons as are hopelessly disqualified or the duties of life", but "not to interfere with the endeavours of existing charities but to take action precisely where their action ceased". Originally based in Carshalton, Surrey, in 1857 it moved to a more spacious house in Putney finally moving patients to its present site on West Hill, Putney in 1865. In 1919 the organisation received its Royal Charter and became the Royal Hospital and Home for Incurables. The hospital had been founded for long stay patients as opposed to those with curable diseases and hence its initial title of the Hospital for Incurables. In 1988 the name changed again to the Royal Hospital and Home, Putney but, because its name did not give an accurate description of its function, in 1995 it became the Royal Hospital for Neuro-disability. From the beginning, distinguished doctors visited the hospital and its first neurologist, Dr James Collier in 1934, was soon followed by Derek Denny-Brown who later became Professor of Neurology at Harvard in Boston, USA; multiple sclerosis and stroke were the main neurological disorders necessitating admission. By 1979 the hospital became research-minded and, more recently, developed units for severe brain injury (persistent vegetative state) and respiratory paralysis as well as its well-recognised work in the management of disability, biomedical engineering, stroke rehabilitation and electronic technology. Speech therapy, physiotherapy and occupational therapy were pre-eminent and there were close links with the National Hospital. In 1988, I was asked to serve on its Research Committee, which I did for several years. Dr John Wedgewood FRCP served as Chairman of the hospital from 1976 to 1979 and was Director of Research from then until 1987 when Dr K Andrews took over, becoming Director of the Institute in 2003. In 1994 it was here that my introduction to His Royal Highness, the Prince of Wales, took place when he visited the hospital and met members of the research committee.

The Real Age Initiative
Over lunch at the Savile Club one day, another member overheard me discussing how people were living longer and healthier lives. Although the biblical "three score years and ten" for life expectancy is well-known, it was now more usual and a generally recognised phenomenon to survive into the eighties and beyond. In America, discrimination on the grounds of age is illegal, partly due to the successful lobbying of more than 30 million members of the American Association of Retired People, otherwise known as the "Grey Panthers". My lunchtime neighbour was a public relations man and not only did he agree with me, but went further and suggested we formed an organisation to be called the Real Age Initiative, where a distinction was made between chronological age (the number of birthdays achieved) and the biological age, meaning how well one was functioning. This interested me when two 65 year old doctors were dismissed from examining clients for an insurance company, not because of incompetence but because of their age.

We suggested assessing biological age by ability to perform various tests but my agreement to be co-chairman of this new organisation was dependent on my co-founder's promised ability to collect funds for organising a conference of various gerontologists who would collate what was already known regarding the aging process. He consequently introduced me to another PR person who was also confident that funds could be found, but the plans came to nothing. Resigning as co-chairman proved to be a correct decision on learning that my colleague was going to charge individuals for assessment of their "real age" – a sort of MOT test, which would include blood pressure, muscle strength and tests of intellectual function. Our final disagreement was when he actually published a note about "...his friend's Great Aunt Edda who is 102 and lives in Paris with her 75 year-old lover. The last time I saw her...she was in a bad mood because her lover could manage sex only three times a week". Later, gossip had it that the name of his putative new organisation had been sold to an American company which had benefited financially.

Association for Research into Multiple Sclerosis (ARMS)

It is not infrequently the case that, for any disease, there is more than one charity existing to raise research funds. Multiple sclerosis was no exception and, although the Multiple Sclerosis Society is a much bigger and older organisation, the Association for Research into Multiple Sclerosis was started by a lay person who felt it could act as a "ginger" group to the larger Society, which fought shy of supporting measures that were not scientifically proven. Hyperbaric oxygen was such a treatment and, in spite of the expenses for providing this costly treatment, ARMS had about thirty centres where the therapy was given. The only accepted scientific condition for oxygenation was in deep-sea divers to avoid getting the "bends" on coming into normal atmospheric pressure too rapidly (when gases could be released from the blood and trapped in the nervous system). My hesitation at accepting their invitation to serve as Chairman was therefore understandable, but nevertheless, I served in this capacity from 1987-1991. The fund-raiser attempted to obtain research funds from tickets to football matches, which turned out to be unsuccessful and it was clearly an appropriate time for my resignation from this honorary appointment.

University of London

In 1973 I was asked to be an examiner in the final MB,BS (London) for Applied Pharmacology and Therapeutics at the Middlesex Hospital, one of London's teaching hospitals, but this was because the regular examiner was not available. There was a certain candidate who had failed several times at his qualifying attempts. Later he had done a temporary job in general practice for two weeks where he performed highly satisfactorily. Although he may not have had the academic book knowledge to get through a particular part of his final exams to become a doctor, after much discussion, and bearing in mind his proven clinical ability, the examiners agreed to let him pass. The fact that his father was a consultant at a London teaching hospital was not necessarily relevant.

Chapter 8

HEADACHE

Although my connections with migraine have already been summarised, association with headache patients has been part of the whole of my professional life, although in the mid-1960s the general view was that there were far more serious conditions for doctors to consider. Exposure to increasing numbers of headache sufferers soon disabused me of this attitude which had been widespread among colleagues, and by a movement in Italy which played a significant role; this was because headache clinics were found in all the main towns of that country and their practitioners always had a significant presence at meetings dealing with these disorders. This became even more obvious when the Italian Society for the Study of Headache, founded in 1976, held an International Conference in Florence entitled "Headache 1980" which helped to promote the European Headache Federation in Venice in April 1991, of which I was a founding member; its remit was to improve awareness of headache disorders, and I became Assistant Secretary of the WFN Research Group on Migraine and Headache in 1977, Associate Secretary in 1978, European Secretary in 1979 and Chairman in 1990.

As a founding member of the International Headache Society in 1982, Chairman of its Clinical Trials Committee from 1984 to 1987 and its Classification Committee from 1984 to 1988, I was elected an Honorary Life Member in 1993, which meant its monthly journal, *"Cephalalgia"*, is still sent to me free of charge.

The Princess Margaret Migraine Clinic
In 1982, AASH awarded the Princess Margaret Migraine Clinic its annual Harold Wolff Award for our work on a certain group of blood chemicals in migraine. As founding Director of this clinic, my visit to Washington DC to accept the award was enhanced when a cousin of Angela, on hearing of the trip, asked me to visit the Women's Art Gallery because she was involved in trying to set up a similar gallery in London, which, more than

thirty years later, has not yet materialised. When going to the Washington museum, a group of women welcomed me as a "stranger visitor" but were not particularly interested in the purpose of my visit.

In 1983, a visit to Copenhagen was at the behest of the Ciba Geigy pharmaceutical company who had organised a Swedish Neurotoxicology Symposium featuring headache. In the following year, Angela and I again visited Palm Springs for a headache meeting. Following Palm Springs, the Annual Meeting of AASH was held in San Francisco, and this time the Harold Wolff Award was for work on a blood chemical in cluster headache, a condition now recognised as being quite distinct from migraine. Following my first sojourn in 1960 as Visiting Assistant Professor, it was a pleasure to meet up with old friends, one of whom had been a librarian in Delhi but was now divorced from her journalist husband. These two visits were capped in 1986 when AASH gave me the Distinguished Clinician Award at their Annual Meeting, which that year was held in Chicago, where my talk was entitled "Headache Research: Past, Present and Future".

A Danish neurologist visited me at the Princess Margaret Migraine Clinic in Charing Cross Hospital in 1985 to decide on what type of migraine clinic he should set up in Copenhagen. He too wanted to see patients during acute attacks, which was routine at the Princess Margaret Migraine Clinic. This neurologist, Professor Jes Olesen, later organised annual migraine research meetings in Copenhagen and asked me to talk at some of them, the first being in June of 1985. In 1986, as Chairman of the organising committee of the 6th Migraine Trust International Symposium; the meeting was held at the Tara Hotel, Kensington, and Professor Jim Lance of Sydney, Australia chaired a symposium on "Recent Trends in the Management of Migraine" sponsored by Sandoz Pharmaceuticals. In 1988, as Chairman for the 7th MTIS, I asked Lord Perry of Walton, who was one of the Founders of the Open University, to start the proceedings as he was a Migraine Trustee, as well as a member of my London club, where we came to know each other well whilst lunching there. In that year, my co-worker from Charing Cross Hospital, the neurochemist Jackie de Belleroche, accompanied me to the VIIth National Congress of the Italian

Society for the Study of Headache in Cagliari, Sicily where she read a paper on the chemical, choline, in cluster headache, showing there was a good response to treatment with lithium, perhaps because it raised blood levels of choline significantly in this rare type of headache. Another paper on "Diet and Migraine", with biochemical colleagues from Queen Charlotte's Hospital, showed that red wine, but not other alcoholic drinks, affected a particular enzyme in the gut that caused headache.

The name of the Princess Margaret Migraine Clinic was given by the Migraine Trust to the facility at the new Charing Cross Hospital. Having become a Trustee in the early 1980s and succeeding to the Chairmanship in 1988, my help was needed to organise the biennial Migraine Trust International Symposia and edit the proceedings; in spite of these Symposia being held every other year, they were not sufficiently frequent to satisfy the need for researchers reporting their findings and, for this reason, the World Federation of Neurology, at its quadrennial congress held in Kyoto, Japan in 1981, sponsored a symposium entitled "Headache and Migraine". It was about this time that the International Headache Society was formed and its Classification of Headache, which listed over 100 causes of headache, gave a firmer basis for diagnosis by indicating precise criteria. This Classification produced by a Committee of twelve, of which I was one, met for two years and proved useful by giving a standardised basis for clinical trials (where one specific type of headache could be used to compare different treatments); it was also valuable in studying the genetic approach to migraine. In considering books based on work of the Princess Margaret Migraine Clinic, the volume on "Headache" of the huge multi-volume reference encyclopaedia called "Handbook of Clinical Neurology" (second edition) is worthy of mention. Another honour given me was at the Migraine Trust International Symposium of 2004; Alan Bartle, the director of the Migraine Trust, named the VIP suite at the conference centre "The Frank Clifford Rose Suite".

The need for the Migraine Trust to inform patients and relatives in simple everyday terms about causes and treatments was soon apparent, as evidenced by the number of telephone calls and letters received. Lay persons had a differing emphasis on how to manage migraine without taking drugs, so that complementary techniques e.g. acupuncture, were included in the Migraine Newsletter. These articles were criticised by some members of the Medical Advisory Committee on the grounds that they had not been scientifically proven to be efficacious, and one member of this Committee – a Nobel Prize Winner – resigned on this issue. It was the need to inform patients that induced the Oxford University Press to publish a book for sufferers, a task which my Research Registrar, Dr Marek Gawel, undertook with me; the book, entitled *Migraine, the Facts,* was published both in hardback and paperback. A second edition, much revised to include in layman's terms the striking advances, was brought out nearly a quarter of a century later, but the only changes were an additional chapter on headaches after head injury with a final chapter called "Headache Clinics and the Future". Another research registrar, Dr Paul Davies, was instrumental in a further book for lay persons entitled "Answers to Migraine", published between the two editions of "Migraine, The Facts".

An example of the Trust not being controlled by the pharmaceutical industry was a Symposium held in 1981 (between the two Migraine Trust International Symposia of 1980 and 1982) at the University of Sussex. At that time, the question of lack of oxygen to the brain as a cause of migraine was being investigated, and this meeting was jointly under the auspices of the Janssen Research Foundation (of Belgium) and the Migraine Trust. Janssen's new product, Flunarizine, was postulated as a preventive remedy of migraine following several scientific papers, but our report on a trial done at the Princess Margaret Migraine Clinic reached the conclusion that "further studies are required to confirm the drug's efficiency". Although Flunarizine has been much used on the continent of Europe, it was not in the UK, probably because of its side-effect of increase of weight. In 1988, I joined the Sumatriptan Clinical Trials Committee, this drug being the most efficacious treatment for migraine attacks.

In November 1991, I gave a seminar to the Pakistan Medical Society of the UK as part of the continuing Medical Education for General Practitioners, and the title given to me was "Differential Diagnosis of Headache and

Management of Migraine in General Practice". Whilst my recollection of the seminar is not good, I remember the meeting was held at a splendid Indian restaurant in Westminster where the dinner following my talk was an excellent curry. In 1992 my talk at the Annual Meeting of the American Academy of Neurology held at the Marriott Hotel in San Diego, California was to the wives and daughters of its members who have an annual auxiliary meeting, my talk being on "Women and Headaches". In June the following year, I was invited to Kiel, Germany for a meeting of the WFN Research Group on the "Organisation and Delivery of Neurological Services" where I talked on "The position of Sumatriptan in the treatment of headache", an anti-migraine drug recently introduced by Glaxo. This was under the joint chairmanship of Klaus Poeck, the Professor of Neurology at Aachen, Germany and Helmet Lechner, the Professor of Neurology at Graz, Austria. Starting by saying this was my first visit to Kiel, my embarrassment was profound when, at the end of the meeting, the Professor of Neurology at Kiel quietly told me of my lecture there on a previous occasion; this may be the reason why I now remember Kiel as the home of Beck's Beer. In September 1993, the Section of General Practice of the Royal Society of Medicine held its 13th London Forum for General Practitioners when my talk was again on "Headache".

A joint meeting of the British and American Neuropsychiatry Associations asked me to talk at St Catherine's College in Oxford. Not being happy with the term "neuropsychiatry", as it is difficult enough to master the individual specialties of psychiatry or neurology without attempting to do both, my lecture was on "Migraine as a paroxysmal disorder"; this was the only occasion where there was a public disagreement with one of the organisers but the day ended amicably enough with a group of singers entertaining us at after-dinner coffee in the Dining Hall.

In November 1995 the 6th International Headache Research Seminar was held in Copenhagen with my introductory lecture on "History of the methodology of headache trials". As the opening was scheduled for 2.00p.m., it was considered that a morning flight would get me to my destination in time, but Copenhagen airport was closed by snow and we were diverted to Gothenburg in Sweden. Making the acquaintance of several fellow-travellers who worked for the famous Carlsberg beer company, and were in a similar predicament, needing to get to the Danish capital, when told their beer was one of my favourites they took me "under their wing" and showed me the way to Copenhagen by ferry. In spite of this, my late arrival meant that the "introductory" lecture had to be given much later in the afternoon but, as the whole meeting was on clinical trials, it fitted in well.

With the introduction of new anti-migraine remedies, two financial companies in the City of London invited me to talk on migraine; their estimate at that time valued the migraine market as approximately 160 million dollars. Happy to reply to any questions, at both meetings it was asked whether I had shares in any company producing the new drugs, to which my answer was "No".

On 4 March 2008, I received an invitation from Stephen O'Brien MP and the officers of the All-Party Parliamentary Group on Primary Headache Disorders to a Reception on the Terrace Pavilion of the House of Commons to promote Headache Research. This MP had suffered from headaches which were not due to migraine but to cluster headaches, so we heard about OUCH, which stands for "Organisation for the Understanding of Cluster Headache". Delighted that a meeting on headache was held in parliament, which was the first sign of governmental interest in headache problems - except for a study many years previously, when the Migraine Trust analysed the number of MPs with migraine. This "Owch" meeting was before the first European Headache and Migraine Trust International Symposium in London in 2008, a combined meeting of the Migraine Trust, founded in 1965, and the European Headache Foundation, which was founded in 1992. A further joint meeting was held in Nice, France in 2010.

I was pleased to be invited to the launch of a book entitled "Migraine" and co-written by two of my previous registrars, Dr Russell Lane, consultant at Charing Cross Hospital and Dr Paul Davies, consultant at the Radcliffe Infirmary, Oxford University. They dedicated this book to me and I hope, dear reader, you will not think it inappropriate to end this chapter with their comments:

"We are pleased to dedicate this book to a special friend and colleague, Dr Frank Clifford Rose. We both owe him a great deal in terms of our careers, and it was Frank who kindled and nurtured our interest in headache. Frank spent most of his career as consultant neurologist to the Charing Cross Hospital in London, and we worked in his department in the late 1980s and early 1990s. This was a time when there were relatively few neurologists in the United Kingdom, and hardly any had an interest in headache. Frank was already a pioneer in British neurology and had a particular interest in conditions that were rather unfashionable or neglected, such as motor neurone disease and stroke, in addition to headache. For example, he instituted an emergency domiciliary stroke service in the early 1980s, a concept that may perhaps resurface one day if safe protocols for acute thrombolysis in the community are developed.

He had a talent for getting things done and for involving and inspiring people. He would often suggest a solution to a problem that might be unconventional, but was nearly always effective. Perhaps our witness to his challenge to establishment views has been part of the inspiration for our work. The seed to some extent was sown twenty years ago and has grown steadily. *Migraine* represents the culmination of our experience and thinking about headache to date.

It is difficult to do justice to Frank's achievements. His entry under "Who's Who" is a full A4 page of small print! He has a huge number of publications to his credit, including some 70 books on various neurological conditions. The following is but a brief précis, concentrating on the headache side of Frank's work.

Frank was born on August 29, 1926 and was educated at King's College and Westminster Hospital Medical School. He worked at the National Hospital, Queen Square and was consultant neurologist to the Medical Ophthalmology Unit at St Thomas' Hospital between 1963 and 1985. He then became Physician in Charge at Charing Cross Hospital, where he formed the Department of Neurology, and over time, he developed the Academic Unit of Neurosciences, which was officially opened by Princess Anne in November 1986. This was to evolve into the present Department of Clinical Neurosciences of the Hammersmith Hospital NHS Trust, affiliated to Imperial College and one of the largest departments of neurology in the United Kingdom. It was in the Academic Unit that he established the Princess Margaret Migraine Clinic, which has been the starting point for a number of neurologists from the United Kingdom and across the world, who went on to specialise in headache.

Some of his achievements in headache include the Harold Wolff Award of the American Association for the Study of Headache (1981 and 1984); the Distinguished Clinician Award (1986); Senior Editor of the American Association for the Study of Headache; and co-Editor of Headache Quarterly; and Trustee and Chairman (1988-1996) of the Migraine Trust in the United Kingdom. Frank also helped in the formation of the International Headache Society and the European Headache Federation. Some of his other neurological achievements also cannot go unmentioned. In 1989, he became Secretary-Treasurer General of the World Federation of Neurology (WFN) and Editor of the WFN newsletter *World Neurology*; he was President of the Section of Neurology of the Royal Society of Medicine, edited *Historical Aspects of the Neurosciences*; and the Founding Editor-in Chief of the *Journal of the History of the Neurosciences*, receiving its Lifetime Contribution Award in 2002.

How did he do it all? We don't really know, but if you arrived early in the department, you always knew Frank had been there for at least two hours! He had probably been jogging beforehand as well. It was fantastic to train in a department with such a dynamic driving force. It was inspiring, but it wasn't all work.

Frank is also an extraordinary *bon viveur* and raconteur, an expert on wine and champagne, and his regular Friday lunches, at which we as juniors were invariably guests, are among our fondest recollections".

Suffice to say this encomium is not exactly accurate but few could have been so highly praised in an Introduction to a book, especially to such an excellent book.

Chapter 9

SOCIETIES

The Eighteen Club

In 1949, all those who qualified with me as doctors at Westminster Medical School agreed to have an annual meeting in March, because this was the month we began our studies at Westminster. As there were eighteen of us, we called ourselves the "Eighteen Club" and had a club tie designed consisting of a maroon background with a gold portcullis and crown motif, which we wear at our annual meetings - originally dinners but eventually lunchtime gatherings. Dress was always informal, absent members were toasted and it was agreed that the last two surviving members would toast the other 16 in champagne.

The first to disappear from this scene was my closest friend, Chris Hoyte, who died climbing in the Himalayas on Mount Minapin in the Karakorum, the first attempt ever. On 7 July 1958 at about 11 a.m., Chris was last seen with the expedition leader only 300 feet below the summit of Mount Minapin. Born in the Belgian Congo where his parents had been medical missionaries, Chris had taken me climbing in Snowdonia. Whilst working at the National Hospital in 1958, a Westminster Hospital surgeon, Harold Ellis, telephoned to discuss Chris's death, assuming someone had already informed me. In 2011 eight members of the 18 Club met for the annual lunch. Of the eighteen, one emigrated to Southern California to become the professor of anaesthesiology at Stanford University in California; another became professor of psychiatry in Edinburgh while another spent his working life as a cardiac surgeon in Bristol. The eventual tally for specialists and general practitioners was roughly equal, which was the approximate division of all doctors in the UK, but in 2011, there was only one G.P among the eight attending the lunch meeting. Of the specialists, four were anaesthetists, the explanation being that this department at Westminster Hospital was exceptional and staffed with well-known leaders in the field. In 2008, we celebrated our sixtieth anniversary lunch but it was rather subdued, as one of our members, Bill Pallister, had died two weeks previously from complications following a fall; he had been an anaesthetist at the Middlesex Hospital and had funded several memorial chairs at the Royal Society of Medicine, each named after a well-known British anaesthetist, one of whom was Sir Ivan Magill, with whom Bill had trained. Bill was predeceased by his wife and had no children. My fondest memory of him is when we sang a duet together on a skiing holiday; it was "Any Old Iron" and it didn't matter to either of us that we couldn't sing.

The Eighteen Club 1955

Back row: Geoff Woods (dcd), Charlie Westbury, Doug Pearce,
Norman Kreitman, Chris Hoyte
Front row: Pete Roberts (dcd), FCR, Barry Fairley
Bill Pallister (dcd), Pat Hynes

Osler Club

In 1928, two medical students at St Bartholomew's Hospital, London discussed the history of medicine, when Willie Bett persuaded Alfred White Franklin that they should found a student's club for its study. Being a Cambridge University man, Franklin favoured naming it after Sir Clifford Albutt, but following a visit to the previous home of Sir William Osler at Norham Gardens in Oxford, they agreed to call it the Osler Club, which was promoted by the publication of Harvey Cushing's biography of Osler. Although the two founders had tea with Sir Henry Wellcome, the American millionaire and philanthropist, he could not be persuaded to support the Club. The first meeting was in May 1928 when six members attended to hear Dr (later Professor Sir) George Pickering talk on Louis Pasteur; also present was Dr Charles Singer, who was particularly interested in the subject, and Hal Mansell, a friend of Lady Osler and an Oxford graduate, who was a first-class pianist with an urge to translate Vesalius, but died early during the Second World War. The Osler Club did not function in the Second World War but in 1947 a meeting to restart it was advertised in the *Lancet*. Since my interest in general history began as a schoolboy, it was inevitable that, as a medical student, I should join the Osler Club of London which promoted the historical study of medicine. White Franklin's brother, John, was a consultant dermatologist at Westminster Hospital who taught me "skins" when a student. Dr Alfred White Franklin became Consultant Paediatrician at his own teaching hospital; Dr Walter R Bett was Honorary Secretary of the Osler Club from 1928 to 1959. Its two-fold purpose was to keep alive the memory of Sir William Osler (1849-1919) as well as encourage the study of medical history. No President was appointed until 1950, when the first was Sir Zachary Cope.

On 5 November 1959, a dinner was given by the Osler Club in the Council Chamber of the Royal College of Surgeons, London in honour of Dr Bett who was emigrating to the USA with his wife. Willie had a slight accent with a characteristic rhythm of speech which lasted all his life and he was well-known for his secretarial minutes, which were always amusing.   My first written contribution to the Club was on "viper wine" which was filched from translating in the mid-fifties an article from a French medical journal (for a small payment). The London Pharmacopoeia of 1746 recommended this wine for weakness, as it was considered nutritious, and live vipers were available at that time. My second historical contribution was in 1958, jointly with a psychiatric registrar (Dr Richard Hunter) on Robert Boyle who had written a paper entitled: "Uncommon Observations about Vititiated Sight"; this was when we were both working at the National Hospital where the serious advice of one particular mentor was "avoid history", which meant keeping quiet about my attending a part-time course on the History and Philosophy of Science at University College London.

Initially keen, my first paper was on "The History of the Salpêtrière Hospital" on my return from Paris in 1960 but it soon became obvious that the history of general medicine was too large a subject so thereafter my historical studies were confined to the neurosciences, and in May 2003 at a joint meeting of the Osler Clubs of London, America and Japan held at the Royal College of Physicians of Edinburgh, my contribution was on "The Beginning and End of a Japanese Disease: SMON". At the end of my talk there was little interest in the condition, largely because it disappeared soon after our first studies in 1971.

Royal Society of Medicine

Having joined this society in 1949, the year of my qualification, I regularly attended the meetings of the Neurological Section and was elected to its Council in 1976 and was the Representative of the Neurological Section on the Library Committee from 1980 to 1989. Because of my interest in neuro-ophthalmology, having been a clinical assistant to Dr Swithin Meadows at Moorfields Eye Hospital for four years, it became necessary to join the Ophthalmology Section and I served on its Council from 1969 to 1972. Although also joining the Clinical Section, I only attended a couple of the meetings as they were held on Friday evenings, when I drove from London to our country cottage.

My Presidential Address to the Section of Neurology of the RSM in 1990 was on Migraine. After delivering this, a dinner was held for all those who had co-authored or co-edited those books published with my name on the spine, of which, at the time, there were more than sixty. Held in the RSM Conservatory, the guests were divided into three groups, each standing to share a toast with me and, and it was a delight to see such a large crowd enjoy the evening. Although my Presidential Address on "Migraine" was published in the Society's Journal, it was in a much abbreviated version and probably not generally understood. In my Presidential year, it seemed a good idea to have joint meetings with other Sections of the Society, which meant that, instead of having perhaps five meetings on

Neurology during my year of office, that number was more than doubled. As Secretary-Treasurer General of the World Federation of Neurology at that time, my suggestion to its President, Sir John Walton (now Lord), that we send a copy of the year's programme to neurologists abroad, resulted in a flood of applications to join and the Section of Neurology became the largest Section and the membership secretary pleaded with me for no more applicants as she was being overworked. As the Section of Neurology included all the neurosciences, its name was changed in 1997 to the Section of Clinical Neurosciences, reflecting its widening sphere of interests.

Other medical societies joined were the British Medical Association in 1949, the Harveian Society from 1952 to 1988, although I rarely attending its meetings which were held at Lettsom House, owned by the Medical Society of London. At the request of the President of the Association of Clinical Pathologists, I became an Extraordinary Member from 1974-1985 but never attended any of its meetings. From 1976-1987, as a member of the City of London Medical Book Society, they were not best pleased on receiving my resignation. The Academy of Aphasia, an American Society limited to 200 members elected me from 1976 to 1987, but the Atlantic Ocean meant I only ever attended only two of its meetings.

On 22 November 1999, the Secretary of the **British Medical Association** wrote to me as follows:

> "I am delighted to tell you that you have completed 50 years as a member of the BMA. This means that, from 1 October, you will be able to continue in membership without payment of any subscription. On behalf of the Council I offer you congratulations and sincere thanks for your loyal support through so many years. I enclose a permanent membership card as a token of your special status".

They continue to send me the BMJ free of charge!

Medical Society of London
1954, the Dean of Westminster Hospital Medical School proposed me for
Fellowship of this Society, the oldest continuous medical society in the
world, having been founded in 1773 by John Coakley Lettsom who was a
Quaker. Being a religious dissenter, he could not be admitted to Oxford or
Cambridge Universities and therefore qualified as a doctor from
Edinburgh. As he was not even allowed to use the libraries of those two
ancient universities nor indeed the library of the Royal College of
Physicians, his main purpose in founding the Society was to build a
medical library and he donated many of his own books; it later became
the custom for Fellows to donate further scientific works. Until its
foundation, the three groups of men who treated the sick, namely
physicians, surgeons and apothecaries, did not associate with each other
but this new Society incorporated all three in equal numbers, initially
thirty of each. At the beginning of the nineteenth century, when the
current elected President stayed in office for over twenty years instead of
the usual one or two, a group of Fellows left to form the Medico-
Chirurgical Society which, a century later, formed part of the basis for the
Royal Society of Medicine.

After two decades as a Fellow and about to resign, Dr Geraint James, a
senior member of the Society, asked me to stand for its Council in 1972,
followed by my election as Junior Secretary in 1977 and Senior Secretary
in the following year. In 1980, the Council elected me Lettsomian
Lecturer, which consisted of two lectures on "Stroke: the Third Killer", so-
called because heart attacks and cancer were the first two. A famous
Professor of Medicine, (later Dame) Sheila Sherlock, the wife of Gerry
James, interrupted the first of these two lectures with a question to which
my reply was: "I'm so pleased you asked that question which I shall be
talking about in my Second Lettsomian Lecture", which she did not
attend. As Vice-President from 1979 to 1981, and then Editor of its
Transactions from 1981- 1984, progression to President followed in 1984.
After becoming Treasurer from 1984 for five years until 1989, my next
position was as the Secretary for International Affairs from 1995 until
2008, after which this post was no longer considered viable as mail from

abroad gradually petered out and the position was removed from the Council.

During my Presidential year, a crisis occurred over the Medical Society of London library; many of its valuable old books were housed in the Wellcome Institute for the History of Medicine, since the Society was unable to look after them well enough. The decision with Sir James Watt, chairman of the library committee, was to sell rather than loan our library to the Wellcome Institute, who initially offered £250,000. Since this offer undervalued the library, a Los Angeles expert in antiquarian medical books was invited to London and gave a valuation of £800,000, a sum with which the Wellcome agreed; the Californian antiquarian received 5% (£4,000) for his invaluable help and the Medical Society of London Library is now permanently kept in the Wellcome Institute's library.

In the academic year from 1983- 1984 as President, my subjects for the fortnightly meetings started with my Presidential Address on "The Medicine of Art" showing classical paintings of medical interest, a talk specifically aimed at non-medical people as Fellows of the Society would bring guests, usually wives or other family members. The second meeting on "The Hand" was given by my old Westminster chief, Dr Dudley Hart who talked on rheumatism, whilst the next was on "Eating Disorders" by Professor Arthur Crisp, my house physician from Westminster Hospital days, talking on "Anorexia Nervosa" of which he had become a world expert. My Presidency was in the period following the Falkland Islands conflict so it was natural the Council agreed to a meeting on "Naval Medicine" where surgeon commanders on "Ajax Bay" and "Uganda" spoke, as well as Surgeon Vice-Admiral Sir John Harrison, who was on "Canberra". The following meetings included such colleagues from Charing Cross Hospital as Eric Arnott on eyes, (later Sir) 'Tiny' Maini on the immune system, and the Lettsom Lectures by the Professor of Surgery from Charing Cross Hospital, Roger Greenhalgh, regarding diseases of the blood vessels. I could not resist having a joint meeting with the Assurance Medical Society which gave me the opportunity to wear *both* Presidential necklaces, an occurrence that had never happened before – or since; my sense of humour was not appreciated and it produced no comment. A fellow Trustee of the Migraine Trust, Lord Perry, who had helped in the founding of the Open University, gave the Annual Oration on "Leadership" whilst the final meeting, which was with the Osler Club, was given by the past President of the Royal College of Physicians, Sir Douglas Black on "Medical Specialisation".

The Annual Dinner was held at the Savoy Hotel where all the speakers in my Presidential year were invited. Previous to the sale of the Medical Society of London's Library to the Wellcome Trust, the occasional book had been sold to help the Society's finances but, following my Presidency, and then becoming Treasurer for five years, it was agreed that the capital sum resulting from the library sale should be invested, annual inflation added and, only after this, would money be used for the Society's needs. It did mean that the annual fee for Fellows was rarely raised and the Society had an ideal lecture theatre with excellent furniture and projection facilities.

In 1975, the Society was left a Bequest by Mrs Florence Alice Mansell, "to promote neurological studies", and to commemorate the name of her husband, Dr Harry E Mansell FRCP, who died from motor neurone disease at the age of 41 years, leaving a widow and two children. He had joined the Society in 1937, while working as consultant cardiologist at Lambeth Hospital, and already mentioned in this book as an early member of the Osler Club. There was discussion in the Council as to how the Bequest of £34,558 could best be used and, although a suggestion was made for it to fund a researcher for a year or two, I pointed out that this would not serve Mrs Mansell's purpose to keep her husband's name remembered. My suggestion was to initiate international symposia, like those organised by the Ciba Foundation funded by the Ciba pharmaceutical company, where experts in a special field would be funded to come to London for a conference and the proceedings published. Since the terms of the Bequest were to apply the sum to "expand neurological studies", Council chose me to organise these gatherings. My first choice of subject, because it was the cause of Dr Mansell's death, was motor neurone disease; there had never been a meeting on this rare fatal disease in the UK, although there had been one in France, where Professor Jean-Martin

Charcot had first delineated this condition. Only twelve experts could be gathered for the first symposium with just a few papers being highly relevant. In spite of this lack of interest, the Proceedings were published in 1976 and there were new volumes published on neurological subjects until I retired from this position in 2008. My decision to give up organising the Mansell Bequest Symposia caused some problems for the Society since few of the Fellows were neurologists. A book on the History of the Society states: "The Mansell Symposia constitute one of the Society's major contributions to the dissemination of up-to-date medical research and knowledge".

The Mansell Bequest Symposia were generally on topics which a commercial publisher would not find suitable or profitable (see table). The second Symposium was on neuro-immunology, a topic I chose to learn about immune conditions that could affect the nervous system. My preface to the published book on these Proceedings was: "The ancient Chinese first used an immunological principle when they inhaled dry small-pox crusts to prevent the more serious disease. It was not until 1718 that any interest was taken in the western world until Lady Mary Wortley Montague, the wife of the British Ambassador in Turkey, had her three-year-old child vaccinated with material from mild small-pox cases, which she had witnessed locally. Later in that century, Edward Jenner, a country physician in England, used cowpox in the same manner; the scientific basis of immunology came later with Pasteur's observations on rabies". The then President of the Medical Society of London, Sir Francis Avery Jones, wrote the foreword in which he stated that the Society was founded by Lettsom, who was born in the West Indies and sent to the UK for schooling at the age of six years. On returning to his home country, he released his family's slaves, and returned to Britain to qualify as a doctor. This Society celebrated its 225th anniversary in 1998 with a dinner held in the Painted Hall of the Royal Naval College, an opulent venue for a Mansell Bequest Symposium dinner, especially as the contributors reached Greenwich from Westminster Bridge by boat.

The Gordon Holmes Society

After the Gordon Holmes Symposium of 1976, a Society was founded in his name which would meet annually. As President, I organised a clinical meeting at Charing Cross Hospital where colleagues and registrars from the Department of Neurology could show their paces with talks on modern advances or rare cases. This Society did not survive long after my retirement in 1991.

In November 1985 I went to Lisbon for a meeting of the **Hydergine Club**; its final meeting was in the following year in Vienna. This Club was supported by the pharmaceutical company that produced hydergine (Sandoz) and included all specialists who were studying this drug. Its final meeting indicated that no useful purpose was ever discovered.

On 2 October 1997 I was admitted as a founding Member of the **Expert Witness Institute** but although occasionally undertaking medico-legal work, I did not attend any of its meeting..

Independent Doctors Forum (IDF)

Having returned to Harley Street after retirement from the National Health Service in 1991, the Independent Doctors Forum (IDF) beckoned as it was restricted to doctors in full-time private practice. The IDF began in 1989 and represented doctors practicing independent medicine, a term chosen advisedly because its members were not only private practitioners but also others, such as company doctors and those in pharmaceutical medicine, whose work does not necessarily depend on NHS contracts; this meant that the IDF also had to deal with governments and insurance agencies.

Originally started by four private GPs who came together to advise other GPs wishing to become private practitioners, few hospital consultants were members, since most of them conducted their private practice on a part-time basis, seeing this type of patients for only a few hours weekly. Within a short time of my joining the IDF, these founding members invited me to dinner at a restaurant in the Harley Street area; it took me some time to realise that the reason for this meeting was to get me to become a member of the Council of the IDF. Quickly pointing out that my membership was very recent, they persuaded me that my only function would be to attend the monthly Council meetings, all held at a local private hospital. The next Council meeting was to be held at Lettsom House, the home of the Medical Society of London which, having been its President and knowing the secretary well, I arrived early to chat to her. Soon after, the next early arrival was a consultant member of the IDF who, after initially wondering why I was there, realised it was because of my recent election to the Council, of which he was also a member. We knew each other from patient referrals but he soon pointed out that this Council meeting was important because it was to elect a new Chairman of the IDF, which he expected to be himself.

After the acting Chairman called Council to order, the first item of business was election of the next Chairman and, when asking for nominations, the only name proposed was mine, which was immediately seconded. On asking for further nominations, there was a deadly silence which meant I was duly elected as Chairman. I only discovered later that this was pre-arranged by the four founding GP members who had invited me to dinner, because they did not like this other consultant, partly due to his intention to appoint, if elected, a PR person to increase publicity of the IDF, because of its important task of making private practice respectable and responsible.

Sir Reginald Murley, the distinguished surgeon who became President of the Royal College of Surgeons, was at my suggestion, the first Honorary Member of the IDF, partly because he was one of the founders of the FFM (Fellowship for the Freedom of Medicine), an organisation that has been claimed to be a forerunner of the IDF. The second Honorary Member was Dr Geraint James, husband of Dame Professor Sheila Sherlock. Gerry was a keen supporter of private practice, and had helped me when I started seeing private patients in Harley Street; both were made Honorary Members during my Chairmanship. In 1993, The Independent Doctors Forum held a Spring meeting abroad with eight talks where my contribution was on "Headache and its management". Study weekends abroad have been a regular feature of the IDF since then and on another such meeting in Madrid I spoke on Goya's illness.

A senior cardiac surgeon at a London teaching hospital joined the IDF, sending his cheque of £60 for the annual subscription. To my surprise, he resigned shortly afterwards, the reason he gave was that there were two classes of membership and those who were only part-time in private practice did not have the full vote. Appalled to hear this, looking at the Rules for the Forum clearly confirmed his point which was raised at the subsequent Council meeting, when it was eventually decided that there should be a debate by the whole membership with a motion proposed by me to admit equally as full members those in part-time practice; this motion was defeated, the GP members fearing they would be overwhelmed by new young consultants. Having pointed out that the IDF had little future if it maintained its existing constitution excluding those who worked part-time in the NHS, I resigned from the chairmanship at the end of my second year in 1994 rather than stay for the full three years term, adding that there may well be a new Association for part-time private consultants if they were not treated equally by the IDF. My warning was soon realised by the formation of the London Consultants Association, after which the IDF constitution was revised so that the Council of the IDF had twelve members, four of whom had to be GPs and four consultants, the other four serving in various capacities e.g. one from outside the M25 motorway to represent those working privately beyond the London area. The IDF were given two places on the Private Practice committee of the British Medical Association, one of which I held for two years from 2000-2002.

It is well over ten years since these events and, although retired, it gives me great satisfaction to report that the IDF is now a respected organisation with about eight hundred members (200 GPs and 600 consultants) and plays a pre-eminent part in private practice within the UK. In 2009 it changed its name from Independent Doctors Forum to the Independent Doctors Federation. After my two years as chairman, I stayed on the Council serving as Chairman of the Constitution Committee until November 2005 when they very kindly gave me a retirement dinner at which all members of the Council attended.

The Royal College of Physicians is not a Society but a professional body. Although obtaining the MRCP by examination in 1954, I became FRCP in 1967. Elected to the Council of the College in 1985, I remained until 1988, serving on the Working Party on Stroke from 1987 to 1978.

FOREIGN SOCIETIES

The International School of Neurological Studies, Venice

Documents have shown that there was a monastery on the island of San Servolo in the Venetian bay in the eighth century, a religious complex which survived to the eighteenth century, when designated by the Venetian Republic as a military hospital, which it needed because of wars with Rome. In 1725, a mentally deranged nobleman was admitted which was how San Servolo's function as an asylum for wealthy insane men began; by 1800, mental patients of every class were admitted so that it became the psychiatric hospital for the Veneto Region. The hospital was closed in 1978 when the Regional Council eventually decided it was to become the International School for Neurological Studies, with myself as the UK representative.

In 1981, I was elected an Honorary Member of the **Société de Neurologie Française** and in the same year joined the **American Academy of Neurology** which was open to all American neurologists, then more than 20,000 and, in the following year became a corresponding member of the **American Neurological Association**, a much older organisation than the Academy and restricted mainly to academics, such as university professors and lecturers. Their annual meetings were usually held in October whereas the Academy's meetings were held around April. The last meeting of the ANA I attended was in 2003 when Professor Srinivas from Madras (now Chennai) was awarded the Honorary Membership of the ANA. Over the ensuing years, my travels to America became less frequent but were always enjoyable. The American Academy of Neurology met every year at a different venue which had to be in a large city since this annual meeting consisted of teaching courses and lectures on every conceivable neurological subject, attracting neurologists of all ages worldwide.

In April 1988 I went to Prague, Czechoslovakia, to attend the First International Symposium on Neurological Emergencies, which was under the auspices of the Research Group on Intensive Management Neurology of the WFN. This was part of the First European Congress of Neurology which was one of the precursors of the European Federation of Neurological Societies (EFNS).

 In July 1988, the New York Academy of Sciences, which had been founded in 1817, elected me as an active member of the Academy.

The European Federation of Neurological Societies (EFNS) was founded in September 1995, its first Congress being held in Marseilles, France, although there had been a preparatory meeting in Poznan, Poland in the previous year. At this 1995 Congress, it was decided to have scientific panels to cover the major subfields in neurology; there was no panel on History of Neurology but the idea was suggested and eventually accepted with myself as its first Chairman. The principle was to bring European experts in the field of neurohistory to get together at the Annual Congress where the Chairman of the panel reports to the Scientific Committee; my chairmanship was for three years when my successor was Dr Christopher Gardner-Thorpe, of Exeter, UK.

Prior to the EFNS annual symposia, from 1957 graduate education in neurology was held quadrennially at the World Congress of Neurology but in the USA there had been annual Easter meetings of the American Academy of Neurology and autumn meetings of the American Neurological Association. The motivation for the EFNS was to give post-graduate education to neurologists in European countries but another organisation, the European Neurological Society (ENU), was for individuals and not national societies. Lord Walton of Detchant made an effort to amalgamate the EFNS and the ENU by inviting three representatives of the EFNS and three from the ENU together at the House of Lords, but without success.

The third EFNS Congress in 1997 was held in Prague with a meeting on "Difficult Headache" where my talk was on "Chronic Cluster Headache". In 1998 there was a focused workshop on the History of Neuroscience in Seville, Spain but not a single Spaniard attended my talk on the Arabic contribution to the medieval period. The 4th EFNS Congress of 1999 was in Lisbon where my talk was on "The Neurology of Galen of Pergamon". The Fifth EFNS Congress held in 2000 in Copenhagen had a focussed workshop on the History of Neuroscience where my talk was on "Historiography". At the EFNS Congress of 2002, held in Vienna, Dr Christopher Gardner-Thorpe gave the first Clifford Rose Lecture on the History of Neuroscience. In the following year, 2003, the Congress was held in Helsinki when Professor Matti Haltia gave the second Clifford Rose Lecture on the History of Neuroscience. The third Clifford Rose lecture was given at the 2004 Paris meeting by Professor Goetz of Chicago on Charcot.

MEDICAL SOCIETIES

Medical Society of London

Fellow	from 1952
Member of Council	1972 – 1975
Junior Secretary	1977 – 1978
Senior Secretary	1978 – 1979
Vice President	1979 – 1981
Lettsomian Lecturer	1980
Editor of Transactions	1981 – 1984
President	1984 – 1985
Treasurer	1985 – 1989
Secretary of International Affairs	1994 – 2008

West London Medico-Chirurgical Society

Fellow	from 1967
Secretary	1969 – 1970
President	1976 – 1977

Royal Society of Medicine

Fellow, Section of Neurology	from 1949
Member of Council	1976-19
Library Representative	1980 – 1989
Member of Council	1989 - 1991
Honorary Life Member	2004
Section of Neurology – President	1990 – 1991
Section of Ophthalmology	1969 – 1972
Member of Council	

Association of British Neurologists

Member	from 1967
UK Delegate to W F N	1977-1989
Member of Council	1983 – 1985

EEG Society	1960 – 2006

International League against Epilepsy

Academy of Aphasia	1976 – 1987

Eye Physic Club, Founder Member   1964 – 1981

British Medical Association

Member   from 1949

Private Practice Committee of the BMA   1995 – 1997

Osler Club   from 1947

Harveian Society   1952 – 1955

City of London Medical Book Society   1976 – 1987

Ophthalmological Society of the U K   1964 – 1985

Association of Clinical Pathologists   1974 – 1985

Extraordinary Member

Hunterian Society   1952 – 1988

Assurance Medical Society

Fellow   1965 – 1991

President   1985 – 1986

FOREIGN MEDICAL SOCIETIES

American Association for the Study of Headache   1977-1991

European Association of Science Editors   1978 – 1984

Société de Neurologie Française Honorary Member   1981 –

American Academy of Neurology Corresponding Member 1982-1991

American Neurological Association

New York Academy of Science   1988 – 1989

Thai Neurological Association Honorary Member

Chapter 10

HISTORY

On a train journey to London in 1978, Dr Bill Bynum discussed with me the possibility of restarting the WFN Research Group on the History of Neurosciences which Macdonald Critchley had originally founded. As it was going to be Critchley's 80th birthday in 1980, my suggestion of holding a meeting in his honour and publishing the proceedings as a "Festschrift", entitled "Historical Aspects of the Neurosciences", edited by Bynum and myself, was agreed. Before that time, publishers were reluctant to produce books on the history of neurology so it is likely that the American publisher, Raven Press, accepted this suggestion because Critchley was on their Editorial Advisory Board; since then there have been many such historical meetings followed by publications. After this festschrift, the Research Group on the History of Neurosciences did restart in 1980 and after acting as its Secretary in 1980, I became Chairman in 1981 until 1989. Bill Bynum went on to become Assistant Director of the Wellcome Institute.

The first meeting of this group was on the History of European Neurology and held in 1986 in Milan, followed the next day in Pavia, Italy. My talk, "The first textbook in neurology?" was given in the presence of Professor Zülch of Germany who had previously nominated Romberg's book of 1840 for this distinction, but my contribution was promoting the claim for John Cooke, an Englishman who had produced his work in 1820; Zulch's reply was that he had never actually stated Romberg's was the first. This initial meeting was convened by Renato Boeri of Milan and followed in successive years in Venice/Padua, Annecy, Graz, and Oslo. The International Society for the History of Neurosciences was founded in May 1995 in Montreal, its second meeting being held in Leiden, The Netherlands; and in 1997, jointly with the 6th meeting of the European Club for the History of Neurology, founded by Boeri.

Early in the 1980s, Dr Geraint (Gerry) James had asked me to give an historical introduction to a meeting on Parkinson's disease which he was organising, as Dean, at the Royal Northern Hospital, London. Seeking for something new, I remembered Dr Arthur Morris, another member of the Osler Club, who had been the Superintendent at St Leonard's Hospital, adjacent to St Leonard's Church, where James Parkinson had been baptised, married and buried. Morris had taken a special interest in Parkinson and Macdonald Critchley remembered him, but thought he was no longer alive. Not entirely convinced, the Medical Directory revealed a telephone number in a South Coast retirement town; his wife answered the 'phone and, after explaining the purpose of my call, replied "You had better hurry to see him as he is very ill". On arrival at their house, he was in semi-coma and the memorabilia that he had on Parkinson was in total disarray. Pointing out that all this collection was worth saving, I recommended its transfer to the Wellcome Institute for the History of Medicine, but Mrs Morris persuaded me to take on the task which, seven years later, resulted in a book "James Parkinson: His Life and Times.

In 1983 Dr Purdon Martin, a distinguished neurologist, complained that the grave of Dr Hughlings Jackson, the "Father of British Neurology", in Highgate Cemetery was overgrown and difficult to find and contacted the two official British neurological societies, the Association of British Neurologists and the Section of Neurology of the Royal Society of Medicine. Serving at that time on the Councils of both these bodies, it was no surprise to be asked to investigate; visiting Highgate Cemetery, Hughlings Jackson's grave was indeed untended and difficult to find. After arranging for restoration work to be done, I telephoned Purdon Martin's home to tell him the good news; a male voice answered and on hearing the purpose of my call, replied "I'm terribly sorry but I'm his son and he died yesterday".

In 1985 there was an Osler Club meeting in Edinburgh with Japanese and American Oslerians where my talk was on "SMON: the beginning and end of a Japanese disease"; there was only one question from the Japanese contingent, presumably because my lecture was then fifteen years after the epidemic, which most doctors, including the Japanese, had long forgotten.

In March 1990, Francois l'Hermitte, the son of Jean l'Hermitte, the leading French professor of neurology, wrote to me regarding the upcoming centenary of Charcot's death in 1893, as he felt it should be celebrated under the auspices of the WFN. He suggested that we meet before, or after, the Symposium on the History of European Neurology which was to be held in Lyons that year. It soon became clear that Charcot's centenary would not be celebrated under the auspices of the WFN, since the French neurological establishment was keen to do this. Part of the proceedings took place at Charcot's house in Paris but, as the only Englishman who attended, it seemed to me that less attention was paid to Jean-Martin Charcot than Charcot's son, who had given up medicine and become a sailor-explorer, Commander Charcot. The plaque placed outside the house mentioned both father and son but the son's name came first; Rue Charcot in Paris was said to be named after the son, since the average Frenchman knew of the Commander, but not his father, Professor Jean-Martin Charcot, the first Professor of Neurology in the world.

In May 1991, the Third European Meeting on the History of Neurology took place at Veysier-du-Lac, the headquarters of the Fondation Marcel Merieux, just by Lake Annecy. Angela came with me and we stayed at Le Père Bise, a hotel/restaurant which had 3 Guide Michelin stars. We returned there a year or two later in order to learn which wine should be drunk with sweetbreads, the reason being it was a question in the *Daily Telegraph* wine competition where I had passed the first written paper but failed miserably in the final section on wine-tasting, as did a well-known wine-loving cabinet minister; the competition was won by a garage-owner, who had an excellent nose and later switched to the wine trade, reportedly with such success that he gave up his garage. My failure may be due to asking the sommelier at Père Bise which wine he would recommend, and his reply was "comme vous voudrez" – which was not a great deal of help!

It seemed odd that there were history journals for many specialities, not least psychiatry, but not one catered for neuro-history. My suggestion to Smith Gordon, one of my publishers, was accepted and we started the *"Journal of the History of Neurosciences"* in January 1992 with me as

Editor-in-Chief. It was never expected to have a large circulation and it took a few years to be 'legitimised' in 2000 by university libraries which then included it in MEDICINE and the INDEX MEDICUS. This journal continues to be published quarterly; I gave up the Editorship after five years, when it was co-edited by two neuro-historians, an American psychologist and a Dutch neurologist, joined later by an Australian psychologist. Its circulation is still steady in the low hundreds and continues to serve a useful purpose. On the occasion of the 500th anniversary of Columbus' voyage to the New World in 1992, the Spanish government held a series of festivals on every conceivable subject. The meeting on neurology was held in the Canary Islands, from whence Columbus had set sail, and was entitled "Encuentro Neurologica" (neurological encounter). The topic chosen for me was "The History of Neurology *before* 1492". John (later Lord) Walton thought that my talk would not last longer than a minute but, in the event, it was a huge topic, largely because of the ancient Greeks, whose work was translated by the Arabs, and returned to Europe in Latin.

In May 1993, the 4th European Meeting of the WFN Research Group on the History of Neurosciences met in Graz, Austria. Another neuro-historian, Professor Ragnar Stien of Norway, organised a similar meeting in Oslo at the time of the Norwegian Independence Celebrations on 17 May; the symposium dinner was held on a boat sailing around Oslo harbour with shrimps and beer served all night and bonfires lighting up the shores, emphasising the nationalistic tendencies of the Norwegians as well as their propensity to enjoy life. Later the same month it was a pleasure to hold a dinner at the Savile Club for Doctor Najoua Miladi who had kindly invited me to lecture at the Second National Meeting of Tunisia, an opportunity to see the fascinating Museum of Carthage. Whilst in Tunis, I asked a taxi driver if he knew of a nearby military cemetery facing the sea and he took me there, less than a mile away. On entering the cemetery, its caretaker, an American, offered assistance. I asked if he was surprised that I was Englishman visiting an American Military cemetery, but he told me many British visited and there were several British graves. It transpired that he had been a top sergeant in the United

States Marines and his son had suggested he apply for this job. When told the reason for my visit was memories of a scene in my favourite film, Patten, he confirmed that it was the same cemetery, and we had a long chat, cut short by my tears (the only time in my adult life up to that time) and a hasty return to the waiting cab.

In April 2000 the ABN met in Exeter, where my friend, Christopher Gardner-Thorpe, the consultant neurologist, had organised a history session. Angela came with me and we then spent a few days at Tresanton, Lord Forte's daughter's hotel (Olga Polliti) in St Mawes, Cornwall, but were quite disappointed with it and have never been back. We spent a day in St Ives, but this pretty fishing village has become much commercialised and lost a lot of its "olde worlde" charm, although there are still many interesting small art galleries and also a branch of the Tate Gallery.

At the June 2001 World Congress of Neurology, where I chaired the historical session on "clinical diagnosis", the initial paper was read by my friend, George York from California, on the "Structure of the nervous system" followed by his colleague David Steinberg, talking on the "Function of the nervous system", but confining himself to the discovery of reflexes from Whytt to Sherrington, both British neurologists. Gardner-Thorpe talked on the concepts and descriptions of nervous disease starting with Thomas Willis who was born in Wiltshire and was the founder of neurology, being the first to use this word, meaning the "doctrine of the nerves".

Rhea & Louis D Boshes Lecture
Professor Louis D Boshes was a loyal member of the Northwestern University, having grown up in Chicago where his subsequent career as a "renaissance man" brought distinction to the University. He amalgamated his clinical work in neurology and psychiatry with other diverse interests, one of which was neuroscience history. Because of this interest, he initiated a new lectureship at his university named after him, the Louis Boshes Visiting Lecture on the History of Neurology. Sadly, Rhea Boshes, his partner in marriage for over 50 years, died just a few

weeks before I gave the first endowed Lecture in October 1993. This was the first named lecture in neuro-history in Academia and included provision for travel and lodging expenses, as well as an honorarium of 1,500 dollars. Benjamin Boshes, the brother of Louis, had also been a well-known professor of neurology in Chicago. When invited to give this talk, they asked me for a list of possible lectures on neuro-history; giving three titles, somewhat to my surprise they chose "The History of Greek Neurology". The Dean of the medical school introduced me with this flattering encomium:

> "Today we are very pleased to launch this lectureship with one of the most distinguished neurologic historians of our time. F Clifford Rose is a distinguished English Neurologist. His illustrious career is also summarised in the programme. He also is a renaissance man. His interests in Neurology have encompassed many specialty areas: stroke, neuromuscular disease, headache, physiology. He is very widely travelled and a familiar figure on American turf. He has been a leader in the World Federation of Neurology. His interest in history came early. In an unusual move, he joined the Osler Society during medical school. He too has written widely on neurological history. His Festschrift for Macdonald Critchley, entitled *Historical Aspects of the Neurosciences*, is particularly notable and interesting. Recently he founded a journal devoted exclusively to the history of neuroscience".

Towards the end of this talk, suspecting it may have been boring, I asked the student audience if they would like to know something of more recent neuro-history of Chicago: "In 1934, there was an outbreak of acute poliomyelitis (infantile paralysis) in Chicago. For advanced cases where the respiratory muscles were paralysed, this cause of death required the life-saving treatment of "iron lungs" (positive-pressure respirators). The nurse in charge of these iron tanks, of which there were ten in this hospital, rang the on-duty resident to say that there was a ten-year old girl dying from respiratory polio who urgently needed assisted respiration but all the machines were in use; the resident considered and then ordered that the oldest patient in a respirator should be replaced by the little girl. Within hours, men burst into the resident's office, held *revolvers* to his head and ordered him to "put our father back in his 'iron lung'". These of course were gangsters in 1930s Chicago and the resident had no alternative but to comply. On the *same* evening, the *same* resident was asked to attend the morgue urgently, an unusual request for a mortuary. On arrival there, the resident found men in Fedora hats, looking at the body of a white man with three neat bullet-holes in the back of his head. The dead man was John Dillinger, Public Enemy Number One, proving that any story of a shoot-out was not accurate." My concluding sentence was to give the name of the resident - Louis B Boshes - after whom the lecture was named and who had told me these stories the previous evening at dinner. Years later, I received a letter from him:

> "I'm sending a copy of this letter to Frank Rose. He will tell you how I have contributed to his delinquency by indoctrinating him into official Al Caponean Chicago crime. He now boasts a complete dossier on Al Capone, John Dillinger, Pretty Boy Floyd and other illustrious gangsters that made Chicago famous far above the accomplishments of our 7 medical schools." It may be worth repeating the dossier he sent to me:

> "Not to lag behind in the underworld arms race, the South Siders (now led by Al Capone) and the North Siders (now led by Hymie Weiss) quickly obtained Thompsons (machine-guns)of their own and started using them against one another in spectacular shoot-outs. By 1929, the Thompson's worldwide notoriety had inspired the rumour that the Auto-Ordnance Corporation was giving the weapons free to gangsters for promotional purposes. In fact, the company was nearly bankrupt, with most of its guns gathering dust in a Colt's warehouse. Repeal ended the Chicago beer wars, but not the gun's evil reputation. By 1933, John Dillinger, Baby Face Nelson, Machine Gun Kelly, and other Depression outlaws were either buying Thompsons on the black market or stealing

them from police stations, and otherwise driving nails into the Auto-Ordnance coffin. In 1939, the nearly defunct company was forced to sell to a shady Connecticut industrialist named Russell Maguire for only $529,000 – about the wholesale value of the 4,700 guns still in their inventory, with manufacturing equipment thrown in."

My interest in neuro-history continued and when our three sons went as boarders to Marlborough College, Wiltshire, we bought a cottage nearby, in Little Bedwyn, where they could come for the weekends. We also used it as a weekend "bolt-hole" and one Friday afternoon in 1993, going for a walk, just at the end of our little road there was a man taking a photograph of a thatched cottage. Saying to Angela "That chap looks like Jim Toole", an American colleague from the World Federation of Neurology (and later its President); on approaching, I added "It is him", and realised immediately what he was doing. Without any preliminary, my first words to him were "You're taking the wrong house"; knowing of his interest in stroke, I guessed he was giving the annual Willis Lecture in the United States and wanted a photo of the birth place of Thomas Willis, the Founder of Neurology. After his surprise at seeing me in this out-of-the-way village, he replied that he had already looked for Willis' birthplace in Great Bedwyn but had been told it was in Little Bedwyn. We then arranged for him to visit our friends who lived in it (in Great Bedwyn). Willis published the anatomy of the brain and its vascular supply, the drawings being done by Sir Christopher Wren, the famed architect of St Paul's Cathedral. Jim Toole and his wife had difficulty in believing we lived where we did, *not* because of Willis' birth place but because our three sons all attended nearby Marlborough College. This incident made me determined to have a blue plaque put on Willis' birth place and the unveiling took place in May 1994. Members of the Osler Club from the United States were present as were the three living biographers of Willis: Bill Feindel, an eminent neurosurgeon from the Montreal Neurological Institute, Hans-Rudi Isler, a clinical neurologist from Zurich, and Trevor Hughes, a neuropathologist from Oxford; each biographer gave a short talk. My unveiling of the plaque is recorded in my capacity as Secretary-Treasurer General of the World Federation of Neurology. We had lunch at the local pub, The Harrow Inn, which has since become the top restaurant in the area, and was awarded a Guide Michelin star in 2007.

Unveiling the plaque at Willis' birthplace, The Castle, Great Bedwyn

The story of this pub is not without interest. When we first moved to Little Bedwyn in 1977 it was, and still is, a hamlet rather than a village as it had lost its school, shop and vicarage with only a tiny post office remaining; the only other survival was the Harrow Inn which was owned by a very old lady, Mrs Lance, who allowed me and our three small sons go through her kitchen to the bar (strictly illegal); we would help ourselves to drinks and pay on the way out. When Mrs Lance died, it was taken over by a couple who made a lot of improvements, but when they split up and decided to sell there was a suggestion that it might be sold as a residence. The village was upset at the thought of losing their pub, so about 100 local people clubbed together to buy it. A local young couple, Louize (the daughter of Bill and Dawn Bacon who lived in Willis' house) and her husband Sean , who had trained in catering, ran the pub with a Board of Directors made up of village folk, including Angela as the token woman, ostensibly for advice on décor. This pub-restaurant was successful for several years until Sean and Louize moved to set up their own establishment a few miles away. The Harrow Inn kept going with successive managers, none of whom proved successful; finally it was losing money and it was decided to sell to a couple whose plan was to phase out the pub element (no draught beer and no sandwiches or crisps for walkers and boaters on the nearby Kennet and Avon Canal) and transform it into a first class restaurant. They have been supremely successful, although few locals can afford to dine there.

In 1996 I went to Buffalo, New York, for the First Annual Meeting of the International Society for the History of Neurosciences (ISHN) which was founded to stimulate interest, education and research in the history of neuroscience. The initial meeting, prior to Buffalo, had been in Montreal, Canada which I attended as founding Editor of the *Journal of the History of Neurosciences* in 1992, and in Buffalo there was general agreement that the *Journal* should become the official organ of the Society. After my 5-year term as Editor-in-Chief, my successors were Peter Koehler, a neurologist from the Netherlands and Stan Finger, the Professor of Psychiatry at St Louis University and, later, an Australian Professor of Psychology. The annual meetings of the Society alternate between the United States and Europe. My talk in Buffalo was on "The history of head injuries; an overview". Never having been to this city before, Angela saw me off at Heathrow Airport telling me there was no need for an overcoat as summer was approaching. On arrival in Buffalo, it was snowing heavily, necessitating a visit to the nearest clothing shop where I was sold a long, thick raincoat which stood me in good stead in all weathers; although still in my possession, it has been shortened and no longer reaches my ankles. The University at Buffalo is a campus of SUNY, the State University of New York, and one of the associate professors of neurology asked me to referee his upgrading for permanent tenure; knowing only of his historical work, my testimonial was not as comprehensive as usual, but tenure was granted nevertheless. After Buffalo, the second meeting of the ISHN was in Leiden, The Netherlands, the third in Annapolis, Maryland; the fourth in Zurich and Lausanne was disappointing, in my opinion because it was held jointly with psychiatrists. The Tenth Annual Meeting of the ISHN in 2005 was held in St Andrew's University, Scotland, a city I had not previously visited but with a very impressive history and architecture; my eldest son, Sebastian, who lives with his family in the Scottish Borders, came up to St Andrews for a celebratory dinner with me.

Later in 1996, I was asked to serve on the Advisory Committee for the History Section of the American Academy of Neurology but this entailed little work. In the following year at the International Epilepsy Symposium in Dublin, Ireland I was asked to help choose a scientist for the Ciba Epilepsy Research Award which, on this occasion, was Professor Mattson of the USA.

In September 1999, the EFNS Panel on the History of Neurosciences had a focussed workshop in Lisbon. My talk was on the "Neurology of Galen of Pergamum (c.129-210)", who was mistakenly called Claudius Galen because of his initials CL but those initials stand for Clarissimus; five of his 22 volumes of medicine concern neurology, and he initiated the naming of apoplexy, hemiplegia and meninges; although he used the word autopsy, there is no evidence that he performed any. It was when he was physician to the gladiators for four years, that he learned how to treat head injuries. In 2000 the European Federation of Neurological Sciences had its Fifth International Congress on "The History of the Neurosciences" which was organised with speakers from Copenhagen, Aarhus and California; their subjects included objectives, how to write and read biographies and other historiographical problems.

In 2002, it was a surprise to receive an invitation to lecture at the Institute of Ancient History and Archaeology of Birmingham University by its Director, who was not a doctor of medicine; the subject was trepanation, the very ancient art of making holes in the skull. The conference was to last for three whole days, which was rather long; my intention was to give my talk and then leave, but this did not happen, not least because the speakers had come from all over the world, including Mongolia. On the last evening, at the Symposium dinner, a lady came and sat next to me, the only neurologist present. She was not a doctor but had been included in the programme to show a video of herself making a hole in the front of her head which was bleeding; she had made this video years before in the belief that it would "expand her consciousness". Listening politely to her rationale, she gave the impression that more recently she had taken her husband to Mexico to undergo a similar operation. By the end of the evening, she had learned that my wife was interested in gardens and invited us to visit hers. Her house, near Oxford, was a listed building having originally been the site of a castle with a moat. Both she and her husband were titled aristocrats but evidently short of money, complaining bitterly about the price of the strawberries served at lunch. On arrival, we were separated, with my wife taken to look at the gardens by the husband, while his wife engaged me in conversation. Carefully explaining that "expanding consciousness" was meaningless from the medical point of view, she tried to get me to agree that some addictive drugs should be graded more lightly. By way of reciprocation, I invited her for tea at my club but subsequently refused to join her group, a decision never regretted.

When attending the eighth Annual Meeting of the ISHN in Cumberland House, Windsor Great Park in 2003, it was a delight to accept its Life Achievement Award. The reasons given by Professor Karenberg of Cologne, Germany in his flattering commendation are as follows: "Mr President, Members of the Society, Dear Colleagues, Ladies and Gentlemen: What usually happens in a situation like this is that all the merits of the lifetime award winner are recalled: Steps of the academic career, list of publications, scientific achievements etc, etc. Tonight, it's simply impossible to follow this procedure. Not that I'm not willing to pursue this regular path, but it would need at least two hours just to enumerate the winner's outstanding contributions, not to mention his regular work. So please be so kind to permit me to deviate from the ordinary procedure and to focus on my personal encounters and impressions. When I decided in the late eighties of the last century to do some work in the history of neurology, there was just one book listed in current major bibliographies: "Historical Aspects of the Neurosciences", edited by Frank Clifford Rose. In a perfect combination of chronological and topographical arrangement, many topics were presented on a high intellectual level – the perfect introduction for a novice in the temple of historical neuroscience and very useful for seminars with students at medical schools. A few years later, when I completed my first paper about a neuro-historical topic at the University of California Los Angeles, my advisor told me: Well, you know, there is a new Journal in the field, and your paper could nicely fit into this frame, so why don't you write a letter to the editor? I looked at the first issue of the newly founded "Journal of the History of the Neurosciences" and who was the founding editor? Frank Clifford Rose. I wrote the letter, got a very friendly and warm response and was delighted that Frank accepted my paper for publication. A few months later, I learned that there is something like a European Club for the History of Neurology, and the next meeting was to take place in Oslo in summer 1995. Who was the speaker of the club and the person to address about the possibility of participating or of giving a paper? I think I don't have to answer this question. In Oslo we met for the first time and Frank had time for a long personal conversation. He advised me to continue my work in the field and to join the Club – exactly what I did. But what left the most powerful impression on my mind was Frank's presidential address at the Banquet of the Oslo meeting. Within a few minutes, he gave an intellectual tour through past and present of the Neurosciences, spiced with a special dosage of British humour. It was this ability to talk elegantly and nevertheless full of meaning about history which was, at least for me, one of the true signs of a true scholar. I could go on endlessly, but I will stop here and just remind you, that the lifetime contribution award is an honour bestowed on a colleague for his long-lasting and wide-ranging contributions on the scientific, on the educational, as well as the organisational level. I am not able to select one of these levels as the most prominent one in Frank's career, because his contributions are eminent on all of them. At least six of his about 50 books are dedicated to the history of the neurosciences. The "Historical Aspects" of 1982 were followed in 1989 by "James Parkinson: His Life and Times" and by "Neuroscience Across the Centuries", in the very same year by "ALS: From Charcot to the Present" in 1994, and by two books on the British contribution to World Neurology in 1999 and 2000 – not to mention all the historical papers and articles that Frank has published over the last five decades.

Just a few remarks on the educational and organisation level - many in this room know that you, Frank, were among others the leading figure in putting together a framework in which serious work in the history of the Neurosciences could be carried out on an international and worldwide level. It was your spirit who was instrumental in founding the European Club, and it was your enterprise to lay the grounds for the Journal of the History of the Neurosciences. For many years, you served as its first editor, and for everyone working on the Journal's board it is a very welcome stimulus for excellence to see your name under the heading "Founding Editor" in every issue. To put it short: that this group of neuro-historians meets here today and publishes in its own journal, is to very great extent due to the paving and untiring efforts of you and your colleagues. You are the true nester of our field, and, in one way or another, almost everybody in this room is indebted to you. At the end, it is not only the scientific, educational or organisational effort which is important, but mainly the personal attitude: we desperately need more, younger top clinicians with the same ardent enthusiasm for their discipline's history in their heart, an enthusiasm which you lived and demonstrated for many decades. Let me conclude with a quotation from one of Frank's papers which is a perfect bridge into the society's future. In 1993, at the end of one of your articles on early neurology, you made the following comment on the chance of future work in the history of the neurosciences: "There are ripe fields to be harvested, and much more research has to be done". I couldn't think of a more deserving winner of this year's Lifetime Contribution Award and, Frank, thank you for all what you have done for us. Let's all raise our glasses to Frank Clifford Rose. *Axel Karenberg, Cologne*". In my acceptance speech, my theme was that two genes were necessary for this Award, the first being an interest in history of neuroscience but the second for longevity. Later that year, there was a conference at the Wellcome Trust Centre, London on "Anglo-American Medical Relations: Historical Insights" where my talk was on "The Medical Society of London Library at the Wellcome Institute". Here was recounted the sale of the Society's library to the Wellcome Institute but still retaining the name of the Medical Society of London Library.

In 2005 the World Congress of Neurology was held in Sydney, Australia. The History of Neuroscience Symposium was organised by Dr George York III of California and was on the History of Cerebral Localisation for which my talk concerned its origins in Antiquity. Among British colleagues was Christopher Gardner-Thorpe who succeeded me as Chairman of the History of Neurosciences Panel of the European Federation of Neurological Societies (EFNS). Before this meeting, we had a wonderful few weeks in Australia starting in Perth and driving down to the South, visiting the vineyards of Margaret River on the way; then to Ayers Rock and on to Adelaide and Kangaroo Island finishing with a wonderful drive from Adelaide to Melbourne. Altogether this was a marvellous climax to our days of long-distance travel.

Chapter 11

WORLD FEDERATION OF NEUROLOGY

Working as a junior at the National Hospital, Queen Square, the professor of neuropathology, Dr William Blackwood, was keen on research into the muscles of the body and their nerve supply, a junction which could then be studied using the relatively new technique of staining with the pigment, methylene blue. Since it was possible to locate electrically the connection between nerve and muscle, he let me go to Brussels to learn and perfect this technique from a Belgian neurologist, a visit that coincided in 1957 with the First World Congress of Neurology, when the worlds' neuroscientists could meet for the first time after the Second World War. This congress was jointly organised between neurologists, neurosurgeons and neuropathologists producing a large attendance of four thousand, including most of "the great and the good" which, as a tyro, intrigued me enormously. A very tall Englishman, Dr John Swithinbank, who had been taught by me in London, also attended the Congress and suggested one evening a visit to a night club where we were encouraged to drink champagne at exorbitant prices, with the result that we ran out of cash, but it was impressive to see John post the money owed through the letter box on the following morning.

The World Federation of Neurology Council has a representative from each member national society, including the UK. It may have been because of my presence at this World Congress that my election as the UK representative to the WFN meetings resulted; the Council considers the venue for the following World Congress and also meets in the intervening two years to choose subjects and speakers. Some years later, a video of this 1957 WFN meeting, filmed by an Australian neurologist, was given to me, which, 50 years later, I presented to the Archivist at the National Hospital, along with other historical artefacts.

The second World Congress of Neurology (WCN) in 1961 was held in Rome, when my chief at St George's Hospital attended, introducing himself to unknown delegates as the Editor of *Brain*, which did not ring a bell with most of the foreign neurologists, who possibly never read this British neurological journal. My failure to attend the third Congress in Vienna in 1965 was due to my appointment that year as consultant neurologist to Charing Cross Hospital. Several American neurologists did not go because the proposed Austrian President of the Congress was said to have played a part in Austria's Nazi period, but their preferred President was a Dr Cohen. In 1969, the fourth World Congress was held in New York when my paper was on work at the Moor House School for Speech Disorders. The Chairman of this session was from France and introduced me in French; it seemed appropriate to begin my lecture by apologising in French that the rest of the proceedings would be in English resulting in much laughter. My travels that year had begun in Asia with Angela and, when returning to Europe, we parted in Italy for her to return home whilst my journey continued to Spain to read a paper on the Japanese disease, SMON. The sixth WCN was held in Amsterdam with its preparatory meeting two years earlier in Newcastle, England.

The seventh World Congress in 1981 was held in Kyoto, Japan where a neurological friend from San Francisco, Ted Norris, gave a party for colleagues in a Japanese restaurant, where we ate sitting on the floor in the traditional manner, which was not very comfortable for the European guests but was nevertheless most enjoyable. As we then had a few days before setting off on a lecture tour of China, we decided to move from our western-style suite to a Japanese style room in the same hotel; this was not a great success as the Japanese custom was to roll up the beds during the daytime which meant we could not have an afternoon siesta. Another problem was that the internal walls were made of paper and I managed to push a suitcase through one of them; also the bath was a wooden "box" and one was meant to shower with soap first, and then sit in the box after washing!

Following the Congress, we were invited to join a group from the American Neurological Association on a lecture tour of China, led by my old chief from San Francisco, Professor Robert Aird. The "Neurological Study Tour of the People's Republic of China" was from 26 September to

11 October, during which time we visited the tourist sites of Beijing, Shanghai and Xian. This was soon after the "Gang of Four", Chinese leaders who opposed the learning of foreign languages, which meant our guides spoke very poor English and our talks had to be given in short phrases which were then translated into Chinese - not an ideal way to give lectures. In Beijing we stayed at a VIP Government "Guest House" where one evening we had a vegetarian banquet made to look like meat. This was the year following President Nixon's visit but, in spite of staying at the same hotel for a night, we had damp sheets and an uncleaned bathroom. Nevertheless, it was fascinating visit: there was an opportunity to see how acupuncture helped in anaesthesia even for major operations. One of the reasons Angela and I had accepted the invitation to join this group was because we love Chinese cuisine but, because of widespread poverty, the food in China was not at all as anticipated and we were pleased to end our tour in Hong Kong, where the food delicious.

The social side of this 1981 trip was organised by Joyce, the wife of Dr Oscar Kofman, a neurologist from Toronto, Canada. On arrival in Beijing (then called Peking) it was snowing and Chinese women were clearing the streets swinging long, straw brooms. Of the five cities visited, the first was Shanghai where we settled into a Guest House for four days during which time we toured and lectured; our first visit was to the Tombs, which has been well restored with artefacts from the Ming dynasty. From here we went to the Great Wall of China, which had been completed in the 3rd Century BC by Emperor Quinn Shir Huang taking 300,000 men ten years to finish; its 1500 mile course across northern China has an actual winding length of 3,500 miles and is apparently the only structure on earth seen by astronauts. In Beijing we were taken to Tian-tan, the Temple of Heaven where the emperors prayed, but this was not as opulent as the Imperial Palace in the Forbidden City, where its grounds cover 250 acres in the centre of the capital; the Winter Palace overlooking two man-made lakes, gave an excellent view of the city. All Chinese seemed to be dressed in grey, dark blue or green with identical shoes and the only variation was in the shirts, which were coloured or patterned; it seemed that the whole of China was one mass of bicycles. We visited Mao's

Mausoleum in hushed silence and saw his body in a crystal coffin, but ahead of the Chinese visitors. In Tiananmen Square pictures of Mao, Marx, Stalin, Lenin and Trotsky were still displayed.

Later we were delighted to see the pandas, the baby in its play-pen and three adults performing summersaults, apparently to amuse us. We went next to Xian which was the ancient walled capital of China and the beginning of the Silk Route; shortly before our visit, they had found in an archaeological dig of three vaults, over 8,000 figures of 10ft high horses, and warriors, each with different faces and military dress, a sample of a few were exhibited in London more than 25 years later. We also visited Guilin, a beautiful tourist town surrounded by mountains, the highlight being a boat trip on the River Li. Angela described her visit to a chopstick factory as follows: "Unfortunately the initial process of actually producing the chopsticks was not revealed. What we saw were raw undecorated bamboo (not plastic) sticks piled high in boxes in darkened rooms. There the sticks were inscribed in Chinese 'The Beautiful Sights of Kweilin' and individually fed into a machine". Our last stop was Canton (Guangzou), a busy metropolitan centre near the Hong Kong border; nevertheless, accommodation for the Chinese was still primitive by western standards. One member of our group, a professor of neurology from Texas, was a keen jogger who, in spite of not speaking any Chinese, would go off running at all our stops, producing relief when he returned safely to the hotel. Another member, a neurosurgeon from Los Angeles, was a keen buyer of ancient Chinese crockery, and acquired countless dinner services. Not having returned to China since then, we have been informed conditions are now much improved, as expected from a booming economy, but I declined to lead a similar American group, later learning that the Chinese professors were disappointed by my refusal.

Later in 1981 I went to Beerse, Belgium for a conference on stroke held in a brewery, where we were given samples of its products on leaving (similar presents were given on another occasion at a migraine meeting in Bordeaux, where our farewell gift was a bottle of claret). In October, Belgium was again my destination, this time to Knocke, to discuss an ongoing European trial for the prevention of stroke.

The eighth WCN was held in Hamburg, Germany and in 1989 the ninth was held in New Delhi in the Taj Palace Hotel, under the Presidency of Professor E P Bharucha; it was at this meeting that I was elected Secretary-Treasurer General of the World Federation of Neurology. It soon became clear to me that this organisation was amateurish without any office or professional secretarial support. Initially after my appointment, Angela did the secretarial work but later a designated secretary was employed by the WFN to work full-time in my Harley Street consulting rooms: some time later a WFN office was established at the Medical Society of London with an Administrator (Keith Newton) and a Secretary (Susan Bilger); Susan already knew the ropes as she had been working at my consulting rooms for more than a year before the new WFN office was set up. Susan retired in 2008, and the WFN moved to brand-new offices in Richmond, on the Thames south-west of London. Finance for these developments came from the profits made at the World Neurological Congresses, which were shared equally between the host country's neurological society and the WFN. Another function of the WFN was to publish a Newsletter, edited by me, which went to nearly every neurologist in the world (over 20,000 at that time).

The tenth WCN was held in 1993 in Vancouver, Canada. Helping with arrangements necessitated my going each year for four years to British Columbia, firstly to approve the venue, secondly to help with the funding, thirdly to learn about tourist attractions in order to encourage possible attendees and, finally, to use my expertise in running congresses; my only upset with the Canadian organisers was how little they charged pharmaceutical companies for exhibition space. On one occasion, the Canadian organisers arranged for a small sea plane for me to visit Saltspring Island and then land near Vancouver airport for my return to London. As the Congress venue and the tourist attractions were superb, it was felt that the time was ripe for educational courses to be held before the Congress and we arranged a short course on a huge cruise liner going north from Vancouver to Alaska. Sad to report, the educational side was a failure because of the more dramatic attractions of the passing scenery;

falling glaciers and wild life. It is a pleasure to relate the educational side of these Congresses have now become more profitable.

In 1995 a letter was written to the WFN from the President of the Taiwan Neurological Society telling us of their change of name from the Neurological Society ROC (Taiwan) to the Taiwan Neurological Society. The background was that they wished to emphasize that Taiwan was "an independent country with our own sovereignty" and was not part of the Republic of China (ROC). This was emphasised to me by a delegation of Taiwanese neurologists who hoped that the WFN would not follow the United Nations, making China one of the five members of the Security Council instead of Taiwan, which was eventually excluded from the Security Council. I promised that this would not happen during my term as Secretary-Treasurer General of the WFN. A comparable misunderstanding had taken place in Tokyo at the seventh World Congress in 1981; all delegates had been issued with a printed name badge giving their name and country; the Taiwanese delegation had applied to attend the Congress early so that their name-plates were pre-printed, but because of the lateness of their application, the small Chinese delegation were issued with *typewritten* name badges, which they took as an insult and promptly returned to China. At that time, the Chinese Neurological Society had not yet become a member of the WFN.

The 16th WFN Congress in 1997 was held in Buenos Aires which necessitated my travelling there on each of the three preceding years to help the Argentinian organisers with the programme. One highlight of World Congresses of Neurology was an award for the best neuroscientific work in the preceding four years, and my advice was needed when they were deciding on an Argentinian-born doctor rather than an eminent Nobel prize-winner. Going to a different part of this huge country in order to advertise its appeal to possible Congress attendees was particularly interesting since Argentina has been called the country of six continents, because of its diverse geographical areas such as Patagonia, including Bariloche where Welsh immigrants had settled many years ago, Ushuaia and the North. At the planning meeting of this Congress Angela and I were invited to the opera in Buenos Aires to hear Tchaikovsky's "Ace of

Spades"; it was sung in Russian with Spanish surtitles. The usual split of profits of the Argentinian Congress allowed the host country to establish a national neurological building with its own library. At this I had to make a speech in Spanish at the end of the Congress. Having visited Spain many times, it seemed possible to learn enough of the language during four years of preparation. Although trying private tuition, adult evening classes and listening to CDs, this was all to little avail and I finally sought help from the head waiter of my London club who came from South America: he taught me to pronounce each syllable as if it was a separate word and after much practising, it began (my translation):

"Ladies and Gentlemen,
I hope you will forgive this attempt to speak your beautiful and musical language but I promised Leonor Gold four years ago that I would say a few words in Spanish. I would first like to thank her and the organising committee of Professors Muchnik, Sica and Bauso Toselli for all their hard work in making the eleventh World Congress of Neurology such a success. This is my fourth visit to Argentina in successive years and I have thoroughly enjoyed exploring your magnificent country. In recent years I have been invited to lecture in other Latin American countries such as Mexico and Peru, nor can I forget the recent Pan-American Congress in Guatemala. You will know that the next Pan-American Congress will be in Columbia and I was delighted to visit Cartagena last year to confirm it as a superb congress venue. My job has been a difficult one, chiefly because the President of the World Federation of Neurology – and everyone else – thinks he gives the orders and I obey them. Please do not tell him that the opposite is the case but I am glad he does not understand Spanish. Please accept my apologies for ruining your beautiful language but it was a way of thanking you, my Argentinian colleagues, as well as all Latin American neurologists, for their endeavours on behalf of World Neurology. Many thanks." After my speech, a *Spanish* neurologist from Madrid came to offer congratulations on my talk, saying "I understood every word, but you spoke with an Argentinian accent".

Marco Medina wrote to me asking how the Nicaraguan Neurological Society could become a member of the WFN and I replied in August 1997:

"Dear Marco, Thank you for your email of the 2nd August. The requirements of Nicaragua would be: a letter of application to join the WFN; a list of their members (minimum of 5), £3 or US $5.00 per head annual dues and a copy of their statutes. If this can be processed immediately we may be able to get them to become members in Buenos Aires in September at the World Congress of Neurology". He replied in October 1997:

"Dear Dr Clifford Rose, it was a pleasure to see you at the World Congress of Neurology. I want to know about the status of Nicaragua, I will send to the president of the Nicaraguan Society of Neurology the details about our conversation in Buenos Aires. On the other hand, I want to confirm your invitation to participate as professor during the Central American Federation of Neurology meeting in San Pedro, Honduras (*November 4-6th, 1998*). We want a lecture from you about "Headaches: Classification and Treatment", 45 minutes. We will pay your air ticket and the hotel accommodation. San Pedro is near our important Maya City: Copan (the Paris of the Mayan world according to the National Geographic Journal), three hours in good paved roads and near the Bay Islands (the second largest coral reef of the world). Our Central American Federation of Neurology was founded during the 80s and the members are: the Guatemala, Honduras, Salvadore, Nicaragua, and Costa-Rican Societies of Neurology; in the near future the Panama Society of Neurology will be the next member. We would appreciate any help from the WFN. I want to know your opinion about our Honduran journal of Neurosciences. Also I want to know the name and address of the new Editor of the Journal of Neurological Sciences (WFN)". My reply was on the following day: "Dear Marco, Thank you for your email. I am delighted to accept your very kind invitation to participate in the meeting of the Central American Federation of Neurology in San Pedro, Honduras from 4-6 November and deliver a lecture on "Headaches: classification and treatment" for 45 minutes. I understand you will pay for my air fare and accommodation. I shall be bringing my wife but I will pay for her air fare. I hope to arrive two or three days before the meeting, in order to recover from jet lag; we will stay on for two or three days holiday afterwards. During that time we can discuss the Honduran Journal of Neuroscience, the formation of a WFN Regional Group etc. I look forward to hearing further from you". Marco also responded immediately: "Dear Dr Clifford Rose, thank you very much for your last email. We are very happy that you will come to Honduras, in San Pedro Sula, on *November 4-6 1998*, during the Central American meeting of Neurology. We will pay for your air fare and for the accommodation of your wife and yourself. Do you want to go to the Mayan City Copan? We can go with you in our car (about four hours from San Pedro and "c'est magnifique!"). We agree that during the Congress we can discuss the Honduran Journal of Neurosciences and the formation of a WFN Regional Group, etc. My best regards to you and your wife. Looking forward to hearing from you, sincerely, Marco T Medina", to which I responded immediately: "Dear Marco, many thanks for your reply and we have now made travel plans as follows: Thursday, 30 October arrive San Pedro Sula 1805 flight Iberia IB6135 (from Miami) Saturday, 8 November depart San Pedro Sula 1025 flight TACA TA390. We wondered about spending the weekend prior to the Congress in the Bay Islands, returning to San Pedro on Monday 3 November. Do you think this is a good idea, and, if so, could you recommend the best place to stay? We would, of course, be very keen to go to Copan and thank you for your kind offer. If we do go to the Bay Islands before the Congress, would it be possible to go to Copan on Friday 7 November – the day before we fly home? Could you please send me a copy of the programme, and in particular when I am speaking. Also, I will need to have the address, tel/fax/email of the hotel we will be staying in – when you have this information. Finally, do we need to take any anti-malaria tablets? With kind regards, F Clifford Rose".

Marco also responded efficiently: "Dear Dr Clifford Rose, we are very happy to know that you have your reservations. The best hotel in the Bay Island is Fantasy Island Hotel and if you want we can make your reservations here and obtain a discount and we can prepay your air fare here in Honduras. The hotel in San Pedro is Hotel Copantl and we will make your reservations. About the programme, your lecture will be on November 5, at 14:00 hours (45 minutes), I will send you the preliminary programme in the next few days. We can go to Copain (the Mayan city) on November 6 (Friday). We can plan to have a meeting with the presidents or delegates of the Central American Neurological Societies, in order to organise the regional group of the WFN, this group will include: Guatemala, El Salvador, Honduras, Nicaragua, Costa Rica and Panama. What is the actual status of Nicaragua? Looking forward to hearing from you, with kind regards", to which I replied: "Dear Marco, many thanks for your email. Your arrangements are eminently satisfactory and we would be delighted if you could make reservations and air fares to Fantasy Island Hotel as well as Hotel Copantl. We are also delighted to be able to go to Copan on Friday, November 6 and look forward to the meeting with the Central American Neurological Societies. Nicaragua is now a full member. Looking forward to seeing you. Kindest regards, yours sincerely, Clifford Rose" and then, on the 30 October 1997: "Dear Marco, we arrived this evening at Copantl Hotel but there was no reservation for us. Unfortunately, we do not have your telephone number. Please call us here as soon as possible (room number 204). The hotel telephone number is 56 94 12. We will look forward to hearing from you. Frank Clifford Rose". I had arrived a year *early* but we were royally entertained at the home of Caroline and Nelson Chinchilla, who told me that the actual Congress was the following year. Nevertheless, I was able to give my usual lecture, as there were only eight neurologists in Honduras. It must have been fate that desired me to see all the countries of the Ruta Maya, that is to say Chichen Itza, Mexico, Tikal in Guatemala and Copan in Honduras; because of Hurricane Mitch the meeting the following year was cancelled, so if that mistake had not been made, I would never have achieved the completion of the Mayan route.

After eight years in my WFN post as Secretary-Treasurer General, the new President, Jim Toole, asked me to stay for one more year after retirement to prepare for my successor. Professor James Toole, of the Wake-Forest University, North Carolina, was elected President of the WFN in Argentina and sent me the following email on 28 January 1998: "I have looked through Recent Advances in Tropical Neurology and noticed the (Mansell Bequest) series began in 1977. What a sequence of titles. When I saw them on your mantelpiece in your hideaway rooms I didn't really appreciate the effort that they entailed. Many thanks for the volume. When next we meet I would like to learn how you accomplished so much, Jim". However, three months later, he sent another one: "Dear Frank, your silent treatment must stop because it is dangerous for the WFN and its members. No matter how you feel about me, the management of the WFN requires our close and continuing interaction. Now we are at a potentially dangerous place with a meeting scheduled in a location where the US State Department has issued formal warnings for US people to stay away, and our colleagues from Mexico and Argentina tell us informally that both organisation and safety are in question. You are the only one of management who has visited. The World Neurology newsletter has front-paged the meeting probably with your input and pictures. I have asked Ted Munsat as chair of Continuing Ed(ucation) committee and management committee member to decide with you whether we should, as WFN, continue to recommend this meeting to our membership or should the next issue of World Neurology contain a warning. This is a management committee decision and must be acted upon with information, supplied by you to the management and the Steering Committee with appropriate notation in the July issue of World Neurology. In order to assure that action is being taken expeditiously, please acknowledge receipt of this memo and send copies of your findings and recommendations to Steering Committee and Management Committee. I have no memory of management authorising $10000 loan for this meeting. When was this done? With kind regards, Jim".

Another email arrived later in the year, on 21 December 1998: "You beat me to it! I wanted to write first to congratulate you for your nine years of toil in the vineyards of World Neurology. That, plus registrarship, consultantship, managing Charing Cross Unit, private practice, the Migraine Trust, innumerable books and research papers, gives you the droit de seigneur. Your spectacular career is unlikely ever to be equalled and for all these accomplishments and your steady hand on the tiller of the WFN, I congratulate you. We toasted you and Angela at the 28 Sept.,

Garrick Club meeting and wished the two of you lasting health and good fortune. With warmest regards, Jim".

The 10th Pan-American Congress was due to be held in Cartagena de Indias on Columbia's northern coast. As Secretary-Treasurer General of the WFN, I had been deputed to approve the Congress venue; it proved to be an ideal place with excellent facilities and, unlike Bogotá, was comparatively safe. The husband of one of my patients arranged for us to stay for a few days with his parents in Bogotá and whilst there we were taken sightseeing in their bullet-proof car accompanied by armed guards in another car. The most memorable visit was to caves at a defunct salt-mine. During a previous planning visit, I was entertained in Cartagena on a yacht in the bay with a lobster dinner where one of the guests (the owner of a hotel) gave me a Havana cigar that Fidel Castro had given to him. The Congress venue proved to be eminently acceptable and the meeting was a great success.

On 19 June 2001, Angela and I celebrated our past travels by having a dinner party at the Savile Club for all those neurologists from abroad who had hosted us in their own countries and were in London for the 12th WCN. Amongst those present at this dinner were David Steinberg and George York from northern California, prominent neuro-historians, the latter becoming my successor as Chairman of the WFN Research Group in the History of the Neurosciences. Bob Daroff of the USA was another eminent neuro-historian who proved a very good colleague as Chairman of the Finance and Publications Committees of the WFN, thus making my task much easier. Another American, Don Dalessio, a doyen of American migrainologists organised a meeting of the WFN Research Group in Headache and Migraine in 1981 at San Diego near his base at the Scripps Clinic, La Jolla, California. Africa was represented by Professor Michel Dumas who worked part-time in Dakar on Tropical Neurology and kindly invited me to Limoges for a meeting on the same subject, a topic later used in a book I edited; *"Recent Advances in Tropical Neurology"*, Elsevier, 1995.

On my retirement from the WFN, several colleagues very kindly wrote flattering farewells in "World Neurology", the newsletter of the WFN. One wrote: "Dr Clifford Rose is a remarkable man, an individual of consummate efficiency and boundless energy, whose friendship I have been privileged to enjoy for many years". An Indian professional colleague wrote: "Until a few years ago he was physician in charge of the Department of Neurology and Director of the Academic Unit of Neuroscience at the Charing Cross Hospital and Westminster Medical School in London, UK. There he built up one of the most outstanding departments of neurology in London, staffed by many able neurologists with broad and diverse interests in basic and clinical neuroscience. His own distinguished career has included appointments in the National Hospital, Queen Square, London (UK), the University of California, San Francisco (USA) and the Salpêtrière in Paris (France). His research, particularly in the field of headache, has won him a well-deserved national and international reputation. He has delivered many eponymous lectures in the UK and abroad and was formerly President of the Medical Society of London. He had received the Harold Wolff Award twice in his career and, in 1986, the Distinguished Clinician Award of the American Association for the Study of Headache. Innumerable scientific papers have flowed from his fertile pen and he has written and edited more than 60 books on many aspects of neurology. He has also had a lifelong interest in medical history and was founding editor of the *Journal of the History of Neurosciences*".

Lord Walton wrote: "When I was elected President of the World Federation of Neurology (WFN) in 1989, I had no hesitation in inviting him to become Secretary-Treasurer General as I knew that his incomparable organisational skills and his energy and dedication made him an ideal choice. This was at a time when the WFN's responsibilities and influence, due to the excellent work of my predecessor, Dick Masland, and of James Toole as his Secretary-Treasurer General, were clearly escalating. No-one could have wished to have a more capable colleague. Not only did he establish a WFN office in his consulting rooms in Harley Street in London, where the WFN's database of 23,000 members of its affiliated societies across the world was up-dated but he also took on the editorship of *World Neurology*, the WFN's window on the world. He prepared the contents of this quarterly newsletter almost single-handedly and he and I together were successful, first with Eldred Smith-Gordon and subsequently with Cambridge Medical Publications (current publisher of the Newsletter), in persuading pharmaceutical and other companies across the world to sponsor its printing and distribution, so that we did not need to use the WFN's own limited funds. When Armand Lowenthal retired as Joint Secretary-Treasurer General and Secretary of the WFN's Research Committee, he willingly shouldered the additional responsibilities of that office. In organising meetings and in preparing agendas and minutes of WFN committees, his work has been immaculate, perhaps above all, the friendly liaison that he has developed with neurologists across the world, and especially with those responsible for organising regional and world congresses, has been particularly notable. He has been an inveterate traveller, covering thousands of miles, whenever necessary, in order to ensure that WFN-sponsored meetings would be successful both scientifically and financially. His stewardship of the WFN's finances has been immaculate throughout. Throughout all these responsibilities he has had the unfailing support of his wife, Angela, who has often acted as the WFN's unpaid finance officer, but who has also helped with secretarial work when required. There can be very few neurologists attending WFN-sponsored international meetings who have not encountered Angela's smiling face at the WFN stand, persuading them to attend meetings and to buy WFN ties and scarves. The man who served for nine years as Secretary-Treasurer General claims that congresses are not always hard work. I regarded it as an exceptional privilege to have presided over the WFN during 8 years of unprecedented growth and development and am delighted that the Federation now has a permanent office with an administrator and secretary, in London. It is difficult to find words to express our gratitude and the thanks of the worldwide neurological community for all that he has done for the WFN and for world neurology. He has left an indelible mark upon this organisation which he has served so faithfully and effectively. Lord Walton of Detchant, Immediate Past-President of the WFN".

Professor James Lance of Sydney, Australia wrote on contributions to headache:

"As well as encompassing the dual responsibilities of being Secretary-Treasurer General to the World Federation of Neurology, running a Department of Neurology and maintaining a busy consultant practice, Frank has sponsored and participated in research and education in the field of headache throughout his professional life. His breadth of interest is demonstrated by his publications on stroke, speech disorders, multiple sclerosis, neuro-ophthalmology and many other topics. When Frank was appointed to Charing Cross Hospital in 1965, it did not have a Department of Neurology and there was no neurological staff. When he left 25 years later it was the largest Department of Neurology in the UK, in which he headed Research Units in stroke, amyotrophic lateral sclerosis and neuro-epidemiology, as well as migraine. At the request of the late Macdonald Critchley, he founded a Migraine Clinic at Charing Cross Hospital, which became the Princess Margaret Migraine Clinic, and soon developed an active research programme. He became trustee, and later Chairman of Trustees, of the British Migraine Trust and, until recently, organised the biennial Migraine Symposium in London, which attracted about 1,000 participants, mostly from overseas. He was involved in the formation of the International Headache Society and the European Headache Federation and, for many years, chaired the WFN Research Group on Headache and Migraine. He and his colleagues won the Harold G Wolff Award of the American Association for the Study of Headache in 1981, on their study *The Effect of Infused Prostacyclin in Migraine and Cluster Headache*. He received their Distinguished Clinicians Award in 1986. Among the 60 books that Frank has written or edited are 15 on migraine. It is not sufficient simply to list Frank's considerable achievements in the field of headache and other aspects of neurology".

In 1998 my stint as Secretary-Treasurer General came to an end and *World Neurology* (1998, 13, No.4) the newsletter of the WFN gave me a page:

"Tributes from the Neurological Community

Throughout his career, and especially in his 9 years as Secretary-Treasurer General for the World Federation of Neurology, Dr Frank Clifford Rose has made many neurological friends worldwide and built up an excellent reputation. Now that he has come to the end of his term in office, as both Secretary-Treasurer General and Editor of World Neurology, some of those friends and colleagues would like to express their deep gratitude and respect for all he has done for the field of neurology. The following dedication is testimony to the high regard in which he is held by many.

The department he built up and the many organisations promoting education and research in neurology, both at home and abroad. His talents extended beyond the clinic and the lecture theatre. He enjoyed choosing the menu and selecting the wines for dinners in elegant surroundings. His obvious pleasure in the company of his wife, Angela, his characteristic laugh and general good fellowship made social as well as scientific gatherings relaxed and enjoyable. I am sure that Frank will continue to lend his enthusiasm and expertise to all who seek it, from the wings if not from centre stage".

Professor Marco Medina of the National University of Honduras, where I had arrived a year earlier than expected, wrote: "When I met Dr Clifford Rose for the first time in La Habana, during the Pan-American Congress of Epilepsy in January 1995, I realised immediately his humanistic soul. He visited Honduras in November 1997 with his charming wife, Angela. They both have a magnificent sense of humour and a profound respect for other cultures. Dr Clifford Rose has been helping us establish a Training Programme in Neurology in Honduras, and we have been very glad of his support with this. I am proud to be able to call as my friend such an influential neurological leader". On 17 November 1998, Marco Medina sent us an email: "Thank you again for your support. I think God changed our plannings and during your last visit to Honduras, HE gave us the opportunity to know you two wonderful human beings. With my best regards, Marco".

Indian colleagues who wrote in World Neurology included Professor Krishnamoorthy Srinivas, Consultant Neurologist in Madras: "I first met Dr Clifford Rose on 1 August 1961, when I joined the Atkinson Morleys Hospital at Wimbledon, which was part of the St George's Hospital, London (UK). I was Medical Registrar and Dr Clifford Rose was the First Assistant to the Neurological Unit. The lasting impression I have of the early stages of our friendship is the help he gave me in settling into the job. I had spent over 2 years in Montreal and Saskatoon (Canada) and had come to this job to hone my skills in clinical neurology. Dr Clifford Rose helped me train for Membership of the Royal College of Physicians of London. He was overjoyed at my success and was proud to be a part of it. In 1978, when I had settled very comfortably at Madras (India), I had the pleasure of welcoming Dr Clifford Rose to India as Chairman of the Department of Neurology at Charing Cross Hospital in London. It was a wonderful reunion and I could see that he was very impressed with India. In 1982, we met again at the Medical Society of London at the Motor Neurone Disease Symposium. There, for the first time, I witnessed his superb organisational skills. Usually, the British do not attempt several things simultaneously. We in India do this very often, partly by habit and partly by circumstance. Dr Clifford Rose has this Indian quality of doing many things simultaneously and doing them all well. This is why he has left a legacy of superb skills as Secretary-Treasurer General of the WFN. In this job, he had a perfect foil in my former Chief, Lord Walton, himself a brilliant all-rounder. I am proud and privileged to have been Dr Clifford Rose's close friend for over 37 years, and I am sure the WFN will feel his absence strongly".

Noshir Wadia of Bombay, India wrote: "It is with great pleasure that I write in this testimonial issue of World Neurology to record the immense service that Dr Frank Clifford Rose has done for the WFN, and to honour him. My association with him has been a close one for over a quarter of a century, and I am pleased to call him a friend. Although I had heard of Frank earlier, we were brought together in 1971 when we were both part of a group formed by Ciba to study, investigate and advise the company on the problem of subacute myelo-opticoneuropathy (SMON), alleged to be caused by clioquinol (marketed by Ciba worldwide), which had afflicted nearly 10,000 Japanese patients. This is the longest compensation case in medical history. We travelled all over Japan to see patients on a very delicate mission which could have easily upset and antagonised the Japanese colleagues caring for these patients. It became instantaneously clear that we needed a spokesman, and who could be better than Frank with his tact, managerial skills, erudition and command of language. In our meetings with Japanese neurologists and lawyers Frank was discreet, pacifying and, at the same time, honest. Subsequently, we had many meetings elsewhere with a slightly larger group to study more cases and, even after long hours, Frank would take on the task of drafting consensus reports ready for the next morning. Evenings and dinners were enlivened by his wit and conviviality. If there was an after-dinner speech, it was Frank who made it with humorous anecdotes. Visiting Angela and Frank's home in England, I realised that he was a 'bon vivant' with European tastes in old wines, which I saw in an amply filled cellar. Over the last years, we have had many occasions to correspond and meet in the service of the WFN, and I have come to realise how much he has done for the organisation. Its re-organisation and the establishment of the permanent secretariat in the building of the old Medical Society of London must be due, in no small measure, to his vigorous efforts. He and Lord Walton formed a formidable team. The publication of *World Neurology* and finding of sponsors to finance its liberal and free distribution to over 20,000 neurologists worldwide is another feather in Frank's cap. We need more people with Frank's untiring energy to make the organisation grow even further to meet its avowed aims and objectives. Knowing Frank as I do, there will be no retirement just yet. My wife, Piroja, and I wish Angela and Frank well in all they wish to do".

Jagjit S Chopra, Vice Chairman of the WFN Finance Committee wrote: "Frank has been a great personal friend over the years, and a great champion of promoting neurology in the developing world. A clinical neurologist par excellence, he made frequent visits to India, and other countries in this subcontinent and in the Far Eastern region, where he advised in the setting up of neurological services and upgrading of teaching and research facilities. I have known him for almost three decades, from when he visited the Department of Neurology at the Postgraduate Institute of Medical Education and Research (PGIMER) in Chandigarh in the early 1970s, as visiting professor. The postgraduate students and the entire faculty appreciated his clinical acumen and teaching skills. This relationship was further strengthened between the new Charing Cross Hospital in London, where Frank worked, and PGIMER due to his subsequent visits to Chandigarh and India, and because of my visits to London as visiting professor. His love for the development of neurology and his excellent organisational mastery are amply reflected by his organisation of symposia on various aspects of neurology, under the Mansell Bequest of the Medical Society of London since 1977 (12 in total). I had the privilege of participating in three of those symposia – on motor neurone disease in 1977, advances in stroke therapy in 1982, and recent advances in tropical neurology in 1995. The proceedings of these symposia were published under Frank's skilful editorship. He has helped the careers of many in the developing world and certainly inspired me, and many others, to achieve what I have today. He readily accepted my recommendations for training some of our postgraduates in London, who are now holding very important positions in neurology. Frank encouraged me to organise the XIVth World Congress of Neurology in New Delhi (India) in 1989, and it was at this Congress that he was elected Secretary-Treasurer General of the WFN. Along with Lord Walton (the then President), Frank was instrumental in bringing many developing and Latin American countries into the WFN fold. Not only is this a great achievement but it also reflects his love for such countries. He has steered the WFN for 9 years, and I have watched his skills from close quarters as a member, and later as Vice Chairman of the WFN Finance Committee, which is now making further progress under the dynamic leadership of James F Toole. In the last decade, the neurological services and their awareness have increased, particularly in the developing world. There are now better interactions between the World Health Organisation and the WFN. The Decade of the Brain, as declared by the USA, was equally matched by the WFN in its performance for proliferation of neurology in developing countries, for which the credit is equally shared between Frank Clifford Rose, Lord Walton and James Toole. The mouthpiece of the WFN, *World Neurology*, has come a long way with Frank as Editor. It has become instrumental in the dissemination of knowledge and achievement in neurology, particularly under the various Research Groups of the WFN, to neurologists in developing countries. Frank's 'better half', Angela, is a charming, cheerful lady who has wholeheartedly supported her husband in his career. They have made very good friends during their travels, and I am pleased to count myself and my wife, Amar, among them – Frank and Angela even participated in the wedding of our daughter, Roby, in 1994. I pay tributes to him for his extraordinary work for the WFN and wish him to continue serving the cause of neurology, particularly in the developing countries, after he lays down the office of Secretary-Treasurer General".

Leonor Gold of Buenos Aires, Argentina wrote: "Frank Clifford Rose … in Spanish we say 'un personaje' … I met him through the organisation of the XVIth World Congress of Neurology, held in Buenos Aires in September 1997, and grew very fond of him and his wife, Angela. Frank's interests are extensive and he is knowledgeable about everything from the history of the neurosciences to bird watching. He has an adventurous spirit and has travelled Argentina more times than any Argentinean, including myself. Dining out with Frank always includes delightful descriptions of wines and exotic food from all over the world. He has an unquenchable curiosity – he always wants to know more about everything and what a prodigious memory! Dear Frank: I had the greatest time working at the World Congress and with you. I wish you and Angela all the best for the future. More than anything else, I hope you both enjoy your latest but greatest accomplishment, being grandparents".

Gustavo Pradilla, President of the 10th Pan-American Congress of Neurology wrote: "Old soldiers never die, they simply fade away. I have known Dr Frank Clifford Rose since the XIIth World Congress of Neurology in Kyoto in 1981. He first caught my attention through his pioneering editorship of works such as *Clinical Neuro-epidemiology* and, later, *Historical Aspects of the Neurosciences: a Festschrift for Dr Macdonald Critchley*. Headache is also one of his principal fields of research. He is the founder of *World Neurology*, which has been an important link between the WFN and its members throughout the world. In Guatemala, during the 9th Pan-American Congress of Neurology in 1995, he represented the WFN when Cartagena de Indias in Colombia was chosen as the venue for the 10th Pan-American Congress of Neurology in 1999. In November 1996, following his visit to Buenos Aires, we had the great opportunity of sharing several days with him in Bogotá and he was one of the principal speakers during the First Colombian Congress of Headache. It was during these few days that I came to know him as more than simply a scientist and master of English neurology; I also came to appreciate his lucidity, honesty, moral principles, his ethics and his fervent desire to encourage neurology in developing countries. At times, I felt like a son receiving wisdom and knowledge from his father. Seeing him in Cartagena de Indias, wearing a Panama hat, smoking a Cohiba cigar, eating two lobster meals a day – and simply enjoying the land that was never conquered by the English nation but will be conquered by an English neurologist in 1999 – it is easy to believe that he must have been the inspiration for many of Graham Greene's novels. Frank Clifford Rose will always be a friend of Colombia. The 10th Pan-American Congress of Neurology is lucky to have the involvement of such an exceptional human being".

Pan-American meetings have flourished since then. While in Cartagena, the locals were keen to show me the statue commemorating the victory over British sailors years before (a battle of which no-one in Britain has heard). They showed me the house where Gabriel Garcia Marquez lived on his holidays (those unfamiliar with his name should know he wrote his book, *One Hundred Years of Solitude*, which sold millions of copies and he has been described as "the greatest Spanish-language book writer since Cervantes": he won the Nobel prize for literature in 1982). It was also suggested that we visit Medellin which, knowing its drug reputation, we declined.

James F Toole, President of the WFN, wrote: "Mrs Angela Rose has been stalwart at every Congress of the World Federation of Neurology since 1989. It was she who created and attended the WFN booth, from where she distributed materials and publicised our cause, and sold ties and scarves featuring the WFN logo. With her cheery nature, she has been an ambassador of goodwill for the WFN and its members, especially among exhibitors when others were attending scientific meetings. Over the years, she has worked with her husband to maintain WFN financial records, send the dues statements, and handle much of the correspondence. The Rose partnership has successfully managed all WFN affairs; while her husband was travelling the world and interacting with his professional colleagues, Angela was doing the background work to keep the organisation running smoothly and solvent. She has helped in the co-ordination of business meetings, accomplished the computerisation of the WFN membership list and provided invaluable help with *World Neurology*. Angela has travelled the world with her husband. Wherever she went, she greeted people enthusiastically, never showing signs of jet lag or fatigue. She is a charming lady, who has cheerfully and graciously served the WFN for many years and donated enormous amounts of time to ensure its prosperity. A lady of remarkable talents, she is a pianist and piano teacher, and is an expert at threading her way through London traffic in her multicoloured Volkswagen Polo. For all her work and support of her husband, we all owe her a deep debt of gratitude". A British GP wrote the final word: "If they say things like that about you whilst you are still alive, what will they have to say when you pop your clogs".

On 26 July 1998, Andrew Blakesley, who had been a financial adviser to Lazard Brothers, agreed to act as unofficial (unpaid) adviser to the World Federation of Neurology and wrote to me: "Thank you for lunch and for the briefing on affairs at the WFN. I am glad to hear that the plans you had to establish a permanent secretariat have been successful and that the requisite staff and offices are now in place. That will certainly help the WFN to carry on smoothly after you hand over the reins. The other side of the coin is of course that the WFN's cost base has increased considerably as compared with the years when you dealt with most of its administration via your office. Against that background I think I should repeat the advice that I gave in my letter last April, namely that the WFN needs to be especially frugal with its other running costs now that the permanent overhead base has increased. It would obviously be unattractive for a charity to absorb all its annual income in running costs leaving little or nothing available for the charitable purposes which are supposed to be its chief objectives. I hope to see you at the club before too long, perhaps at the bridge table. With best wishes, Andrew".

Because of my part in organising international medical meetings, I was asked by IAPCO (The International Association of Professional Congress Advisors) in 1995 to speak at their meeting in Earls Court, London. As they sent me an entry badge, I talked on my experiences of World Neurological Congresses, but suspect it was superfluous, although it was about "sponsorship support to neurology congresses and the extent to which support from industry brings participants" – a subject that still provokes doubt.

On the occasion of the 17th World Congress of Neurology held in London in 2001, I served as one of the Patrons and arranged a visit to Westminster Abbey where Dr Thomas Willis, the Founder of Neurology and the first to use the word, is buried. The Dean of the Abbey at that time suffered from a neurological illness and, when asking him for permission, arranged a time for the visit when no other tourists were at the Abbey except those attending the WCN. Westminster Abbey was built in 1245 in the English Gothic style and there is no church more intimately connected with British history. Every coronation has been held there and many of the medieval kings and queens lie there, including Queen Elizabeth I, daughter of King Henry VIII. Among the 1800 men and women interred, there are tombs of Charles Darwin, Sir Isaac Newton, George Frederick Handel and Charles Dickens. I gave a short talk on the life of Thomas Willis by his tomb.

I gave a Valedictory Address to the 17th WCN: "There are nearly 7,000 participants at this congress. At the last (16th) WCN held in Buenos Aires, Argentina there were 5,500. The President (of that Congress) was Solomon Muchnik and I assisted by visiting Argentina every year for four years. The previous (15th) WCN was held in Vancouver, Canada under the aegis of Don Patey whom I visited every year for the four years prior to that Congress, which was attended by 3,500 participants, so that the number of attendees in each Congress has steadily gone up, a trend that may well continue." Professor Vejjajiva was representing Asia and Professor Fieschi Europe. I was asked to help organise a meeting on the Neuro-epidemiology of Asia and, although the meeting was in Bangkok, all the speakers were taken to the beautiful seaside island of Pukhet where, whether as a result of these endeavours, I was rewarded by being made an Honorary member of the Thai Neurological Society, an honour given to only one other British neurologist.

The most generous donors to the World Congresses of Neurology were Dr Victor and Clara Soriano who hailed from Montevideo, the capital of Uruguay. For many World Congresses, they donated sums for two awards used to pay the fees of invited contributors. The first was an early morning talk given as the Fulton-Soriano Lecture and the second was the Victor and Clara Soriano Award Lecture delivered by the most prestigious neuroscientist of the preceding four years.

Sydney, 2005

The last World Congress of Neurology I attended was in Sydney, Australia and we took a seven-week holiday to see more of the country not previously visited on our previous shorter trips. After two weeks in Western Australia driving down the West coast from Perth, we spent a few days at an amazing hotel in the desert looking across to Ayers Rock and then took the Ghan (the name of the train and short for Afghan) from Alice Springs to Adelaide, a two day trip which proved rather disappointing. After a couple of days in Adelaide, where we saw my old friend and colleague Dick Rischbieth, we went to Kangaroo Island with its amazing kangaroos and koalas in the wild. We then drove through the Grampians, staying in a wonderful bed and breakfast, to Melbourne to see Angela's ninety-three year old uncle; he admitted wanting to die (as he had cancer) but promised to stay alive until after our visit. This he did, leaving this earth only weeks after we had left.

At the Congress in Sydney the historical symposium was on localisation in the brain and it fell upon me to open this session with a talk about the views of the Ancients. Believing that if a neurologist knows only neurology, he is no more than a technician as opposed to someone who is "groundedly learned", my aim was to try and interest specialists in their history. The symposium was published in the *Journal of the History of Neurosciences* which was started in 1992 and edited by me for its first five years.

On 7 August 2007, I was invited to the 50th Anniversary Reception given by the President and Trustees of the WFN which was held in the Ballroom of the Royal Hotel, Brussels; I may well have been the only one present who was at the first World Congress of Neurology in Brussels in 1957. Professor Johan Aarli, of the University of Bergen, was the President of the WFN at that time and gave a brief history of the organisation and how it had grown to encompass 102 national neurological societies. These congresses are held every four years and the only one I missed was Vienna in 1965, having just been appointed consultant neurologist to Charing Cross Hospital. The congresses held were as follows:

1957	BELGIUM, Brussels
1961	ITALY, Rome
1965	AUSTRIA, Vienna
1969	UNITED STATES, New York
1973	SPAIN, Barcelona
1977	HOLLAND, Amsterdam
1981	JAPAN, Tokyo
1985	GERMANY, Hamburg
1989	INDIA, Delhi
1993	CANADA, Vancouver
1997	ARGENTINA, Buenos Aires
2001	UNITED KINGDOM, London
2005	AUSTRALIA, Sydney
2009	THAILAND, Bangkok

Chapter 12

ASIAN TRAVELS

My first lecture tour of the Indian sub-continent was in 1968 and involved eighteen 'plane flights in twenty-one days, starting in what was then Ceylon (now Sri Lanka) and ending in Nepal. This trip was under the auspices of International Cultural Exchange, an organisation founded by Dr Hingourani who came from Sind in Pakistan. We were a group of seven consultant doctors from London teaching hospitals all in surgical specialties with myself as the only physician. The leader who invited me was the ear, nose and throat (ENT) specialist at Charing Cross Hospital. In Ceylon, which was more developed than India or Nepal, all the local consultants had trained in Britain where they had obtained their diplomas; my lecture to the Ceylon Medical Association was on "Recent Advances in Neurology". The arrival of our British medical group had been reported in the local newspaper and one evening, while resting in my hotel room recovering from jet-lag, there was a very loud knocking on my door which, when opened, revealed a whole family with a child who had a large head due to hydrocephalus (water on the brain), for which they hoped an immediate magical cure might be possible.

Spouses were not invited on this tour and, in any case, mine was eight months pregnant at the time. One of the local Singalese ladies kindly took me to a jeweller to buy a present for Angela; this was a large brooch in the form of a bouquet of flowers made from a mixture of differently coloured local gem stones; initially she did not like it at all, but over the years changed her mind and came to love it.

The group visited several large cities on the way north to Delhi, and in one of these a British expatriate, who had "stayed on" after India became independent in 1947, asked me to see a young Sikh who was paralysed from the neck down. He had been fully investigated with all available tests giving negative results so I suggested a special X-ray of the spinal cord. It was only years later that I realised he had *lathyrosis* due to excessive consumption of cheap meals containing the chick pea (*lathyrus sativa*), a condition I had never seen before, or since. Another stop-over was in Madras (now Chennai) where a British trained Indian neurologist, Krishnam Srinivas took care of me; on later trips Angela and I visited him several times. On one occasion, when unable to give a prestigious named lecture at his centre, he chastised me, pointing out that I was the only European speaker ever to refuse such an honour.

At our stop-over in Bombay (now Mumbai), my lectures were at two of the four medical schools, where I also participated in ward rounds at King Edward Memorial and J J Hospitals. I stayed with the family of my friend Dr Eddie Bharucha, who had trained in neurology in London; we first met in 1959 when he was admitted as a patient to the National Hospital where , having examined him, I thought he might have a brain tumour as there was evidence of pressure on the left side of the brain. Commiserating with his wife, Piloo, who was also a doctor; my fears luckily were unfounded and he just had a clot of blood due to head injury. He made a complete recovery and we remained good friends; staying with him and Piloo in Bombay was most enjoyable, but it has to be confessed that curry for breakfast proved to be somewhat of a challenge.

In Delhi the main post-graduate centre was the All-India Institute of Medical Sciences; the Director had trained at Charing Cross Hospital but, when the group from the UK were welcomed by the whole faculty of medicine, one Indian doctor referred to my youth, being the youngest of the visitors, albeit aged 41 years. The last country visited was Nepal which was the most backward having then only 250 doctors for a population of 11 million and without any neurologists. My lecture in the Municipal and Mission Hospitals was on headaches and, as the Nepalese Queen suffered from these, Dr Hingourani was asked if I would see her; without mentioning this request to me, he replied this could only be arranged if all the other doctors in the visiting group could be introduced to Her Majesty, a condition refused so that I did not see her. A memorable incident in Kathmandu was going to the hotel lavatory to find someone combing their very long hair; quickly retreating with apologies, a man's voice told not to worry as we were in the men's toilet and the long-haired person was in fact a man – this was of course in the 1960s when "hippies" with long hair were less well-known than now.

In 1971, a letter appeared in the correspondence columns of the *Lancet* written by Dr John Spillane, the senior neurologist of the University of Cardiff, in which he reported a case of a young girl with a visual disturbance, adding that he had just returned from Japan after seeing patients with SMON, a condition affecting the eyes as well as other parts of the nervous system. Because of my interest in the optic nerve, this Japanese disorder, which did not occur in the UK, was known to me and Spillane's diagnosis did not, in my opinion, fulfil the requirements for patients with this disease. In discussing the *Lancet* letter with my senior colleague, he advised against my challenging Spillane because he was a reputable neurologist with a well-travelled knowledge of geographical disorders. After further thought, as this diagnosis in Wales would alter the current attitude to the disorder, which was then considered as being peculiar to Japan, and only Japan, I wrote a letter to the editor of the *Lancet* gave the reasons for doubting the diagnosis, ending with "although my conclusion is not geographically apposite, the Scottish verdict of "non-proven" would seem appropriate". To my surprise, Spillane followed with another letter diagnosing SMON in an older man in Wales; again not satisfying diagnostic criteria, but there seemed little point in my writing a further letter. Shortly after this, a representative in England of a large Swiss pharmaceutical company, Ciba-Geigy, invited me to join a small group of four European neurologists who were going to Japan to see patients with SMON and report whether we had seen any such condition in our own countries; these other three experts were the professors of neurology from Basle, Zurich and Bombay.

The background of SMON was that in the nineteen-fifties a new disease was described in Japan, which affected the optic nerve, spinal cord and peripheral nerves in different combinations and of variable severity; the patients complained of pins and needles in the hands and feet spreading up the legs; the name SMON tripped off the Japanese tongue much better than its medical name, subacute myelo-optic neuropathy. Because the disorder reached epidemic proportions with about 10,000 people being affected with blindness or paralysis, the SMON Research Committee was set up in 1969 by the Japanese government, with a virologist as its chairman because it was suspected that, as the disorder occurred in clusters, a virus was the most likely cause. In 1970 this Committee laid down diagnostic guidelines, since there was no laboratory test for the disease. It was only after the Japanese Society of Neurology was founded in the nineteen-sixties that this speciality in Japan steadily became as good, if not better, than in many countries of the developed world. Our group of four was taken to the main medical centres in Japan to see several patients with SMON and had many discussions with those investigating the condition. As there was widespread interest, some meetings were attended by a politically orientated lay person, often a journalist, to report our deliberations.

While in Tokyo, a scientific paper was published in the *Lancet* on SMON occurring in Sydney, Australia - the first definitive report of cases occurring outside Japan. It was therefore decided that one of our group, who had seen confirmed cases in Japan, should go to Sydney to ascertain whether these patients really had the disease. Being chosen to go, presumably because, unlike the others in the visiting group, my mother tongue was English, my proviso was of not returning to Tokyo but going straight home to the UK after Australia. Within half an hour of our arrival in Sydney, the telephone in my hotel room rang from the leading professor of neurology of Australia, Jim Lance, telling me he had a case of SMON that had not been reported, which he would like me to see. Having just arrived after a long journey of thousands of miles, my visit was delayed to the following day when I examined the patient at her home nearby; she was in fact an ex-patriate from England who had been taking a medicine in doses far exceeding those recommended in the West (it had been used for travellers' diarrhoea, but not for longer than two weeks). Taken later to see the other Australian patients reported in the *Lancet*, there was no doubt that they all had SMON.

Because some patients had abdominal symptoms, my suggestion of adding to our group a neurologist who had written a book on the relationship of the nervous system to the gut, Dr Christopher Pallis of the

Royal Postgraduate Medical School, Hammersmith, was accepted. Other specialists included later were Professor Schaumberg, a neurotoxicologist from the United States, Professor P K Thomas of the Royal Free Hospital, London who was particularly interested in the peripheral nerves, and my registrar, Dr Marek Gawel. The importance of identifying SMON in countries other than Japan was that there were law-suits for all patients with the disease and, for four years after our tour, invitations were received to travel to different parts of the world to decide whether reported cases of SMON could be accepted as genuine. On one occasion, the group, now considerably enlarged from the original four, met at my choice of venue, a hotel in Avignon, Southern France. These medico-legal proceedings continued for many years and the sums eventually paid by the pharmaceutical company to patients were even greater than for thalidomide, which up to that time had been the largest ever medico-legal compensation.

While in Japan, I was taken to see a case of Minamata disease, another neurological disorder peculiar to Japan, which occurred on the southern island of Kyushu; from 1932, the Chisso chemical company's plant in Minamata had pumped highly toxic methyl mercury into Minamata Bay which had accumulated in the bodies of the local fish and shellfish, that were then eaten by the local people. In 1956 a ghastly neurological condition followed affecting children; the epidemic was called "cat-dancing disease" and lead to a long campaign by victims, followed by denials from the company as well as the inhabitants of Minamata, which was a company town. There was a four-year trial which succeeded and a Japanese film was made in 1971 lasting 105 minutes (*Telegraph Review*, 4.8.07, p.16) and entitled *Minamata: Kanja-san to Sono Sekai* (Minamata: The Victims and Their World). Keen to see the condition, I was taken many miles through the Japanese countryside to places where I felt that no "white" man had trod before; imagine my surprise when, after examining a patient, he showed me a photograph of himself with Dr J D Spillane, who had been taken to see him on an earlier visit.

When asking Japanese doctors and scientists what they thought was the likely cause of SMON, a percentage said a virus but a similar number claimed that it was due to the pharmacological drug, clioquinol; it seemed to us that part of Japanese culture was individuals with different views would not directly confront each other, so it was decided to have a symposium on SMON where ten contributors would come from Japan, Europe and North America, making thirty expert participants, with the Chairman being a neutral Canadian. Hawaii was chosen as the venue, being outside the areas where any of the participants lived. At this meeting in January 1976, after a long and exhausting flight, we arrived at our Japanese hotel and shown to a tiny room with a very short bed, suitable for small Japanese people; the next day we managed to get a slightly larger room with a normal sized bed. It was hoped this meeting would provide an open discussion but, when the Japanese contingent arrived, they asked to sit together; the Chairman pointed out this was not a political debate but intended to form a consensus as to the cause of a challenging and awesome disease; it was finally agreed that there would be five sets of two Japanese contributors sitting throughout the auditorium. Unsurprisingly, no definitive result was achieved at this meeting but as it was our first visit to Hawaii, we did some sight-seeing and visited the island of Kauai, staying at the Coco Palms Hotel, with its coconut grove of 2000 trees, famous for its celebrity visitors such as Bing Crosby and Elvis Presley. The issue was eventually resolved with a report that some patients with SMON had a green tongue, and a few even green urine or green faeces. A senior Japanese neurologist, Professor Tsubaki of Niigata, took scrapings of the green pigment from patients' tongues and these proved to be an iron chelate of clioquinol. On further enquiry, it was discovered that sufferers had been taking massive doses of medicine containing this drug for their general health but particularly for "inner cleanliness", whether it be constipation or diarrhoea. The Japanese government took immediate action, stopped the production of preparations containing clioquinol, of which there were 200 different varieties sold over the counter, and the disease died out.

In 1973 a lecture tour of Indonesia was sponsored by a pharmaceutical company. We broke our journey in Bangkok, where we stayed at the beautiful Oriental Hotel where we saw traditional Thai dancers performing in the gardens, and went on a sight-seeing trip by boat to see the floating markets and various temples. On arrival in Indonesia we were guided by one of the company's local representatives, a charming Chinese man called Frank Tshai, who told us something of the country's population, which was entirely Muslim, except for the far eastern part which was Christian, and Bali, which was mainly Hindu. At that time Indonesia had a population of 80 million (it has now grown into nine figures); there was widespread poverty and crime and the Army had been sent to the worst areas to take the extreme action of shooting criminals, which proved effective in diminishing the crime rate, but only in the short term. Frank Tshai showed us the sights of Jakarta, the capital of Indonesia, and then drove us to Bandung, about 80 miles away, where my lecture was to be given. On the drive we visited the forests of Indonesia, the Bogor Botanic Gardens and also tried a delicious drink made from avocado and syrup. My task in Bandung was to lecture on the treatment of epilepsy but, looking back, it was probably a waste of time because the modern drugs discussed were not then available in Indonesia, where the standard treatment was phenobarbitone. In Bandung we stayed at the Savoy Hotel dating from Indonesia's colonial days; it had remained virtually unchanged in the interim and still displayed notices in Dutch and the decor very much of the 1920s. The town had not changed greatly either, and there were bicycle-rickshaws in the streets. After my lecture, there was an entertainment by a conjurer who appeared to swallow glass and then pierced his skin with needles, making Angela feel faint so that she had to move from our honoured front-row seats. The next day we went on an outing to the local dormant volcano, a very pleasant walk and a nice change from the crowded city. After this meeting we went on to Bali where we stayed at the Bali Beach Hotel, near the capital, Denpasar.

One of my weekend habits was to walk across Richmond Park from our home to a café where they served delicious chocolate éclairs and coffee. On one fine Saturday morning in the spring of 1976, Angela came running through the park to find me; she had received a telephone call requesting me to go and see a patient at the Neurological Centre in Chandigarh, 150 miles north of Delhi in India. I managed to arrange a flight for later that day but its departure was delayed, meaning that I missed the connecting flight to Chandigarh and was, therefore, met by a car and driven the remaining 150 miles. Having seen the patient, Prof Gulati, the Director of the centre, saw me off and specifically told me not to sit in the front seat of the car which they called the "suicide seat", seat belts not being used in India. However, soon after leaving, the car had a puncture which inevitably took some time to fix and in order to make up time I encouraged the driver to go faster, as I was keen not to miss the flight back to London for my Monday NHS clinic. After this, not having slept for 36 hours, I decided to sit in the more comfortable front seat, and the result of my encouraging the driver to go faster was that he drove into the back of a bus (this was a busy period for traffic on a Sunday evening) which resulted in my sustaining a fractured knee-cap: I was carried onto the 'plane and taken straight to hospital on arrival in London, but missed my NHS clinic. Two years later, when I visited Chandigarh again, I told Prof Gulati what had happened and he laughed, saying never had his advice been ignored and so promptly punished. He also told the patient, who invited Angela and me to a very splendid banquet at his palace – quite a memorable experience.

Towards the end of 1976, I received a telephone call from the House Governor of St Thomas' Hospital telling me that he was advising a medical company which was due to open the first British-managed hospital in Sharjah, one of the United Arab Emirates. He wanted me to find a senior physician to head a team of seven consultant surgeons, and welcome the Ruler of Sharjah to the official opening of the new hospital. Being on the staff of two London teaching hospitals (Charing Cross and St Thomas'), we both thought it would not be difficult for me to recruit someone who would fit the bill; unfortunately, all those approached could not take time off as they were busy with research and Christmas was approaching. On telling the House Governor of my failure, he asked me to consider going myself but this was difficult as we had planned a family skiing trip to Switzerland which included my mother-in-law, whose husband had recently died. The House Governor's immediate response was that his company would fly the whole family to the Emirates and accommodate us in a brand new villa overlooking the Gulf. After some deliberation, we cancelled the Zermatt trip and went to Sharjah, my departure being three weeks before the rest of the family who, on arrival, were treated to such an excellent Christmas that they still have fond memories. The other consultants, all surgeons in different disciplines, had taken the job for a two-year "stint", as their tax free salary would help pay for their children's private schooling.

There was time for me to learn sufficient basic Arabic to examine a patient, but I soon discovered that in Arab countries not all patients are equal and, if there was a queue, "lesser fry" would give way immediately to their superiors; thus it was not possible to maintain British standards, particularly as these "superior" patients were accompanied by armed guards. One patient was admitted with jaundice due to an alcoholic liver and my attempts to reduce his alcohol intake were negated because his armed minions, who were always present, would bring in bottles of whisky. The only way to prevent further alcohol consumption and save his life was to bring over to Sharjah a liver specialist from London who would take him back to hospital in the United Kingdom. This was done but he died soon after leaving the London hospital, not unusual in these cases. As he was closely related to the Ruler's family, a three-day mourning period was held in Sharjah.

When in 1977 all our three sons were at boarding school, I suggested to Angela we could have a holiday anywhere in the world she would like to go, thinking of either South Africa or South America, where we had not been before. To my surprise she chose Indonesia as we had much enjoyed our previous visit there. In those days a British travel company (Swan Hellenic) did air tours of the islands of Java, Sumatra and Bali, and we went on one of these. Our guide turned out to be an excellent woman called Sybil Sassoon, who was related to the First World War poet of the same surname. In Jakarta a very senior neurologist, who was unknown to me, came to our hotel bringing presents; he told me he was fifth generation Chinese in Indonesia but his children were still regarded as foreigners; although he had achieved success, having been elected Dean of his medical school. His decision to emigrate with his family was irreversible, so he wanted to know if there were professional possibilities in the UK. Explaining the highly competitive nature for medical consultancies in our National Health Service, he accepted my view of excluding Britain as a place to go, and emigrated to the USA where he was appointed to the University of California San Francisco in their EEG department.

Our holiday itinerary included Toraja on the island of Borneo and, although our flight was cancelled, Sybil somehow managed to conjure one up. Toraja consisted of a Christian community with strange burial customs that could take place years after death, this long period being necessary to save the necessary funds for the expensive funeral. Prior to concluding our tour with Bali, which we had visited previously, I bought an object at a stall jungle in Sumatra selling souvenirs, having been told that it was a book containing prescriptions from previous centuries of such natural medicines as plants; the script was unreadable so we took it to the Museum of Mankind in London, who confirmed that it was a fake. The second object obtained from this "souvenir shop" was an ornament said to increase fecundity; it would be hung up and the story given to us was that "boiled baby" water would be placed inside, so clearly another fake, but it looks very attractive hanging on the wall in our sitting room, where it provides a never-ending topic of conversation.

In 1978, I did a lecture tour of Indian neurological centres particularly interested in stroke, talking on the latest advances. This was under the auspices of the British Council Division of the High Commission and, on arrival in New Delhi from London, we were met by a British council official who took us to stay at the home of Professor Vimla Virmani, the female Head of the Department of Neurology in Delhi; she was a delightful hostess and we enjoyed fresh chapattis for breakfast. As well as general sightseeing, visits to the Observatory and various temples and gardens, we were puzzled when she suggested we go to the "tank" – but discovered that this was a swimming pool. We then went to Chandigarh, 150 miles north of Delhi, which had a Postgraduate Institute of Medical Research and Education. My reception there, as well as accommodation and programme, was in the hands of Dr Jagjit Chopra who was Head of the Department of Neurology, and he showed us around Chandigarh, explaining how it had been planned by the French architect, Le Corbusier. The city was built in rectangular "sectors" each of which housed different professions; the more senior academics being placed centrally and the less important in the periphery, whether they were doctors or lawyers. A fascinating visit was to the Rock Garden, which had painstakingly been constructed from collected pieces of broken crockery and other waste material.

From Chandigarh we went via Delhi to Madras where Professor Ramamurthy, the senior neurosurgeon and Dr Srinivas, who was the senior neurologist and already a friend, took us to a party in a basement room of the best-known hotel in the city where his junior colleagues smuggled in alcoholic drinks in plain carrier bags, since Madras was the capital of a "dry" state where alcohol was prohibited. Invited to dine with the head of the British Council, two other guests were a couple who had driven with their caravan all the way from the UK, in the days of the Shah when it was possible to travel across Iran. One of the sights not far from Madras is Mahabalipuram, with temples carved into the rocks along the beach and submerged temples that are only visible at low tide. There is a hotel with cottages in the grounds, one of which we were given for the day; the couple we had met at the British Council were also staying there in their caravan. The husband had just retired from the British Board of Film Censors and we invited them to join us in drinking my long-saved bottle of champagne which I had bought at London duty free, knowing Madras to be a "dry" state, and which I had carefully installed in the cottage refrigerator. We ordered appetising warm roasted cashew nuts but I had not noticed the fridge was on a sloping tiled floor and when I opened it the bottle of champagne rolled out and broke into a "thousand" pieces. Somewhat abashed, when my predicament was explained to our guests, they solved the problem by producing a bottle of Scotch whisky from their caravan.

Being supported by the British Council was an interesting experience as each head office in the larger towns had an Education Advisor as well as two or three Assistant Education Advisors. My only chore was to make a report on my three week tour. We were flown to Bangalore, where my lecture to the National Institute of Mental Health and Sciences, of which Professor K S Mani was the head, it was where he taught me about "shower epilepsy" – that is attacks provoked by a cold shower on a very hot day, a lesson that proved useful in later years. Booked into a guest house in a residential area, we moved ourselves the next day to a more salubrious hotel with a swimming pool overlooking the racecourse. From Bangalore, we flew to Bombay where Professor Noshir Wadia was in charge of arrangements; we had become close colleagues as members of the international quartet of neurologists investigating the SMON epidemic in Japan. He had another unusual experience travelling from the USA via Portugal when he was *imprisoned* because the Indian government was taking over the Portuguese province of Goa; included in a rescue plan for our colleague was a successful missive from famous international neurologists to have him released. We were later entertained in Bombay by the Bharuchas, old friends since my help in looking after Dr Eddie Bharucha when he had been ill in London.

An invitation to visit Brunei in 1980, again at the expense of the British Council, came from Rex Lawrie MD, MS, FRCS, FRCP, who was General Physician to His Highness The Sultan, with a letter that included the following: "We have facilities for projection … Our audience is a mixed one, doctors, nurses, technicians. They are Indians, Chinese, British and a few Malay, all English speaking. The population of Brunei is about 220,000, half of whom are under 20 years old. There are about 600 deaths a year, but the causes are mostly guessed at, although probably cardiovascular disease plays quite a part, since a small survey of adults in one area showed quite a number of unsuspected hypertensives; people do get 'strokes' and I think we should benefit from teaching about prevention, diagnosis and management. Polio is now prevented by immunisation but some 18 year-old + are seen and some alas are house-bound; we have a physio and occupational therapy department. There is some leprosy. There are about 200 'new' cases of tuberculosis every year but hopefully now with BCG vaccine we shall see fewer and only older people. There is a plenitude of round worms, no hydatid disease, some hookworm, no bilharziasis and there is some Thalassaemia distribution. Please let me know your itinerary in due course and address in Hong Kong". This was followed by another letter: "The flight Hong Kong to Brunei is a one-class flight. I am arranging a provisional timetable for you and your wife, with two lectures (I hope you do not mind), ward rounds and clinic/seminars in our two hospitals. The second lecture we have billed you for on Saturday, 8 November at Kuala Belait Hospital on 'Migraine' ... the audience would enjoy and benefit most from a down-to-earth practical lecture. The three physicians have written to me to say they fear some lectures may be too high powered. I have replied that I will suggest you pitch the words at a lower level to suit the audience".

Brunei was then the richest country in the world, due mainly to its oil, which provided a record-making Gross Domestic Product. We flew to Hong Kong with Cathay Pacific but the airport reception said that our reservation to Brunei had not been confirmed and so no seats were available. As we were following a fixed schedule, we made a fuss and pointed out that going to Brunei was at the invitation of their government, and seats were duly found. In Hong Kong, my lecture on Stroke Research at Queen Mary's Hospital was under the chairmanship of Professor Todd; impressed with their high standard of medicine, it was disappointing to find it was difficult for them to retain neurologists because of the more advantageous remuneration of private practice. My recommendation was that a new contract similar to one that had recently introduced in the UK, whereby full-time consultants could engage in a certain amount of private practice, should be considered by the University of Hong Kong Medical School, otherwise it would be difficult to keep highly qualified people within the framework of the University.

On arrival in Brunei, we were surprised that nearly all the houses, which were built on stilts above the water and looked poverty-stricken, had television aerials. We took the opportunity to visit the Churchill Museum, which is devoted solely to him, but also houses an Aquarium and post-graduate library. My two lectures included one at a military base where the non-commissioned soldiers were Ghurkas. Following another lecture, we were invited to an official curry lunch at the officers' mess after the

Remembrance Day church service. My three days in Brunei were very busy quite apart from visiting the hospitals and discussions with the doctors, since we also enjoyed a boat trip to Kampong Ayer in one of their typical crafts; having admired the local boats used on the jungle rivers, they presented me with a silver model, which takes pride of place in our collection of ethnic silver boats.

The physician advising on the new hospital in Brunei had trained in Edinburgh as had most of the British specialists who lectured there; the new hospital was going to be a sumptuous affair with money no object. The population of Brunei meant it was not inappropriate to have a neurological service, but not including neurosurgery, as the number of inhabitants was not sufficient to keep an expert neurosurgical team, which would require at least six neurosurgeons; my conclusion was that they would have to continue to send patients requiring neurosurgery to either Singapore or Hong Kong. My report was clear that, in spite of a considerable need, the population of nearly a quarter of a million was approximately the same as the catchment area of a district general hospital in the UK, which would usually have a half-time (five-session) neurologist. While the latter could function in Brunei with the support of EEG and EMG, and their technicians, five years was too soon to consider establishing a complete unit with neurosurgeons and scanning; hence my recommendation of regularisation with neurological visits, either monthly from Singapore or perhaps quarterly from the UK. My lectures were not well received, probably because my talks were too research-orientated and not appropriate for everyday practice.

The "Neurological Study Tour of the People's Republic of China" was from 26 September to 11 October 1981, and was led by Professor Bob Aird from UCSF, who was accompanied by his wife Ellinor. During this trip, amongst other places, we visited Xian and Shanghai. The social side of this trip was organised by Joyce, the wife of Dr Oscar Kofman who was a neurologist in Toronto, Canada. On arrival in Peking (now Beijing) it was snowing and Chinese women cleared the streets swinging long, straw brooms. We visited five cities, the first of which was Shanghai. We settled into a Guest House for four days during which time we toured and lectured. Our first visit was to the Ming Tombs, one of which has been well restored with artefacts from the Ming dynasty. From here we went to the Great Wall of China, which had been completed in the 3rd Century BC by Emperor Quin Shir Huang and took 300,000 men ten years to complete; its 1500 mile course across northern China has an actual winding length of 3,500 miles. It is apparently the only structure on earth seen by astronauts. In Peking we were taken to Tian-tan, the Temple of Heaven where the emperors prayed, which is not quite as opulent as the Imperial Palace in the Forbidden City, which has grounds covering 250 acres in the centre of Peking; the Winter Palace overlooked two man-made lakes and gave an excellent view of the city. All the inhabitants were dressed in grey, dark blue or green with identical shoes and the only variation was in the shirts, which were coloured or patterned. We visited Mao's Mausoleum and passed his body in a crystal coffin in hushed silence, but ahead of the Chinese visitors. In Tiananmen Square there were still pictures of Mao, Marx, Stalin and Trotsky displayed. At the zoo we were delighted to see the pandas, the baby in its play pen and three adults performing summersaults to amuse us. We went next to Xian where at that time they had recently found, on an archaeological dig of three vaults, over 8,000 figures of 10ft warriors and horses, a sample of a few having been shown in the British Museum more than 25 years later. The warriors all had different faces and different military dress. Xian was the ancient walled capital of China and the beginning of the Silk Route. The whole of China seemed to be one mass of bicycles. In Shanghai we observed the uses of acupuncture, in one case supporting anaesthesia for a major operation. Accommodation for the Chinese was then primitive by western standards. We also visited Guilin which is a tourist town and the highlight is a boat trip on the River Li. We also visited a chopstick factory which Angela described as follows: "Unfortunately the initial process of actually producing the chopsticks was not revealed. What we saw were raw undecorated bamboo (not plastic) sticks piled high in boxes in darkened rooms. There the sticks were inscribed in Chinese "The Beautiful Sights of Guilin" by individually being fed into a machine". Our last stop was Canton (Guangzou) which is a busy metropolitan centre near the Hong Kong border. Having stayed at some strange Chinese hotels and guest houses – one where the bedclothes had obviously not been changed after the previous visitors – it was somewhat of a relief to end our visit in Hong Kong, where we also were pleased to eat some really good Chinese food. At that time China was still a very poor country and unable to provide accommodation and food up to the expectations of Western travellers.

In 1984 there was yet another Asian lecture tour on stroke, funded by the pharmaceutical company which produced a drug called Praxilene, tested by us with a clinical trial, but this trip was also partly under the auspices of the British Council; it was embarrassing to be met in Singapore airport by representatives of both groups. One invited us to a "special" restaurant for dinner and when the other group asked us the next day to go to a "special" restaurant, it turned out to be the same one, but we kept this secret to ourselves. We next flew to Taiwan where we visited the Taipei Museum, which has more Chinese treasures than mainland China, largely due to Chiang Kei Shek, the Nationalist leader, who took them when he broke away from Communist China to form the independent state of Taiwan. It has to be confessed that, exhausted by the travel and lectures, sleep overcame me when sitting down in this fabulous museum.

Our next lecture on this tour was in Manila in the Philippines, where we were invited to the Polo Club; before going, they assured me that wives were invited but we were embarrassed when it became evident on arrival that Angela was the only female present. The next day we were by the hotel pool waiting to be taken to the airport when an unknown neurologist appeared and presented us with a large package which we could not take on the aeroplane; luckily the pharmaceutical representative who was looking after us said he would post it on to us. Some six months later we had to pay duty to retrieve this package which contained a lampshade made of sea shells, entirely useless! Our return to the UK was via Kuala Lumpur, the capital of Malaya, where the local physicians were not impressed with my talk, possibly because they too in 1988 were doing a stroke trial. Our final visit was to the beautiful island of Penang for a holiday which was badly needed to recover from the exhausting lecture itinerary.

It was at about this time that the President of the Indonesian Society of Neurology informed me that they were to hold the Asian-Oceanic Congress of Neurology in 1987 and asked me whether it should be held in Jakarta or Bali. My reply was unequivocal, stating that not many people would come to Jakarta but everyone would want to visit to Bali; my advice was taken and the Congress was a great success. At that meeting, my talk was on "Dementia" after which a later President of the WFN congratulated me saying he had taken notes of my lecture. In September 1987 we went again to the Bali Beach Hotel in Indonesia for a Sandoz meeting and, on the way home, stopped in India to attend the planning meeting for the next World Congress of Neurology which was to be held in Delhi in 1989 and to visit neurological friends in Bombay.

In July 1989 the pharmaceutical company, Sandoz, asked me to undertake a lecture tour on stroke to Pakistan and agreed to pay expenses for Angela as well. In Karachi, on expressing our appreciation of the local mangos, we were taken to a mango market and were given two large boxes to take back to the UK and told that as there were two different varieties, they would ripen at different times, but on arrival home found them all to be ripe, and Angela was very busy making mango ice cream and mango sorbet whilst at the same time we tried to eat as many as possible before they went bad. In Pakistan, we visited Lahore, a centre for British activity during the old Empire days, and Islamabad with the largest mosque in the world. Although taken to Peshawar with its large Afghan population, we were not allowed to visit the Khyber Pass for security reasons; we also had a memorable visit to the vast ancient ruins of Taxila where it was so hot that we spent the time seeking shade under the crumbling walls.

 On another lecture tour to India, we arrived at Heathrow airport in a snowstorm, not surprising for an English December. We checked in and boarded the aeroplane as normal at about 10.00 p.m., but there were several other Jumbo planes queuing to take off before us and our flight was delayed because apparently they had to clear the snow from these planes. The flight captain spoke to us periodically, firstly to apologise for the delay, then to tell us that drinks would be served, followed an hour later by food. His final statement, which came in the early hours of the following morning, was that as pilots and cabin staff were allowed to work a maximum ten-hour shift, we only had time to fly to Rome, where we would spend twenty-four hours before setting off again for Bombay. (None of the flights ahead of us had been able to take off and the reason we were kept on the plane all night was that their passengers had taken all the available local hotel rooms). On arrival in Rome, when ringing my contact in Bombay to inform him that we were in Italy, he asked "What the hell are you doing in Rome? You're supposed to be in Bombay giving the opening lecture". Explaining our predicament, we pointed out that we would be in Bombay the next day when my talk could be given later in the meeting as the title of my opening paper was "Global review of stroke". As it was sunny in Rome, we took the opportunity of lunching with friends who were living there and enjoyed the unexpected visit.

Whilst at the conference in Bombay, the largest city in the province of Maharashtra, we decided to visit the caves at Aurangābād in the same province, but about 150 miles to the north-east. We began with the caves at Ajanta where there were Halls of Worship and Buddhist monasteries which had been most active in the years from 200 BC to 600 AD; we then visited the Ellora caves where there were shrines sculpted between the 6th to the 9th centuries AD on a granite hillside by the followers of Jaila (5 caves), Hindu (17 caves) and Buddhist (12 caves) faiths. Nearby was the most famous and beautiful rock-temple, Kaliasa, said to be the holy mountain residence of Lord Shiva.

We then went further afield to the province of Rajasthan staying in Jaipur at the Rambagh Palace hotel, visiting the Amber Fort which we reached by elephant. Jaipur, the provincial capital, is sometimes called the "Pink City" with its myriad of flower and fruit stalls; it also has one of the best observatories, the Jantar Mantar dating from 1728, with the largest sundials and astrolabes; and there was another sight that was new to us – a kite market. We left Jaipur for Delhi by car, as fog prevented air travel, and then took the train to Chandigarh where we stayed at the guesthouse of the Postgraduate Medical Centre. Our host was Jagjit Chopra, the professor of neurology, an old friend and colleague who had trained in

Northern Ireland; we attended his family supper party on the evening of our arrival because our reason for going to Chandigarh was to attend his daughter's wedding on the following day. We had travelled from Jaipur by car and train, a long journey; the car was driven by a young man who wanted to buy my wife's jeans, but she could not spare them as she was wearing them.   The Sikh wedding was a sumptious affair held in a local hotel and attended by hundreds of guest; we were the only Europeans and treated as honoured guests. Although the wedding actually lasted over several days, we only attended the first day. After this we went to Madras, and then to Assam. Whilst my opening lecture had been delivered to neurologists in Bombay, the second talk was to general physicians at the 59th Joint Annual Conference of the Association of Physicians of India, in Guwahati, the capital of Assam on the north-eastern side of the Indian sub-continent. My talk on the treatment of stroke did not go down well because, at that time, the generalist audience treated stroke patients with steroids and had difficulty in appreciating the need for controlled clinical trials. This meeting took place ten days after the one in Bombay and when asking the sponsoring company what we should do during this interval, they gave us carte blanche to tour wherever we liked in India, which is how we came to explore Rajasthan, visit Jaipur and go to the wedding in Chandigarh.

Whilst in Guwahati, it was suggested we take a trip to the Kasirango nature reserve, famous for tigers as well as white rhino. Assam (which wanted independence) was embroiled in political troubles so that, in our small car we had not only the driver, but a military guard armed with an AK40 rifle. We stayed the night at a hotel near the nature reserve. Since we were on a high plateau, it was very cold, and as we had to rise at dawn I kept my pyjamas on under my clothes, an unusual sight which made Angela take photographs of me to show on our return home, when she gave a slide-show of her travels. We started at day-break as the mist lifted, riding on elephants, and saw the white rhinos, which are becoming increasingly rare, but no tigers; later in the day, our guide pointed to a tree which, he said, bore the marks of tigers' claws. Because of the political problems in Assam, we were advised to leave Guwahati early for the airport as all roads into the town were about to be closed as a security measure to protect an expected visiting political personality and we were due to fly home from Delhi that night. This meant spending the whole day at the airport, although initially we had a room at the hotel near the airport gates. When we went into the airport lounge it was crowded with people who had all been there for hours. I realised we had spent all our Indian money, but luckily spotted an Indian physician who had attended the Conference and was also waiting for his flight, and he lent us enough rupees to buy a drink. We arrived in Delhi at the *domestic* airport, which had not been anticipated, and so had to transfer by taxi to the International airport but I now had only American dollars and the taxi driver was not too pleased. It was a great relief when we finally boarded our BA flight for home.

In January 1992 the medical authorities of Thailand asked me to organise an international symposium on "The Neuroepidemiology of Asia" in Bangkok. This was to last three days and included reports on stroke in China, Japan, India, Indonesia and Taiwan as well as Thailand; other sessions included degenerative conditions in these countries as well as epilepsy. The contributors, who were all senior neurologists from these countries, were then given a three-day holiday in a lovely hotel in Phuket by way of appreciation. It should be remembered that in 1992, Thailand was considered to be one of the Asian "Tiger economies". Although it was hoped that the proceedings of the symposium would be published, this did not happen.

In September 1996 Angela and I were guests of the 9th Asian and Oceanian Congress of Neurology in Seoul, the capital of South Korea, where on one evening the local neurologists had arranged separate dinners for men and women; at the former each man had a Korean "lady" by his side; "lady" is in inverted commas because, halfway through the meal, I felt a hand on my thigh which seemed to go higher with an enquiry as to my hotel. Alcohol flowed freely, and it was no surprise to find our dinner was followed by dancing when a very senior British neurologist was seen kissing his dancing partner! The women's dinner had no such entertainment and was a very proper affair.

On one lecture tour in the Middle East, the local organiser asked me to see a middle-aged VIP who had an epileptic attack. As he had been fully investigated, with MRI and EEG, my inclination was to demur to the invitation, and pointed out that there was little more to recommend. Nevertheless, the patient being an eminent politician, my neurological host, as well as the Dean of the medical school, insisted, ending with my reluctant agreement. My first question to the patient was to ask what he had been doing on the day of his attack, to which he replied that he had gone for a swim in the Gulf, as the outside temperature was over 100ºF, and then had a shower which was followed by a major epileptic attack, which he never had previously. The only reason I was able to make an immediate diagnosis was that I had learned about "hot-water epilepsy" (HWE) on a previous visit to Bangalore in India, so it was easy for me to advise stopping his antiepileptic drugs to allow him to drive. The Dean, not being a neurologist, remained unconvinced and asked me how I knew and whether I had seen such a case in the UK; when replying in the negative saying it did not occur in Britain, was even morel doubtful. This type of case confirms the importance of world-wide travel to increase experience.

Chapter 13

JOURNEYS ELSEWHERE

One of my earliest professional trips was to Luxembourg, where the leading neurologist, Henri Metz, who had trained partly in England and partly in France, asked me to see one of his patients. Previously, in 1961, at a meeting of French and British neurologists in Paris, we had gone together to visit the doyen of paediatric neurologists, André Thomas, who was over 90 years of age at the time, but unhappy because most of the people he knew had died. This was a new phenomenon to me at that time but presented itself more frequently as longevity became more common, including my own.

In April 1976 I was invited to lecture at a meeting of the North Pacific Society of Neurology and Psychiatry in Canada, which consisted of specialists from British Columbia and the States of Washington and Oregon; this Society had been founded in the days when it was not easier to journey north or south rather than travel across the Rockies. Because it was customary for specialists to meet and exchange knowledge regarding advances, these consultants rotated their annual meetings between the three areas of the north pacific region. On this trip my whole family of wife and three small sons came with me and stayed at the famous old-fashioned English-style hotel in Victoria, British Columbia where afternoon tea was served at 4.00 pm; British traditions were preserved by the local populace. When asking the Society's President if dress for the Symposium dinner was tuxedo, she huffily replied it was "dinner-jacket" as they did not use the word tuxedo in British Columbia, emphasizing the term British. Although there are Canadian provinces where the inhabitants are bilingual, particularly Quebec, there was no French to be heard in this part of Canada. After Victoria, we went to Edmonton, Alberta where I gave another lecture; we travelled on the Canadian Pacific Railway through the Rockies but sadly missed most of the exotic scenery as it was during the night, although the children did have the excitement of sleeping on a train. In Edmonton I met an erstwhile colleague from Atkinson Morley's Hospital in London, who wrote novels in his spare time and told me that one of his fictitious characters was called "Frank Flower", being modelled on me, apparently because he was a "ladies man".

The Louise van Hess Foundation for Medical Education had its inception in Pennsylvania in 1979 and each year until the year 2000 it would put on a programme in Lancaster County, not far from Philadelphia. The meeting took place in the centre of the Amish country and it was only later when seeing the film, *Witness*, that I learned this unusual religious community has an interesting history and is a tourist attraction. The speakers were mostly from the surrounding area and all but one were American, the visitor from abroad being expected to give three postgraduate lectures. Geraint James, a London colleague, had recommended me.

Another interesting trip was to New Orleans in February 1982, at the time of the Mardi Gras celebrations, to attend the annual conference of the American Stroke Society, organised by cardiologists rather than neurologists. Angela had a wonderful time shouting the traditional "throw me something, mister" at the street parades and collecting many bead necklaces thrown to the crowds from the passing floats. We stayed in the French Quarter of New Orleans and went directly to the airport from this parade, where she amused the passengers on the 'plane with her collection of "jewellery". Four months later, my next visit to the USA was to deliver the George T. Abell lecture at the University of Texas in Houston, which had been arranged by Professor William S Field. Bill Field, at the outbreak of the Second World War, volunteered for the Canadian Army and at the end of his service received an honour from Her Majesty, Queen Elizabeth II; he later also served with the United States forces. He told me of a lecture tour in Russia, ostensibly to improve relationships between the Russian and American governments, when he was asked, just before his departure to see a patient (Shostakovich) who he diagnosed with (fatal) motor neurone disease. On walking to his aeroplane, a government official thrust bundles of dollars in cash into his unwilling hands for seeing this eminent composer. Going on to Washington for the Annual Meeting of the American Association for the

Study of Headache (AASH), which I joined in 1977, it was 4 July, American Independence Day, and there was a tremendous firework display with an excellent view from the top floor of the hotel. As an honoured guest, at the dinner they placed me on the table next to the band, which was extremely loud preventing any conversation, but no one complained, perhaps because the band leader was Ray Charles, the blind pianist.

We returned to the USA in 1982, for a conference held at a hotel near Lake Mohonk in up-state New York, where smoking and alcohol were not allowed, as the building belonged to a religious institution. This was the annual meeting of the Academy of Aphasia, an American group of two hundred people interested in speech disorders; there were only three British members, namely Macdonald Critchley, Professor Zangwill and myself, the other two not being present on this occasion. We took the opportunity to see Niagara Falls from the American side, having previously seen it across the border from Canada. A later compliment was paid to my interest in disorders of speech when asked to give the Mary Law Lecture to "Action for Dysphasic Adults " (ADA) in the UK, but as this was a patient support group, my talk was rather too specialised for a lay audience.

In December 1982 my visit to Basel in Switzerland was for a conference of the Hydergine Club, known mainly by its members who reported any work done with the drug, hydergine, a product of ergot and manufactured by Sandoz, which was undoubtedly the reason why the meeting was held in Switzerland. The chairman of both departments of neurology and psychiatry in the University of Graz, Austria, was Professor Dr Helmut Lechner (sic), as he preferred to be called; as well as training in Graz, he studied in Marseilles, Zurich and London. At this meeting, he invited me to lecture in Graz, which I readily accepted. Due to return to London by changing flights in Vienna; Helmut, who was also a trained pilot and flew his own 4-seater plane, offered to fly me to Vienna, an invitation I politely declined, not liking flying in small planes, having experienced them in several parts of the world, including the Middle East, New Zealand, Vancouver and over the Grand Canyon. However, the problem was that the commercial flight to Vienna was at precisely the same time as Helmut was flying, so it was difficult to refuse his offer. Suffice to say, the exposure to heights sitting next to the pilot made me feel distinctly uncomfortable and it was a relief to finally land at the airport in Vienna. Helmut Lechner died in 2007 and is sadly missed by all who knew him.

In April 1983, an invitation to lecture at a headache conference in Palm Springs was irresistible; the course was organised by an American headache specialist, Seymour Diamond, whose wife, Elaine, was very friendly with Angela. We stayed at Ingleside Inn, a peculiar hotel decorated in "Ye Olde English" style, perhaps because the manageress was English. Following this we went on to Las Vegas which was not a success, not least because the weather was extremely cold and there were no warm clothes available in the shops. We then flew to the Grand Canyon for Angela's first visit; our small plane carried only 30 passengers, mostly Japanese, but the flight was very rough and she was ill and terrified and initially refused to take another plane for the return tip, but eventually changed her mind, which was lucky as the alternative would have been a very long drive. However, our short stay overlooking the Canyon was definitely up to expectations. We ended this trip with a visit to the famous Scripps Clinic in La Jolla, California and then San Diego to see its zoo.

In June of 1984, we went to Palm Springs again for another lecture, taking the opportunity to show Angela Yosemite Park. For the first couple of nights we stayed in a sort of luxury tented campsite, then moving upmarket to the Ahwahnee Hotel, where we were given the suite that the Mountbattens had stayed in previously. We then visited our favourite American City, San Francisco, and watched with some amazement a gay parade of over thirty thousand people.

In June 1986 the annual meeting of AASH was in Chicago after which we visited Milwaukee with its breweries. We stayed at a B and B that had been recommended, but this proved to be a mistake. Angela was returning to London via New York, where she was staying with friends, while my destination was San Diego to lecture on the management of motor neurone disease; to my surprise, she telephoned me from New

York to inform me she was returning to London on Concorde. After my gulping with disbelief, to my relief she explained that British Airways had upgraded her at no extra cost.

Each year, the town of Portland, Oregon in the north-west of the United States but, more particularly its Good Samaritan Hospital, invites an Annual Neuroscience Lecturer and my turn came in 1986. The necessary duty, besides attending a dinner for the sponsors and giving the neuroscience lecture, was to talk at a nearby Liberal Arts College. Whereas up-dates of a neurological disorder could easily be given in clinical talks, the lecture for this university audience had to be largely non-medical; the title of my talk was the "Medicine of Art" which consisted of a series of internationally well-known paintings, giving the background medical stories. The person responsible for my invitation was Professor Robert Dow, an eminent neuroscientist held in high esteem internationally; in the year of my visit, he was in his late seventies but still very impressive with a fishing rod or tennis racket. To travel to Portland, a change of planes was necessary in Seattle, where the brief stop allowed exploration of this fascinating city, the birthplace of Starbucks, Bill Gates, Jimmy Hendricks and many others.

In February 1988, we went to San Antonio, Texas at the invitation of Bill Field, the professor of neurology in Houston; to our surprise the aeroplane was diverted because of snow and ice and we had to drive into San Antonio. Bill and his wife, Alma, where good friends and we invited them to dinner locally; he chose an excellent restaurant but, on paying the bill, my addition of a 10% tip was corrected by the waiter who pointed out the usual percentage in the USA was 12½%. Somewhat taken aback, my guest confirmed this was the usual arrangement because the weekly wages of the waiters took tips into consideration, so my mistake was hastily corrected. Having seen the film, *Alamo* several times we were delighted to visit the actual fortress with its memorial plaques of several Britishers who took part in the battle for Texan Independence against the Mexicans. We also attended a rodeo, which was a very entertaining experience.

Mexico, of course, is always a delightful place to visit, and my first time was in 1960 when working as a Visiting Assistant Professor at the University of California, San Francisco. Asking the locals where to go for a long weekend, they replied Mexico City and Acapulco, which advice was duly followed. After that, my visits to Mexico were frequent because of the kind invitation of Professor Francisco Rubio-Donnadieu, who arranged lecture trips to see other parts of the country, including the excellent Mayan ruins of Chichen Itza in Yucatan. A more recent visit to the New World was for the initiation of the pan-American Congress of Epilepsy in Havana, Cuba. It was an interesting symposium, but upsetting to hear a distinguished professor from the USA criticise his own country for its attitude to Cuba. As an old cigar addict, since cured, it was a fascinating trip and a pleasure to visit Calixto Muchado, and to see cigars being made. Although visiting lecturers are usually entertained by their hosts, this was not the case in Havana, when we invited two poverty-stricken professors to dine at our hotel, a treat they could not possibly afford on their meagre pay.

In October 1986 one of my junior consultant neurologists arranged for Angela to go with me to a meeting in Brac, an island off the coast of Yugoslavia opposite Split, and discuss the latest investigative techniques. Although the island is a delightful holiday resort, I was somewhat disturbed when my junior and his wife joined in communist songs which they appeared to know quite well. In May 1987, Angela came with me to Gdansk in Poland for an international meeting, where we met Dr Uristoff Selmaj, who had been one of my assistants in London before becoming one of Poland's most distinguished neurologists. First going to Warsaw, followed by Krakow, in the latter's magnificent square a young man approached asking if we needed Polish currency for American dollars at an extremely favourable rate. Although previously warned not to undertake this sort of exchange, we were intrigued to see what would happen, so handed the young man a 20 dollar note. Telling us to keep a look-out for police, he counted out the Polish notes and disappeared; it was then that we realised that only the outside notes were genuine – he had palmed other notes which were not legal tender; the money lost was a useful lesson and we could not but admire his dexterity. Gdansk (known before the Second World War as Danzig) was the excuse for Hitler's invasion of Poland and had been destroyed by bombs but the town was later completely rebuilt in its beautiful and original style. We ended this lecture tour by sailing across the Baltic Sea to Helsinki; we had a few zlotys left, but the emigration controller was adamant that we could not take Polish currency out of their country but should spend it in Poland; this meant going back through customs to spend the currency (on chocolate) before being allowed on board ship. Although given a nice, very large cabin, it was adjacent to the noisy engine room with one of the beds alongside the party wall, so they gave us another small cabin to sleep in, although still keeping the large room for daytime use. Finland was entirely another "cup of tea" from Poland, being much wealthier. We hired a car in Helsinki for the two- days drive to Savonlinna for the Finnish Congress; at the castle there, we attended an opera and we went to a concert in an extraordinary cave carved out of the rocks.

1989 was a year that changed the world: the Berlin Wall came down, Russia left Afghanistan, apartheid ended in South Africa and Tiananmen Square in China provoked human-rights protests.

In March 1990, an unusual meeting was organised in Bologna, Italy on "The Rehabilitation of Multiple Sclerosis", where my talk was on "The State of Our Knowledge". My introductory lecture included the fact that it was 34 years since my last visit to Bologna and, whereas the attractions of the old city were still magnificent, the modern metropolis showed huge development. My congratulations were given to the organisers for such an unpopular topic which would hardly be held elsewhere, but was very well attended, and funded by the local communist government. Later the same month Ciba-Geigy, the pharmaceutical company, asked me to go to Copenhagen for a neurotoxicology symposium and, two months later, Professor Eero Hokkanen of Finland invited me to be the guest of the Scandinavian Migraine Society; he first kindly took me on a touristic car journey towards the Arctic Circle, ending up with sleepless nights due to the "midnight sun". My host, who was the senior professor of neurology in Finland, impressed me by recounting how, after the Second World War, he had organised five neurological centres to cover the whole of his country. As these services had been far more recently organised than the UK, we decided to hold a joint meeting later in London, when the two countries' services would be compared.

In May 1992, at the 10th Congress of the Pan-African Association of Neurological Sciences in Marrakech my talk was "Recent advances in the treatment and management in brain ischaemia". As we had never been to Morocco, we decided to see something of the country by having a three-day holiday both before and after the meeting. At the end of our stay, on going to pay the hotel bill, I was told me there was nothing to pay. Pointing out that, whilst the three days of the Congress may well be free because of being an invited speaker, we had spent 3 days before and 3 days after on holiday in the hotel; he checked again and said "You are a guest of His Majesty, King Hassan the Second", a lovely surprise which we have never forgotten. Many years later we stayed at the Mammounia Hotel in Marrakesh for a few days where, quite by chance, my niece Maureen and her husband were visiting during their tour of Morocco, and we invited them to a meal at the hotel. On another occasion, we took a natural history tour in Morocco where, amongst many interesting things, we were lucky to see the Bald Ibis, a bird whose habitat is virtually only in the foothills of the Atlas Mountains. This was our British guide's fourteenth trip to the area and said we would be lucky if we saw this unique bird, which he had never seen mating. Not only did we find these rare creatures but, as the guide left the mini-van to set up his telescope, I spotted a pair of birds mating. Indicating this to the group who were all waiting in the van, they insisted we should tell Martin, our guide, as he would really want to see them. With some hesitation, I pulled the van door open, which made a noise, resulting in the birds flying away. At the time, these birds were in danger of extinction, so I was upset for possibly being partly responsible for their disappearance; it is a relief to report that in the following year, it was noted that their numbers had increased.

In 1992, the Spanish government celebrated the 500th anniversary of Columbus' discovery of America by having meetings on various subjects in different venues. The one on neurology was held in the Canary Islands where the topic given to me was "The history of neurology *before* 1492". My friend and colleague, Lord Walton, on hearing the title, hoped that they asked me to speak for less than one minute but, in fact, it proved to be an enormous subject, largely because of the Ancient Greeks and their Arabic translators.

In October 1993 the Saudis asked my help to organise an International workshop on Headache and Migraine at the College of Medicine, King Saud University, Riyadh, for which I was presented with a certificate by the Dean. Later the same month I attended the ninth Pan-American Congress of Neurology in Guatemala where Mexico and most Central American republics were represented. The same year, Dr Cuba, who was President of the 14th Peruvian Congress of Neurologists, invited me to lecture in Lima, presenting me with a Diploma for lecturing on headache and migraine, and a certificate making me a titular member (Miembro Titula) for talking on "The Neurology of Ancient Greece". This visit gave me a chance to visit Machu Pichu, the old mountain city which is Peru's main visitor attraction. Unlike my son and his then girlfriend (now wife), who walked the three-day trek to this site years after my visit, my journey was by train. On my departure, I was presented with an antique bronze knife used centuries ago to open the skull by making holes in the head (trepanation).

FCR (2nd from left) and Professor Cuba (3rd from left)

In April 1994, Glaxo asked me to go to Budapest in Hungary to talk on treatment for migraine in an Imigran (sumatriptan) symposium with the title of "Recent Advances in Migraine Therapy"; needless to say, entertainment was particularly enjoyable at the typical restaurants with violin music. After three annual visits to Budapest I was appointed to the editorial board of the Hungarian national neurological journal, which was always published in Hungarian, a language completely unknown to me. The 2nd International Conference of the European Headache Foundation was held in Liège but proved to be embarrassing because of two invitations to celebrate the 100th Anniversary of the Belgian Neurological Society, the reason being that there are *two* such bodies, one for the French-speaking area centred on Brussels, and the other in Ghent, where Flemish is the preferred language.

One week in November 1994, there was a course for British general practitioners at La Manga Club, Murcia, Spain which, unbeknown to me, was famous for its golf course. Asked to lecture on neurological disorders, including Parkinson's disease, a twenty minute video of Parkinson's life was completely ignored as the assembled gathering was more interested in the golf, and *not one* came to see the video; they did come to my lectures but this was because there was no golf scheduled for those times.

Italy has always been a marvellous place for meetings and, on one visit in 1994, I went to three consecutive conferences at Lake Garda, Turin and Rome where, after the final session, Professor Cesare Fieschi had organised a meal at a restaurant overlooking the Tiber, and I was seated next the Italian Home Minister. On being asked why Italy hosted so many medical meetings, he replied it was due to the low taxes for pharmaceutical companies. After this, we were due to go to Gibraltar but there were no direct flights to Spain (because of a political ban) so we went first to Tangiers, which was certainly worth a visit.

In the following year, my travels took me to Fyrom, a country unknown to me but I soon discovered that the name was an acronym for the 'Former Yugoslav Republic of Macedonia'. At that time, most people were unaware of the problems of this country, which was accepted by the

United Nations, although Greece strongly objected to its name as they had always considered "Macedonia" to be Greek, e.g. Alexander of Macedonia. As this was the First International Congress of Neurologists in Macedonia, it was a pleasure to accept the invitation, not least because the meeting was at Ochrid, beside the lake of the same name, which separates this country from Albania. Under the auspices of the University of Skopje, the capital of Fyrom, we flew to Skopje airport where we were informed that we could not fly to our destination, so had to drive over the mountains, a journey of several hours. At the meeting there were several international speakers including some from Belgrade, Zagreb, Ljubljana as well as Sofia, Bologna, Paris and Bethesda. The area is fascinating, being full of medieval churches and, understandably, there were a considerable number of Albanians living in this region. The speaker from Belgrade was surprised when I told him that the WFN would be pleased to accept Serbia as a constituent neurological society.

September 1996 saw me attend the Second National Congress of Neurology of Tunisia, held in its capital, Tunis.

1996 Tunisian Congress of Neurology

I was invited several times to Central America, firstly for the pan-American Congress in Guatemala under the Presidency of Professor Luis Salguero, and immediately after to Columbia to inspect the Congress Centre in

Cartagena, a lovely seaside resort; there was no doubt this would be an ideal conference venue. One of the most intriguing invitations was to speak at the Central American Congress in Honduras, where the population in 1997 was five-and-a-half million but with only about ten neurologists for the whole country, even though epilepsy was three times commoner than in the UK, according to Professor Marco Medina of their National University. Having previously been to Guatemala and visited the Mayan ruins of Tikal and also having seen Chichan Itsa in Yucatan, Mexico, Copan in Honduras would complete what is known as the Ruta Maya (The Mayan Route).

In 1998, I accepted an invitation by the Kuwait Neurological Society to give two talks, each of half an hour, at their Conference in November, the formal title of which was the 2nd Neurological Conference and 1st Gulf Meeting in Kuwait. The audience was mixed, including several female doctors I had not previously met in other Arab countries; all were knowledgeable and spoke good English.

Having worked for several years in Norwich Health Education Department, our middle son, Jolyon, resigned to become a volunteer with VSO (Voluntary Service Overseas) teaching health educators in Vanuatu in the South Pacific. His initial contract was for two years, but he was asked to stay on for a third year. Angela visited him each of the three years but I only went once. An extraordinary country, Vanuatu had been an Anglo-French Condominium and years after our visit we met the ex- British Governor who was involved with that country obtaining independence and heard something of the difficulties he had experienced, particularly with the French co-Governor.

Chapter 14

A NEW DEPARMENT

Excited in 1972 by the opening of the new Charing Cross Hospital, I invited Mrs Betty Kenward, better known as "Jennifer", Social Editor of *Harpers and Queen* to visit. Afterwards she wrote in her magazine: "On Tuesday, I spent one of the most interesting mornings of my life, going round part of the new Charing Cross Hospital, which is on Fulham Palace Road, and was officially opened by the Queen last May. It has been built after twenty years of careful and thoughtful planning, by doctors as well as architects, and takes the shape of a cross to the height of seventeen floors, and is, I was told, the biggest one-block building in the world. The government contributed around twenty-five million pounds to building this hospital and, as I made my tour, I felt more and more that here for once, taxpayers money really had been well and wisely spent. The design gives a feeling of light and space everywhere … In one morning it was not possible to see more than a small part of the wonderful work done at this Charing Cross Hospital, or of the up-to-date machinery, equipment and buildings".

My previous application in 1970 for additional help in my department had been rejected by the government department of Health and Social Security on the grounds that they could not permit "any additional posts at senior registrar level, especially in London, in neurology …" adding "… you will appreciate … that approval is exceedingly unlikely". Perhaps the biggest advantage of moving to a new hospital was to have solely neurological wards so that we could again appeal for a senior neurological registrar who would then be trained to become a consultant neurologist. The "independent" advisor from the Royal College of Physicians, a neurologist from Maida Vale Hospital, asked *why* Charing Cross Hospital should have a senior neurological registrar. In spite of pointing out the advantages such a centre, near to the end of the M3 and M4 motorways, with many accidents resulting in head injuries, all my arguments were non-availing but eventually successful when a middle grade medical registrar from the old Charing Cross converted to become a senior neurological registrar in the new hospital, the condition being participation in the general medical intake. My outpatient clinics were so organised that no referral would wait more than a week for an appointment; the local GPs rapidly recognised the usefulness of such a system, but it did mean that an hour (the usual time for a neurological consultation) could not be spent with each patient and complicated cases were admitted to hospital, giving satisfactory time for investigations. The result was that more neurological patients were seen at this new Centre than anywhere else in the North-West Thames Region of London, which proved to have unforeseen advantages.

When appointed in 1965 as a consultant to Charing Cross Hospital, there were no complementary services, such as neuropathology or neuroradiology; these were established in the ensuing years. The department of neurology, on moving to the new hospital, willingly accepted participation in the "on-take" of general medicine, which meant accepting patients with non-neurological conditions, not a problem for me, having previously worked in general hospital medicine for eight years. This later worked out well as stroke became one of our main interests so it was agreed that the neurology department would admit all the stroke patients seen in exchange for the other departments taking those disorders of their special interest. This appealed to general physicians since stroke patients were regarded as "bed-blockers", meaning they tended to occupy hospital beds for a long time. The department of neurology was thus able to set up the first Stroke Group in the UK, which consisted of a nucleus of research registrars and a multi-disciplinary team involving neuro and vascular surgeons, rehabilitation experts such as speech therapists, as well as haematologists, epidemiologists, social workers and others. With the new Charing Cross Hospital there were no general physicians but, instead, seven specialist departments, each undertaking the care of patients with disorders in their particular field. Because of the possibility that early admission of stroke patients could lead to more rapid recovery and increased survival, we devised a scheme where local GPs could contact a dedicated stroke registrar who would visit the patient with an ambulance for urgent attention; we were able to have three registrars each rotating after being on duty every 24 hours. It transpired that the majority of patients called out by the dedicated ambulance did not have strokes so this scheme was abandoned.

In many countries of the developed world, stroke (meaning blood vessel problems of the central nervous system) was considered a neurological problem but not so in Britain, which may explain why there were relatively few neurologists (less than 100 in the whole of the UK in 1957). Perhaps one reason why most neurologists in the UK were not interested in stroke was that they feared that their beds would be occupied for longer than average, which was understandable as about 30% of cases do not make a full recovery. A retrospective stroke survey using the hospital computer linked with the London University computer from the first of January 1973 to the end of March 1974 was the first time a computer had been used for stroke research. We instituted weekly meetings with social workers and other paramedics to explore every avenue for early discharge; one of the important factors was that facilities for patients at home were limited and we found it useful to draw "A Social Network Diagram", which was published in the British Medical Journal.

In 1975, as Chairman of the Division of Medicine, I suggested that each of the seven medical departments should arrange meetings to demonstrate their special services but this idea was not widely supported. In 1984 the Minister of Health approved the transfer of the North-West Thames Regional Neurosciences Unit to Charing Cross Hospital which meant that there would be a link with the Central Middlesex Hospital, and their neuroscientists would also work at the Centre in Charing Cross Hospital. From 1985 until 1988, I served on the Academic Board of Charing Cross Hospital Medical School, which was my second stint having previously served from 1969 to 1973, as well as on the Board of Studies in Medicine of the University of London from 1969 until 1975. The Academic Unit of Neurosciences was formed by the Charing Cross and Westminster Medical Schools in 1985, myself being its first Director; this was slightly embarrassing for me, as I was virtually the only Westminster graduate to be on the consultant staff of Charing Cross. As the creation of this Academic Unit demanded more time, my appointment as consultant neurologist to the Royal Eye Medical Ophthalmology Unit at St Thomas' Hospital was terminated and those two sessions transferred to Charing Cross Hospital which made me a maximum part-time consultant, i.e. working nine sessions each week. Following the re-organisation of the Imperial College School of Medicine to include Westminster, Hammersmith and St Mary's Hospitals, most of the neurosciences have remained at Charing Cross Hospital in the Fulham Palace Road.

HRH Princess Margaret was due to open the Princess Margaret Migraine Clinic at the Hospital in September 1982 but, presumably because of the newspaper publicity surrounding one of her romantic activities, she was obliged temporarily to drop this commitment. Muriel, her Personal Secretary, wrote to me on 12 October 1989 saying that Her Royal Highness would be "… very pleased …" to open the North-West Thames Regional Neuroscience Centre on Wednesday, 22 November and would like to see the Princess Margaret Migraine Clinic at the same time". The announcement of her visit was in the week following that letter.

The first European Stroke Prevention Study (ESPS) showed preliminary results published in 1987 and 1990 of a study of 2,500 patients on aspirin as reducing the risk of stroke after two years by 38%. From 1981 until 1988, I was coordinator of the ESPS, the study being based on thousands of stroke sufferers in sixteen European countries. In October 1986, I lectured to a meeting in the Sofitel Hotel near the Brussels airport on "New Developments in Prevention, Diagnosis and Treatment of Brain Ischaemia" and, two years later, became a member of the Working Party on Stroke for the Royal College of Physicians.

There is little doubt that the pharmaceutical industry has been a great asset for medical research. Not only is this segment of the commercial market in the UK highly successful but, globally, individual laboratories and progressive medical departments have benefited hugely by their long-standing support. It would not be an exaggeration to claim that the creation of the Academic Unit of Neuroscience at Charing Cross Hospital would not have taken off without the continued funding from companies researching new drugs. To take one example, in February 1982, Labaz, a subsidiary of Sanofi, a large French pharmaceutical complex, funded the Medical School to organise a conference on "Progress in Epilepsy". As chairman of this international meeting, it was a pleasure to organise lectures given by Professor Richard Masland, President of the WFN at that time, Sir Desmond Pond, President of the Royal College of Psychiatrists, and Sir Martin Roth, a past-President of the same college. The meeting was wound up by the chairman of Sanofi UK, who talked about the best pharmacological therapy for convulsions. The volume published of this meeting is replete with other examples of financial support for medical research, both in clinical trials and scientific education. In 1986, for two years, I helped with Training in the Pharmaceutical Industry (TPI) which necessitated my chairing a meeting in Paris (in poor French), which was followed by other Courses for the pharmaceutical industry.

The merger between Westminster Hospital Medical School and Charing Cross Hospital Medical School took place in 1997, resulting in the Charing Cross and Westminster Medical School.

The final training to become a hospital consultant was a senior registrar (SR) post. At Charing Cross Hospital, the second doctor to hold this post in the Department of Neurology was Rudy Capildeo, the first being David Park who had been appointed consultant neurologist to Southend General Hospital and Oldchurch Hospital, Romford. At this centre there was another consultant neurologist, Leslie Finlay, who had been my middle grade registrar at Charing Cross. When another appointment for consultant neurologist was advertised for Oldchurch Hospital, it seemed obvious for Rudy to apply. Before this, it was agreed with David Park, who had been a keen oarsman, that he would arrange a picnic lunch at the Henley Regatta with Leslie Finlay, Rudy and me and our wives. On the day of the picnic we set up our table; both Leslie and I had brought champagne and we had a very good lunch but, it has to be confessed, we did not see a single boat race, but Rudy did obtain the consultant post at Oldchurch. David Park and Leslie Finlay became consultants at the Royal London Hospital, the latter with a particular interest in tremor, while Rudy retired early from the NHS to manage his highly successful private practice. David Perkin and Russell Lane were both my registrars and became consultant colleagues at the North-Western Regional Neurosciences Unit at Charing Cross Hospital and other hospitals in that area, now all part of the Imperial College School of Medicine with over 200 neuroscientists. On 15 November 1991, a third annual dinner of the Gordon Holmes Society, named after my eminent predecessor, was held at the Derry and Toms Roof Garden in Kensington High Street, but this Society lapsed after my retirement.

Teaching is a regular part of a teaching hospital consultant's day; students attend outpatient clinics and weekly ward-rounds with question-and-answer sessions a regular feature; although initially enjoyable, this part of my job became less appealing and eventually a chore, except when teaching postgraduates, who were studying for higher examinations. On one occasion, when teaching a group of budding anaesthetists, they were asked to vote for their best teacher after which the head of the anaesthetic department had to ask, "who is 'Rose'?" Although not well recognised, good teaching is considered when merit awards are given; these awards result in increased salaries and pensions. With increased longevity, this turned out to be of great value.

Chapter 15

PRIVATE PRACTICE

Until the early eighteenth century, senior London doctors lived close to the great religious hospitals in or near the City of London – St Thomas' Hospital (founded about 1100) and St Bartholomew's Hospital (founded 1123). When other hospitals such as Westminster (1716), Guy's (1721), St George's (1733), London (1740) and Middlesex (1745) were started, their doctors moved towards Bloomsbury and Hanover Square and north of Oxford Street to Cavendish Square (which was called Oxford Square until 1734). The explanation for the names of these well-known London streets was that the north side of this square was intended for the Duke of Chandos, who was Paymaster-in-Chief to Queen Anne, hence Chandos Street was the turning going northwards from Cavendish Square; further grandiose schemes stopped when the "South Sea Bubble" burst in 1721. The second Earl of Oxford and Mortimer (1689-1741) developed the area as a residential estate, which went to his daughter Peggy, who married William Bentinck second Duke of Portland, and the estate remained in Portland hands until passing by marriage to Lord Howard de Walden. The dignified Georgian houses of Harley Street attracted eminent citizens such as the artist Turner, William Pitt the Younger, Gladstone, James Boswell, Nelson's wife (who died there), and Florence Nightingale.

Within the next century the great London railway termini were built and Harley Street became a medical centre for the "great and the good", particularly those who lived outside London, where the fee for a consultant's visit would be estimated at a guinea for each mile from Harley Street (a guinea being one pound and one shilling). An early inhabitant of Cavendish Square, at the bottom of Harley Street, was Lady Mary Montague Worsley, who in 1717 was the first to use inoculation against smallpox (on her three-year old son), which she had observed in Turkey as the wife of the St James' Ambassador to that country.

My maximum part-time contract with the NHS allowed for two sessions a week of private practice so that initially, after my first consultant appointment, I rented a room for two sessions a week at number 10 Harley Street for £10.00 a session. One patient referred to me by Professor Sorsby, objected to the size of my fee, but when I offered to waive the fee it was immediately paid. It was at this time that a GP, who had inherited his father's private practice in Portland Place, invited me to share his rooms without payment, an invitation readily accepted, particularly as I could work with a colleague on research into eye movement. When I was appointed to Charing Cross Hospital I rented a 5-room flat at 37 Harley Street, where I had a dedicated EEG room as well as consulting room, secretary's office and waiting room; there was also an extra room where we could spend the night if necessary. I gave up this flat when the Academic Unit of Neuroscience was created at Charing Cross Hospital, and saw my private patients in the private wing of the hospital. After retiring from the National Health Service in 1991, I returned to Harley Street to practise privately full-time. A senior registrar in radiology at Charing Cross Hospital told me there was only one house in Harley Street that could accommodate magnetic resonance imaging (MRI), which was a necessary investigation at that time for many neurological patients, and this was at number 110, where consulting rooms were available. I called these rooms the London Neurological Centre and registered the name at Companies House. A brochure was designed to advertise its facilities for diagnosing and treating such conditions as migraine, headache, epilepsy, sleep disorders, movement abnormalities, pain and stroke prevention etc. Although several million people suffered from neurological disorders in the United Kingdom, this was the first private clinic for their diagnosis and treatment where most of the ancillary investigations were available at the Centre. Electroencephalography (EEG), electromyography (EMG), psychometry etc, were also available at the Centre and for a time the retired Professor Sidney Watkins was available to see patients requiring a neurosurgical opinion although few of my patients needed his advice. Sid was a medical friend of Ayrton Senna, the F1 motor racer who died after famously crashing.

Because a percentage of patients came from abroad (at one time a third were from overseas) a successful appeal by a PR agency was made to the Central Office of Information to develop a marketing proposal and business plan with a coordinator for this project printed as follows:

A new initiative in Britain is helping to bring hope to sufferers of neurological disorders, ranging from migraine and Parkinson's disease to epilepsy and stroke, which cast a shadow on the health of populations throughout the world.

Our picture shows one of Britain's leading neurologists, Dr Clifford Rose, examining the brain waves of a patient using an electroencephalography (EEG) machine at the new London Neurological Centre in Harley Street.

Recently opened by Princess Margaret, it is the first private centre in the United Kingdom to bring a comprehensive range of neurological expertise under one roof with direct access to advanced diagnostic equipment.

Dr Clifford Rose leads a distinguished collaborating multi-disciplinary team including specialists in neurosurgery, vascular surgery, clinical neurophysiology, neuroradiology, neuropsychology, nutrition and remedial therapy. The London Neurological Centre, which has an international advisory board with representatives from 12 countries, also houses the headquarters of the World Federation of Neurology whose 23,000 members include all the world's top neurologists.

Dr Clifford Rose, author of 60 books in the field of neurology, set up the centre with support from various organisations, including Britain's Department of Trade and Industry. National Health Service patients are welcomed as well as private clients. About a third of the centre's patients are from countries outside the United Kingdom.

"The widespread incidence of neurological disorders in the world poses a   major challenge to both public and private sectors of health care" comments Dr Clifford Rose, who is Secretary-Treasurer General of the World Federation of Neurology.

He adds: "Undoubtedly more emphasis needs to be placed on patient care in this often neglected area of medicine as well as communicating the remedies that modern research has discovered".

Migraine is one of the most common conditions treated at the centre, where assessment of all neurological conditions can involve using some of the world's most advanced equipment, such as magnetic resonance imaging (MRI) and the use of a transcranial Doppler (TCD) – a state-of-the-art computerised scanning device.

The EEG shown in the photograph is manufactured in Britain by Specialised Laboratory Equipment of Croydon, Surrey. It is linked to the patient by electrodes attached to the scalp which detect micro-voltages caused by brain activity. These are relayed through the machine's 18 channels, giving a graphic trace for analysis.

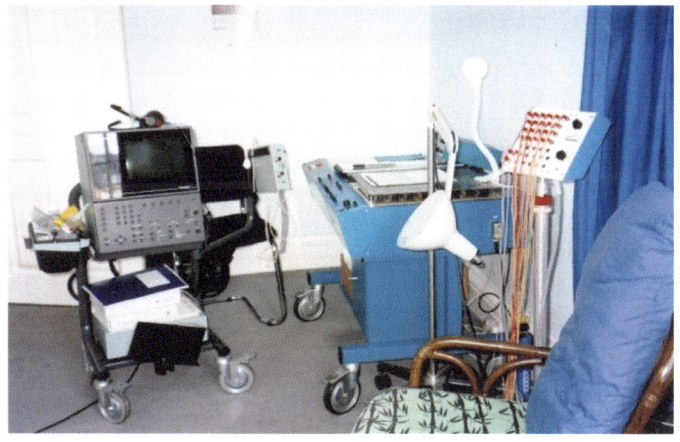

EEG machine

The Department of Trade and Industry (DTI) accepted the report and provided 50% of the costs to spread the word. The London Neurological Centre (LNC) was formally opened by HRH Princess Margaret on Tuesday, 30th November 1993, the press release for this being issued on the previous day. A letter was received in 1993 from the Lord Napier and Ettrick KCVO, Private Secretary to The Princess Margaret, Countess of Snowden, that Her Royal Highness would agree to open the London Neurological Centre. In the Court Circular of the *Daily Telegraph* was printed:

"KENSINGTON PALACE
November 30th

The Princess Margaret, Countess of Snowden, Patron, The Migraine Trust, this evening visited the London Neurological Centre,

110 Harley Street, W1.

Her Royal Highness then attended a reception for the Trustees at the Medical Society of London, 11 Chandos Street, W.1.
Mrs Jane Stevens was in attendance".

I greeted Princess Margaret at the front door of 110 Harley Street and she was taken to the London Imaging MRI Centre in the basement where she met Dr Iain Colquhoun, Consultant Neuroradiologist, and the Magnetic Resonance Scanner was demonstrated, as were the EEG, EMG and evoked potentials equipment; a plaque to commemorate her visit was unveiled, and is still in my possession. This was followed by a Reception where Her Royal Highness met the Trustees of the Migraine Trust, including Lady Schiemann, my successor as the Chair of the Trust, Lord Walton of Detchant and Sir Phillip Orton, who were other Trustees. There were also present members of the Houses of Lords and Commons as well as several celebrities, including Michael Aspel and Nicholas Parsons.

One of the first neuroradiologists to work at the Wellington Hospital was Dr James Bull and, as one of the first to admit neurological patients there, it was a pleasure to support him in his request for new radiological equipment, which has contributed so much to modern neurological diagnosis; the Wellington was also one of the first private hospitals to establish a facility for rehabilitation which included the services of a wide variety of sub-specialities. It was after seeing their wine list that, in spite of doctors being looked after well in NHS hospitals, I took out private medical insurance. My consultations at another private hospital, the Cromwell, began in 1995 with an out-patient clinic every Friday morning, but four years later adding an additional session on Monday mornings, and finally retiring in 2002. There was one embarrassing time when one Friday morning I saw a Wiltshire neighbour at the front reception desk awaiting admission for cancer; she was delighted to see me, thinking I had come especially to see her. On explaining the truth to her husband, he asked me not to tell her.

In 1991, the Charter Nightingale Hospital in Lisson Grove, NW1, was given a licence to admit patients under the description of Neuro-Psychiatry, after which they asked me to see patients there; although the majority had psychiatric problems, some needed tests and investigations which were performed at the LNC.

PATIENTS
While it is well-known that a doctor does not talk about his patients, it is less widely understood that this confidential relationship still applies after a patient's death. A seminal case was with Sir Winston Churchill whose doctor, Lord Moran, published an account of his last illnesses in a book, "The Struggle for Survival". In it he revealed that even in the latter days of Churchill's premiership, the Prime Minister sustained a series of strokes which, in other circumstances, would have prevented him from carrying on working in this high security position. Moran had been a consultant physician at St Mary's, a London teaching hospital, where he had also been Dean of its medical school, he strongly favoured admitting students who had excelled at sports, especially rugby, for which reason the St Mary's Hospital teams often won matches. Moran also played an active role in setting up the National Health Service in 1948 but had been known by some members of the medical profession as "Corkscrew Charlie", a

nickname given before his elevation to the peerage, having previously been Sir Charles Wilson. The publication of his recounting of Churchill's illnesses created a storm of protest, so much so that the British Medical Association and the General Medical Council reasserted the rule that patients' accounts of their illnesses were privileged, even after death. By chance, I sat opposite Moran at a Fellows' dinner of the Royal College of Physicians. Rarely going to these dinners except when serving on its Council, or working for its Stroke Research Committee, these are social occasions with good food and wine; it may be because of the latter's consumption that, during our after-dinner chat, I had the temerity to ask Moran "Why did you do it?" referring to his book on Churchill. He explained: "While working as Churchill's doctor, I had to accompany him on all of his many travels. As a result, I had no time to build up a private practice; the publication of my book meant that this lost income could be replaced, so it was really done for my grandchildren". He told me that the royalties of the book amounted to half-a-million pounds, a very substantial reward in those days. This episode is recounted to emphasise that any mention of patients' names, even when dead, can only be given if the information is in the public domain e.g. the newspapers, so that the well-known confidentiality of the doctor-patient relationship is strictly maintained.

A French Patient

A London GP rang to say that an ex-pat (a Briton living abroad), whose home was in the South of France, had French friends whose son was comatose; on flying to see him, I was told he had meningitis due to an organism which he named, but my confident reply was that this germ does not cause meningitis; the patient was a young man aged 24 who was clearly dying. Having studied in France, my discussion of his case was in French and the doctors had diagnosed AIDS. This was at a time when that diagnosis was just beginning to be made but enough was known that it had a predilection for the nervous system and that meningitis with an unusual organism was recognised. When meeting the boy's parents, the mother was weeping because she had been told the diagnosis but could not accept it as her son had lots of female friends. As my return to

London was the next day, the parents invited me to dinner and my acceptance was out of sympathy for the mother. It transpired that the young man had previously been involved in a car accident necessitating a blood transfusion and they were pleased when told that this could have been the cause of his infection. The ex-pat who requested my visit quibbled about my fee, presumably because the patient had not been cured

Sir Oliver Duncan, Bart

Sir Oliver Duncan, the third and last baronet, was the multi-millionaire grandson of the founder of the Pfizer international pharmaceutical group and died in September 1964 in Rome, where he was living at the time,. He had made a Will in 1960 in Berne, Switzerland leaving his wife as heir, and recognising those who had worked for him as well as medical charity. Between making the Berne Will in 1960 and a Rome Will in 1961, he had developed Parkinsonism. In 1969, a firm of City of London solicitors contacted me because Sir Oliver's general practitioner in Rome had developed cancer and, before he died, they wanted me to assess his medical evidence, with particular reference to whether Sir Oliver's illness had caused him to change his Will in favour of a Miss Elizabeth Marie-Pauline Fay. This hearing was heard not in court but in chambers in April 1969 and lasted about four days. The solicitors asked that my report should deal particularly with the likely effect of Sir Oliver's illness, Parkinson's disease, on his intellectual capacity and emotional stability.

The Daily Telegraph on 17 May 1969 published a column entitled: "Woman's move to gaol editor for contempt"; a move to commit to prison the owners of the *Evening Standard* and its editor, Charles Wintour, because of an article written by Mr Sam White in his Paris column on 2 May, two weeks previously, under the heading "The Will of a Shadow". An application by Miss Elizabeth Marie-Pauline Fay of Monte Carlo was to commit to prison the proprietors and editor of the London *Evening News* in the Probate, Divorce and Admiralty Division because it had been alleged that Miss Fay and others had conspired together to procure the Rome Will by fraud, pressure, importunity, threats and convulsion, which allegations Miss Fay entirely denies. These contempt proceedings failed, as it was likely to prejudice the trial of a probate action over the Will, scheduled to begin in January 1970. Anthony Lincoln QC, acted for the plaintiff, Miss Fay, who sought revocation of a grant of letters of administration of the Will made in Rome in 1961 together with a codicil later that year naming Miss Fay as universal heir to Sir Oliver's considerable worldwide estate, and sought to set up instead the Will made in Berne in 1960. The most serious complaint was "Then he (Sir Oliver) left another large sum to his Hungarian mistress but nothing to his Hungarian wife". "She (Miss Fay) utterly denies and repudiates that she was Sir Oliver's mistress". Mr Lincoln, acting for the plaintiff, added that Miss Fay, in a sworn statement, stated that the article was prejudicial, particularly in writing that nothing had been left to the widow; in fact, as part of his divorce settlement, Sir Oliver promised to pay his wife four million Swiss francs, which Miss Fay carried out on Sir Oliver's death. The article had stated that "Sir Oliver had a passion for Hungary and especially for Hungarian women. He married one and another became his mistress". This was offensive and libellous of Miss Fay, continued Mr Lincoln "What we are concerned with is the effect on the witnesses [in the forthcoming action] who know all about these proceedings and Miss Fay ...". Mr Wintour, the newspaper editor, made a statement saying that Mr White, the author of the article, had informed him that this was based "on reports of proceedings in a French court and also contained matters of public knowledge which had appeared frequently in the press".

My professional view was that no opinion could be given as to whether other circumstances e.g. pressure, played a part. From the medical point of view, there was a statement of a senior British neurologist, who had been a chief of mine, quoting James Parkinson's 1817 *Essay on the Shaking Palsy* that intelligence was unaffected in Parkinsonism. This neurologist was unaware of recent work at that time indicating the opposite, which was my opinion, supported by a recently published volume of the "Handbook of Clinical Neurology" giving the research evidence. This "Handbook" was edited by two Dutch neuroscientists and became an encyclopaedia issued every few months with over 40 volumes.

The one on Parkinsonism shown by me in chambers may have been only one of four in private hands in the UK.

Following this hearing of the evidence of Professor Fieschi, the Rome doctor, the solicitors asked that my fee for the three to four days in chambers should not be higher than the leading QC, with which there was ready agreement; they then asked me to consider continuing the case on a contingency basis, i.e. no win, no fee. Having been recently appointed to the consultant staff of Charing Cross Hospital where my time was fully occupied in building a worthy department of neurology, there was no alternative but to decline. Since those times it is now generally recognised that Parkinson's disease can have an effect on the psyche.

A Portuguese Patient

In January 1985, a GP asked me to see a patient in Oporto, Portugal. As I knew this town, having previously visited it to learn more about the port that was in my cellar, it was a pleasure to make the return journey by air in one day. The patient proved to be the mother of a wealthy merchant, who was happy with my advice. On leaving his house, he offered me a glass of port which, because of my hobby, I willingly accepted. Congratulating him on his excellent taste, he gave me a bottle on my departure. On arriving home, the label revealed it was vintage port of 1880, then over one hundred years old and I kept it in my cellar until the millennial New Year's Eve, December 31 1999; my 13 month-old granddaughter was staying with us at the time so the drinking had to wait for another occasion, when it tasted as good as promised. The patient's father was also happy as he asked me to return to check his mother in Oporto in the following year, but this time without a take-home bottle.

A Portuguese aside

That year ended with another visit to Portugal, but this time to Lisbon, which was home to the Gulbenkian Museum; Gulbenkian had made his large fortune in oil and was known as "Mr Five Percent"; although he loved England, he spent his later years in Portugal at Estoril. His Will, reported to me by a Portuguese citizen, left money for his museum in Britain but this ended up in Lisbon, which was probably more in need of a new museum than London. Although there was some money for a Gulbenkian charity in the UK, it was a more modest sum and intended for the arts, explained to me on my attempting to apply for a science research fund. Gulbenkian's son, Nubar, was keen on fox-hunting and we met at one of these occasions when he wore an orchid in his buttonhole. An overheard comment on this hunt was a critical remark "I've never seen an orchid out hunting" (the allowed buttonhole flower apparently being a violet) to which Nubar's quick response was "No, and you've never been out hunting with an Armenian". (As this took place in my presence, over 60 years ago (in 1952), its accuracy cannot be entirely vouchsafed).

A Saudi Patient

While attending the World Congress of Neurology in Delhi, India in 1989, I received a fax asking me to see a patient in Saudi Arabia. Being committed to reading a paper at the Congress, as well as chairing a session, there was no alternative but to reply in the negative. By return, another communication stated that the patient's private plane was on its way to Delhi to take me to Saudi as soon as my commitments were over. When they telephoned again, my wife answered and the patient's PA asked if she would be coming to Saudi as well; Angela initially refused this offer, not least because at that time women were apparently not very well received in Middle East countries, but an American friend, who was in the hotel room with her at the time of the call, encouraged her to accept on the grounds that she would never have another chance like this; so my wife changed her mind and faxed her passport details as the PA had requested. On the day the aeroplane arrived, its English stewardess came to our hotel to ask what we would like to eat on the flight, saying that we could order anything that the hotel would provide.

On arrival at Delhi airport the following morning, we were escorted by the airport manager to a private waiting room. The plane, a Learjet, had a British crew of pilot, co-pilot and stewardess; there were no customs or security on departure and the two pilots and stewardess welcomed us on board. Although the aeroplane could carry over 20 passengers, my wife and I were the only two. Exhausted by many duties at the Congress, a bed was immediately prepared for me. The plane had sufficient fuel to take us to the Middle East, but as we were flying over Pakistani air space, Karachi airport insisted that we land. On doing so, an airport official came aboard to ask our flight number, presumably because the required landing fee could not be charged without one. Our stewardess promptly replied that we did not have a flight number as this was a private jet, whereupon the official insisted that we must give one. "Very well" said the stewardess "let us say 1-2-3"; the functionary looked at her and said "Well, let us say 1-3-2" after which we were allowed to proceed.

On arrival at the private terminal at Riyadh airport, the stewardess was surprised and impressed by the number of people in flowing robes waiting to welcome us, after which we were taken to a room where we were offered coffee and dates and then driven to the home of the patient's executive assistant, an American with a young Irish wife, where a house-boy ironed my suit while Angela went to bed to recover from the flight. After a short rest the American executive, an ex-Marine top-sergeant, took me to see the patient who was lying in bed and clearly distressed. There was an American neurologist from California in attendance and, familiar with the drugs prescribed, the diagnosis was soon apparent. Having worked in California, it seemed to me that the treatment regime had been the cause of his distress; this was quickly changed and, by the next morning, the patient was much better. While I was out seeing the patient, the executive said to my wife "The boss wants me to buy you a present. Would you like to come and choose it?" Angela, although surprised, naturally agreed but, when asked what she would like she had not idea; asking the executive for suggestions, he replied "Gold". The shopping trip was arranged, and had to be fitted in between prayer calls, the times of which could be found in the newspaper, since all shops closed during these times. She was taken to a gold shop but was still embarrassed as to what to choose; the executive pointed to some necklaces and suggested "make a short list" after which he could then return and make the final choice. She therefore chose three necklaces, one looked cheap (relatively), another expensive with the third in between, so that, depending on their budget, she would be happy with any one of them. On returning home, the executive handed her a plastic bag, rather the worse for wear, and said "Here's your present"; on opening the bag she found all three gold necklaces, two of which had matching bracelets. That evening, all four of us, including the executive's wife, went out for dinner, the ladies clad in neck-to-floor black silk. On the following day we were given a short tour around Riyadh which was, at that time, strictly forbidden.

Travelling back to London in the patient's jet, on this flight we were seated at the back of the 'plane with the American assistant, as the patient was also travelling to London with his entourage. The stewardess asked me "would you like a drink?" As it was a Saudi plane owned by a Muslim who was also on board, there was hesitation on my part but, as she was English, my next query was did she mean "A drink-drink?" which she understood and to which she replied affirmatively. Champagne, my favourite aperitif, was ordered which turned out to be Roederer Crystal and, feeling expansive, I gave its Tsarist history and why the bottle was clear glass and without a punt; the executive, realising wine was my hobby, asked what are the best wines; I named a couple of classified clarets, so-called because they were based on the 1855 classification and were top wines. Every Christmas after that, for many years I was sent a present of two *cases*, each containing a dozen bottles of classified claret; this was in addition to my agreed fee.

With the outbreak of the First Gulf War in 1991, the patient's executive telephoned to say that his boss, being on medication, would like to be checked at the Mayo Clinic, Rochester, USA but would not go unless accompanied by me. Never having acted as a patient's escort previously, this was a first, so I accepted the invitation, not least because one or two of the consultant staff of the Mayo Clinic knew me. At that time, Concorde was still in service and we flew supersonic to New York to connect with the patient's own plane, a Boeing 727, to Rochester where he, accompanied by me, spent five days having check-ups. On the way back to London we landed at Atlantic City since my patient was a gambler; he usually stayed in the Presidential Suite at Donald Trump's Taj Mahal Hotel, but on this occasion it was already occupied, so the executive rang Donald Trump who made the Presidential Suite available to my patient.

On returning to the UK, I discovered that the Boeing had belonged to Trump who, for financial reasons, had sold the plane to my patient. Some weeks later, the patient's executive rang to say he was embarrassed because he thought that his boss had paid my fee for the Mayo Clinic visit whereas the patient thought the executive had paid. I replied that they should not worry that I had not charged a fee bearing in mind the previous fee, gold necklaces and wine presents. However, the executive insisted on a fee being charged but when maintaining my stance, he continued with "Perhaps Angela would like a present?" to which my reply was "there are just so many gold necklaces that a woman can wear" but, at his persistence, I asked her and she replied that, being a pianist, she had had a life-long ambition to own a Steinway piano. My reply was that was far too expensive to charge for an American visit, but she claimed to be saving for one and by also selling her own grand piano, hoped to get a contribution towards a reconditioned piano; she then went to Steinway's in Marylebone to try out these reconditioned instruments. When the executive and his wife came to London, they asked how much she had saved and she had to explain that all her savings had just been spent on fitted bookshelves in a new extension to our home and she only had as much as she would get from the sale of her existing piano. When told she had looked at reconditioned pianos at the Steinway showroom, she was met by the answer "We have no intention of buying a *second-hand* piano". At Steinway's, the sales girl was ordered to remove all the price tags from the pianos so that Angela choose the one she liked bestand this was delivered to our home the following week.

In 1996, this wealthy Saudi patient asked me to organise a meeting in California to which half a dozen of the world's top specialists in his illness would be invited to discuss questions regarding the management of this condition, the whole meeting to be recorded on video. This took place at the San Diego Harbor Beach Marriott Hotel in June where senior neurologists from Toronto, San Francisco, the Mayo Clinic (Rochester) and Scripps Clinic, La Jolla were invited, following which interviews were to be added with two other specialists who were unable to attend in San Diego; one was a Swede video-recorded in London, while the other was an

American, interviewed by video-link at a medical conference in Sardinia; the whole was put together and sent to the patient, as well as to his American GP in Fort Lauderdale, Florida. Based on these reports, the patient decided on a short hospital admission and a letter from his assistant listed his requirements while in hospital as follows:

"His Excellency has indicated that he will wish to occupy a large room (similar to a suite if possible) where he can also receive visitors. He will also require a further room next to his bedroom/suite which will be occupied by his assistants at all times. I await confirmation as to whether they will also be expected to sleep in this room, but I presume this will be a waiting room and the personnel will not sleep there.

His Excellency normally likes to sleep in TOTAL DARKNESS so anything the hospital could do to achieve this in His Excellency's suite/bedroom would be greatly appreciated. We would be grateful if all telephone calls for His Excellency could be routed through his assistant's room. Generally His Excellency's normal meals and diet consist of (although this is obviously subject to any specific diet that may be decided by yourself, sir, or by any of the other participating doctors). His Excellency likes to drink a very low caffeine tea such as best Darjeeling in the mornings or alternatively Lipton tea. His Excellency drinks some Jasmine tea throughout the day (along with Darjeeling and Green tea occasionally). His Excellency drinks Camomile with Anise tea in the evenings. If the hospital cannot provide these teas, we can obviously provide whatever may be required. His Excellency presently has peeled and sliced mango and papaya for breakfast, along with 2-3 cups of the tea as specified above. Occasionally, His Excellency may ask for clear honey and a low (or no) yeast bread. Generally His Excellency does not like food containing garlic or red fruits. Would it also be possible for the hospital to supply a good quantity of Evian water in His Excellency's suite/bedroom.

Would it be possible to put the following newspapers (daily)/magazines in His Excellency's room/suite: The al Hayat, The Asharq al-Awsat, The Herald Tribune, USA Today, British daily: The Times and The Financial Times, Daily Mail and Express. Selection of scuba/diving, yachting, and health or better quality men's magazines and Time/Newsweek. Would it be possible for His Excellency to have a multi-system video in his room along with the TV. Would it also be possible for me to obtain a list of the TV channels/in-house movie guide that His Excellency will be able to view so that I may prepare my usual TV schedules and programme summaries for him".

However, the day before this patient was due to go into hospital, he cancelled his admission, paying the hospital for all the expenses, including the specially fitted black-out blinds for the windows. Not much later, the Mayo Clinic's report to me summarised the findings of his recent visit but there was no evidence that his medication had affected his health. In October 1991, a letter from Glaxo asked how the patient had been on this early use of one of their drugs, which had been prescribed before release and given on a "named patient basis"; having initially seen him in August 1989, this information was first sought in a letter dated 30 April 1991.

While attending a meeting in the Canary Islands to celebrate the 500th anniversary of Columbus' voyage in 1492, a fax on 22 July 1992, read:

"Dr C Rose – Gran Tenerife Hotel, Gulf Stream III Flight. We will soon have you back in sunny England. The changes to the flight arrangements are regretted and trust that this has not caused too much inconvenience. Please check-in at 3.00 pm at the Information Desk and ask for Universal Private Aviation who are the local handling agents dealing with your personal flight. You will of course be met at Heathrow when you arrive and transported to your home and on to the (patient's home)".

Arriving at the latter in central London, I was led into an empty sitting room where there were several paintings on the walls which looked like Picasso prints; they were in fact genuine paintings. The patient arrived shortly after this; he had sent for me from Tenerife because he had not been feeling well at the time but was now better. In fact it transpired that he wanted a personal doctor in permanent attendance, a post that did not interest me, but was eventually filled by his American GP.

Sir Alan Bates

Several actors consulted me in my Harley Street rooms; in the *Daily Telegraph* of 29 December 2003, Hugh Davies looked "at the career of Sir Alan Bates" who was noted for such films as *Women in Love* which was Ken Russell's adaptation of D H Lawrence's book, and *Zorba the Greek*. Bates died from cancer on 28 December 2003, but consulted me in 2001 with a three-day history of a minor headache behind the right ear; a day or two later, both he and his son had noticed his face was lop-sided; he had complained of watering of the right eye and his speech was not quite normal; examination showed muscle weakness of the right side of the face, so that the diagnosis of a Bell's palsy was unequivocal. The problem was that he was acting in a stage play in Guildford which was shortly due to move to a West End theatre. Knowing the usual good recovery of this condition, my reassurance pleased him and he continued with his stage commitments. Seeing him later in the following month, he had made a 90% recovery and told me his Guildford acting had gone well and he rang me the following week to say he was OK and appearing on the West End stage. He died aged 69, one year after receiving his knighthood. It was his obituary that told of his gender preference, although a biography written about him by Donald Spoto was quoted in the *Telegraph Review* of 23 June 2007. The reviewer, Roger Lewis, wrote: "Alongside his furtive homosexuality, there were always "social flirtations" which avoided "carnal compensations ... When Princess Margaret was rebuffed, it is rumoured she personally blocked Bates's knighthood".

Tony Benn

Tony Benn's father was the younger son of a baronet, who was initially a Liberal MP but became a Labour MP and then Viscount Stansgate. Benn himself became a Labour MP after working in the family publishing company, but had to resign his parliamentary seat on succeeding to his father's peerage, but disclaimed the title to again become a Labour MP in

1963. Tony Benn was a Labour Member of Parliament for Bristol South-East from 1950 to 1983 and MP for Chesterfield from 1984, contesting the Labour Party leadership in 1976 and 1988.

On 14 May 1981 he went to see his GP, whom he visited about every five years for tingling in his legs and hands and loss of sensation in the legs; on 4 June of that year his legs were hurting and he had an unsteady gait, and he was driven to Charing Cross Hospital by his son, Hilary. The out-patient receptionist on the first floor rang my office on the 10th floor and asked me to see Tony Benn as an NHS patient. On my way down to the out-patient department, my thought was that, as he was a contender for the leadership of the Labour party, the problem could be psychological. To my surprise, physical examination revealed signs indicating peripheral neuropathy and he readily followed my advice to be immediately admitted to hospital, but insisted that it had to be as an NHS patient; nevertheless he was given a bed in a small side room of the (private) 10th floor (Benn, 1994, p.136). He drafted a statement together with Hilary saying he had been admitted for tests of a viral infection, after which the media descended *en masse* on the hospital. Flowers, telegrams and letters came, one of the latter being from the Joint Shop Stewards Committee at the hospital asking him to address their meeting. In his autobiography he wrote: "From 6 to 20 June, as a result of my stay in Charing Cross Hospital for what was eventually diagnosed as Guillain-Barré Syndrome …"

The hospital security had a terrible job because camera crews and journalists were camped outside the hospital and one of them tried to enter dressed as a doctor in a white coat. Another admitted himself to Casualty with a pain and, when examined, a camera was found in his trouser leg; media folk were offering bribes of £400 to get photographs of me, but without success; to quote Benn again: "I had a very high regard for the security system" (Benn, 1984 p.138). He came to see me again on 15 October when he was told that electrical tests in July confirmed that there had been serious damage to his sensory nerves and it would be up to two years before we would know the extent of his recovery. "I am beginning to realise that I may be handicapped for life. I would like to be able to run and jump about before I die but I've got to face the possibility that I never will. It was a bit of a shock, but I had guessed it" (Benn, 1984 p.159). At the time, he enquired if there was any possibility of poisoning, but this idea was immediately dismissed.

Polly Havers

One of my celebrity patients was Mrs Polly Havers, the wife of actor Nigel Havers, who was the son of a previous Lord Chancellor, Sir Michael Havers. Nigel had met Polly, a former model and actress in 1986; they began their affair when Polly was still married to John Bloomfield, a property developer. After Polly's divorce, she married Nigel Havers in 1989; Polly died of ovarian cancer in June 2004, leaving the bulk of her estate to her two sons, Ben and William Bloomfield. Havers received a share of the marital home in Barnes, South-West London but, when aged 57, claimed he had not been left reasonable financial provision in Polly's Will drawn up in 1989. A compromise gave Havers an immediate £375,000 with £235,500 going to the two sons; he also received the proceeds of the sale of his late wife's Mercedes and her jewellery. The dispute was "a long, drawn-out and painful process" (*Daily Telegraph*), the newspaper article pointing out that Havers was living with Georgina Bronfman, aged 57, a millionaire divorcée in Holland Park, West London.

Lord Weinstock

Lord Weinstock's GP escorted him into my consulting rooms introducing me as the "best neurologist in England"; Weinstock immediately chipped in by saying "What do you mean, England? He's the best in the world" but without revealing where he had obtained this information. The story of his wealth accumulation was given in Sir Kenneth Bond's *Daily Telegraph* obituary of 30 May 2006. In 1957 Bond, an accountant by training, joined Arnold Weinstock at Radio and Allied Industries, which prospered in the manufacture of cheap television sets. In 1963, Radio and Allied did a reverse takeover of General Electric Company which was re-invigorated 5 years later to lead a tripartite merger with English Electric and Allied Electrical Industries, a world class company which was a beacon of strength of the British Industrial landscape in the next two decades. In 1954, EMI took over Sobell Industries which had been built up in the

Rhondda Valley by Michael Sobell, Weinstock's father-in-law, who was named as "one of Britain's greatest industrialists" (*Daily Telegraph 5 June 2010*). Weinstock was keen on racing horses but his companies, renamed Marconi, deteriorated under Weinstock's successors. When he came to see me as a patient, as his company had been valued at £500 million pounds and he was indeed criticised for not making use of this large sum, I asked why he was still working. He told me it was "for the grandchildren", but he was at the end of his career and not keen to survive on a hospital regime which he found decidedly upsetting. Some time after his death, his widow came to see me as a patient but she was much younger than her late husband, and keener on survival.

King Fahd of Saudi Arabia

King Fahd of Saudi Arabia died in 2005, about ten years after having a stroke. The mayoress of Marbella, in Spain, declared three days of official mourning since the monarch's 70-foot yacht was moored there; he first went to Marbella in 1974, booking 100 hotel rooms as his visits there were accompanied by a retinue of 3,000. Ordering the dark carpets to be changed to white and leaving a tip of $300,000, he liked Marbella because "it was a land blessed by Allah", referring to the Arab occupation of Spain from the 8th to the 13th centuries. His father, Ibn Saud, an uneducated Bedouin who fathered 46 sons by numerous wives, was recognised by the British in 1932 as the new Monarch of Saudi Arabia. King Fahd would arrive in his own 747 jet along with other aeroplanes, including a flying hospital. At that time his estimated wealth was £15.7 billion; he had 7 palaces in Saudi Arabia worth at least £6 billion. The Arab princes loved to play roulette in a private room and, in the absence of the Crown Prince, would order Vega Sicilia, an expensive Spanish red wine which they would drink from coffee cups.

When asked in 1995 to go to Saudi Arabia by their Embassy it was thought that I would be seeing the King who had, according to newspapers, suffered a stroke. I was invited to bring my wife with me, and told we would be staying in a luxury hotel with swimming pool, and that the weather would be warm and sunny. On arrival we were taken to a special hotel for VIP visitors, mostly military, and shown to a very large suite. The weather was cold, the swimming pool closed for Ramadan, and anyway women were never allowed to use it. The Saudi Embassy, on requesting a medical specialist does not reveal who the patient is until arrival in their country, presumably for security reasons. In fact the patient proved to be the King's niece, the favourite daughter of Crown Prince Abdulla who, as half-brother to King Fahd, was in control of Saudi Arabia after the King's stroke. On my first visit to see the Princess, I was then asked to see several other friends and relations, rather like an out-patient clinic. When the Princess enquired if my wife had accompanied me, she asked to meet her; the following day Angela was surprised to be ushered into the bedroom with a large bed on a raised dais where the Princess reclined with various children wandering in and out. After introductions and some small-talk, the Princess gave her a ring which she was delighted with. Seeing this Princess several times, it was clear that she was being given too many medications by her ladies-in-waiting and others so that her illness was difficult to control. While in Saudi Arabia on this occasion, there were two American neurologists in the hotel who were particularly interested in stroke; they told me that the King's advisors had asked for a further opinion and although they thought of recommending me, they considered my view would be so similar to theirs that they had recommended a neurologist from Paris. Guessing that this advice would not be taken, I was later asked to see the King, waiting with the American doctors late into the night, as the King rested during the day and did all his business, including medical consultations, well after midnight. Most of his medical advisors were from the USA, but when introduced to an English neurologist, the King continued to shake my hand delightedly, presumably because I was an Englishman and Lawrence of Arabia had been given credit by the Saudis for helping them in the past. His welcome was so effusive that his advisors asked me to return some months later; in fact that year I travelled to Saudi Arabia on five separate occasions and on one of these visits I was to see him whilst he was sitting in the dentist's chair!

Towards the end of my career, the Saudis requested me to help sort out the affairs of the present King's brother. My wife was not keen on my going because there had been reports of Westerners being attacked in

Riyadh. When pointing this out, they immediately doubled the fee and I accepted the invitation

Tiny Rowland

Rowland transformed Lonrho from a small mining company into a huge conglomerate with interests in the *Observer* newspaper, gold mines in Ghana and whisky. Held in high regard in Africa, he rejuvenated Lonrho (the London and Rhodesia mining and Land Company) in 1961, defeating Sir Basil Smallpeace with a vote of 3000 shareholders in 1972. Well-known to African Heads of State, he sold a stake in Lonrho's hotel chain to Libya soon after the Lockerbie bombing. "Tiny" Rowlands was labelled "the unacceptable face of capitalism" by Prime Minister, Edward Heath in 1973. In 1988 Lonrho was dismembered by selling off its mining assets.

His GP rang me from Tiny's yacht near a Mediterranean island saying that he thought Tiny, who was 80 years old at that time, had had a stroke. On hearing the history, it was not at all certain to me that this diagnosis was correct and my advice to the GP was to bring him back to London to be investigated, advice that was ignored as his paralysis had improved. Not long after, he had a recurrence so that my view for his immediate return was strengthened and then accepted. While taking his history in a private London hospital, his wife wondered whether the trouble with Mohammed Al-Fayed of Harrods was the cause (there had been a well-known difference between them) but "Tiny" did not accept this explanation. Both Tiny and his wife admitted to me that, although he lived a long time in Africa, he never took precautions against sunburn; it was soon clear that this was the cause of his trouble and, although there were treatments at that time, he and his wife tearfully considered the options, declining treatment so that he died a short time afterwards.   At the time of his death, it was estimated that at one time he had earned £270 million a year. After his death, his wife continued the legal battle with Al-Fayed and won.

Lady Brocket

Lady Isabel Marie Brocket was born on 16 July 1959. She spoke five languages and thought of being a doctor but became a Vogue model; she had eloped to Las Vegas with her "Englishman", who was eight years her senior. The Brocket family was one of Britain's oldest and her husband, the third Baron Brocket, was the owner of a 5,000 acre Hertfordshire estate; he played polo with Prince Charles and traced his lineage back to the fifth century. She had family worries, one of which was that in spite of three previous troublesome pregnancies, her husband insisted on her having a fourth child. During her third pregnancy her husband seemed "too busy to sympathise with her, although hospitalised for three months and in excruciating pain". After their 12 year marriage had collapsed, she lived in a cottage on the estate.

It was in 1991 that Lord Brocket, whose debts then amounted to nine million pounds, filed a false insurance claim. Although he withdrew this claim before his arrest, his wife accidentally gave him away to the police for allegedly forging a medical prescription when questioned by them (reported in *The Mail on Sunday* of 28.8.1994 by Sharon Churcher). In May 1994 she "had swallowed dozens of sleeping pills and painkillers in a suicide attempt". According to a national newspaper, Charlie Brocket, an Old Etonian, was jailed in 1996 for "stealing" three of his own Ferraris and a Maserati from his stately home Brocket Hall, claiming £4.5 million insurance. He served 2½ years in seven different prisons. Brocket Hall is now leased to a German hotel chain and used for conferences, and I went to my great-niece's wedding reception there in 2007.

Patrick Berthoud

A 63 year old man was referred to me in 1991 by Dr Bernard Patten, an American neurologist whom he had seen in Houston, Texas. The patient had had a heart attack three years previously and was admitted to St Stephen's Hospital in London for a week, as he lived in nearby Hereford Square; he was a bachelor who worked as a stockbroker. His complaint was of dribbling from the mouth with difficulty in speech and swallowing, worsening over the previous two years. On examination, there was no doubt about the diagnosis of motor neurone disease. I saw him several times over the ensuing year during which he deteriorated and eventually died. A Patrick Berthoud Charitable Trust was formed which funded three-year fellowships for neurological researchers in the UK and the USA.

A Columbian patient

In 1988, a man came to see me in Harley Street because his wife had multiple sclerosis but was too disabled to travel from Bogotá, Columbia where they lived; Bogotá is the third highest capital (8,500 feet) in South America after La Paz, the capital of Bolivia and Quito, the capital of Ecuador. After the consultation, my next sentence was: "It will surprise you to know that my wife and I are going to Columbia next week because, as Secretary-Treasurer General of the World Federation of Neurology, I have been invited to help organise the 10th Pan-American Congress of Neurology in Cartagena". His response was immediate "you must both come and stay with us in Bogotá and we will also take you to our club and show you around". This was the first time that this Congress was held in Columbia under the auspices of the WFN and my first visit was to Cartagena to approve the venue. Columbia, under Simon Bolivar's leadership, became the first South American country to obtain independence from Spain, and for its first ten years, was part of Gran Columbia, which also included Venezuela and Ecuador. After initial democracy, there were two civil wars with a long unsettled period, which explained why the US government advised caution. On this trip to Bogota we stayed in the safer northern suburbs, at the home of my patient's parents, which proved to be an interesting experience. By car the entrance to the flats was via an underground car-park so as not to be a target of gunmen and, wherever we went by (bullet-proof) car, another car followed us with an armed guard. When we asked the reason for these precautions we were told two nephews had been kidnapped for ransoms; the first was a young sporting athlete riding a motor-cycle who resisted his captors and was shot dead; for the second nephew they paid the ransom. After this second kidnapping, a meeting of the family was called to decide whether to stay in Columbia or emigrate to Miami, Florida; they (mostly the younger generation) decided to stay in Columbia. As well as going to their club for a meal, we were also taken to another fascinating tourist attraction, the salt mines of Zipaquira, which were also very popular with the locals.

Because of the patient's almost complete invalidism, they asked me about the "Myelin Project", myelin being the substance on the outside of a nerve cell, with its alteration as the putative cause of multiple sclerosis (MS). This project was based on the case of a boy with a myelin illness (*adrenoleukodystrophy*), quite distinct from MS, but he had survived for several decades on "Lorenzo's Oil", portrayed in the 1992 Hollywood film of that name. Lorenzo lived to be over thirty years of age, which was previously unknown for his condition.

Sir Paul Getty

I was asked by a Canadian surgeon to see a patient in the London Clinic; his GP complained that he had not asked for my opinion and my explanation that it was at the consultant's request did not satisfy him and he asked if I had seen his name on the door of the patient's room, which I had not. J Paul Getty was a billionaire and the greatest philanthropist Britain has had (*Daily Telegraph*, 12.04.2000). He died aged 70.

Sir Peter Moores

Another philanthropist, Sir Peter Moores, who had given a £100 million to good causes and spent £6 million in 2006 to save two mid-18th century Canaletto paintings from leaving the UK. His father, Sir John Moores, founded Littlewoods with its Football Pools and chain stores; Sir Peter gave half his inheritance to the Peter Moores Foundation and opened his own Compton Verney art gallery in a Grade I listed 18th century country house in Warwickshire, where his charitable foundation spent £6.4 million to show his art collection to the public in perpetuity. It opened in 2004, the gallery showing mainly German paintings from 1450 to 1650, Chinese bronzes and Neapolitan art from 1600-1800. In addition to art, his foundation supports such projects as young singers and musicians, health care schemes and horticulture in the West Indies. When seeing him as a patient, I emphasised he was not seriously ill.

Osbert Lancaster

Having seen this famous cartoonist as a patient, it was interesting in 2008 to go to the Wallace Collection in Manchester Square, London to see an exhibition of his works on the occasion of the centenary of his birth. The accompanying biographical details stated he died after a series of strokes. It was at this time that he had consulted me and, although his name was well-known, he had not at that time been recognised as a genius. Although stroke was one of my particular interests, which was then unusual for British neurologists, our knowledge of its causes and advice on prevention was not so well understood; research continued but at that time the effects of smoking and alcohol were not appreciated.

Tina Turner

While on the wards in the Princess Grace Hospital, a phone call from my secretary asked me to see a patient called Turner, but replying that I did not know a patient with that name, she told me it was Tina Turner; although not a fan of pop music, the name seemed familiar. She had come to London to perform, in spite of being in her late sixties. She was born Anna Mary Bullock in Tennessee and when still at school she met a band leader, Ike Turner, and sang with him in 1960 going high up in the pop charts. Her husband took cocaine, had violent episodes, and attacked Tina, according to her autobiography. She married Ike in 1976, divorcing him after only two weeks. One of her admirers was the American producer Phil Spector, who was later arrested for murder. In 1974, she was converted to Buddhism by a friend, later chanting for three hours a day while on tour. In 1984, she became the oldest female artist to have a US number one hit with *"What's Love Got to do With It?"* In the following year she appeared with Mick Jagger in Live Aid. Yet another admirer was David Bowie, who sang with her on television ending with a "cosy clinch" (the *Daily Telegraph*, 2.03.2009). In 1988 she broke the world record for the largest paying audience of 184,000 people: she had sold more concert tickets than any solo performer in history, in addition to 200 million records. In 1994 she moved to Switzerland, bought a villa on the Côte d'Azur and announced her 50th Anniversary Tour in October 2008, reaching London in March 2009.

Chapter 16

HOLIDAYS

One of the pleasures of being invited to lecture abroad was to see tourist sites all over the world with expenses paid. Although some colleagues would travel, say to Singapore, for a weekend of lecturing, and immediately return home, my preference was to have one day sightseeing for each day worked. Although most journeys were professional, either to talk at or attend meetings, family holidays free of work were more enjoyable. Following our Tenerife honeymoon in 1963, we did not go abroad until our first son was nearly a year old. Naming him was Angela's decision and she chose Sebastian Zachary; his second name was given my approval thinking that Z was rare and distinguished, but neither he nor anyone else has ever used it. He was born on 29 August 1964, which was also my birthday. .

While Resident at the National Hospital, a budding neurosurgeon from Baltimore, Maryland suggested we take a river trip down the Wye Valley. We drove there in my first car, a Ford Anglia, with his rowing boat tied to the roof.

My first car, with rowing boat on roof

I was disappointed to discover there was little in the way of white-water rafting, but we explored the castles, to the delight of my American friend..

In 1965, we went with Angela's parents to Milano Maritima in north-eastern Italy, where they stayed at a very nice hotel, which conveniently had a small flat that we rented. Arriving a few days after my in-laws, who came to meet us at the airport, Sebastian had cried for most of the flight and, being somewhat hassled, we were anxious to pick up our suitcase quickly. Arriving at our flat, we found it to be locked and closer inspection revealed it was not *our* suitcase, which meant Sebastian had no clean clothes; luckily we had nappies in our hand baggage. The next morning my father-in-law returned with me to the airport to return the case and fortunately ours was waiting for us. This proved to be an enjoyable beach holiday, but we were surprised to hear German spoken in all the shops, our explanation being it was a very popular holiday destination for Germans at that time, perhaps because the Second World War was too recent for them to take trips elsewhere in Europe.

In the winter of 1966 we went on our first "family" skiing holiday to St Moritz but, as Angela was pregnant with our second child and had 16 month-old Sebastian to look after, my skiing was a solitary affair. Later that year we spent a week at the seaside in Felpham, Sussex borrowing the house of Sheila and Mike Gampell; Angela had been a bridesmaid at their wedding and was Sheila's best friend, and Mike had arranged my first research grant. They had three children, but sadly the marriage ended in disaster when Mike, a very successful solicitor in a City law firm, was arrested for embezzlement and served his sentence at Ford Open Prison; they eventually divorced. Another friend of Angela's married a man who became a GP and was later convicted of asking patients to sleep with him in return for private prescriptions.

In 1967, we took an Easter break in Greece, while our two children were looked after at home by our *au pair* girl helped by "Mrs Walsh", who moved in and was a much loved mother figure. Staying in Athens, we saw crowds of marching soldiers and were told this was the "Colonel's Revolt", which had overturned the incumbent government. We then left for a meeting in Israel, where Angela had never been before. Enjoying the tourist attractions of Jerusalem and Eilat, there was again a military outbreak, this time leading to the Six-Day War between Israel and its surrounding Arab countries; we then went to Knossos in Crete to end our "peaceful" holiday. Later we opted for Majorca in the Balearic Islands, where we and our two sons could enjoy the warm sun and sea; our second child, Jolyon Meredith born on 22 March 1966, was named after the character in "The Forsythe Saga", whose author (Galsworthy) had lived near our home and had invented the name. After the book was made into a successful TV "soap", the name became extremely popular, but that was a year after our son was named. When Sebastian was born our pet dog, a Pekinese called Peke Frean (named after the biscuit), became absurdly jealous, taking to "lifting his leg" in the sitting room and sadly had to be put down; later we acquired a new puppy, a Shih Tzu called Tutzi, who was loved by all.

In March 1968, our third son was born, like Jolyon, at St George's Hospital in Tooting, South London where the Obstetric Department had moved from Hyde Park Corner. The entire hospital is now at Tooting and the old hospital has been transformed into a five-star hotel. As we had two boys we were had hoping for a girl – in fact Angela had wanted a girl each time - and had bought pink nappy pins and nighties before Sebastian was born. When we had been in St Moritz in 1966 Angela admired an embroidered baby dress in a shop window; as she was expecting our second baby two months later, I had secretly gone back to the shop and bought it, but then realising I had chosen the wrong dress, I returned to the shop to buy the correct dress. When Jolyon was born, I admitted having bought the dress in St Moritz; Angela was amazed but told me it was not actually the one she had coveted, and gave it as a present to her friend Lucie, who had a baby girl about the same time. The second dress I kept hidden away for another two years and, when Fabian was born in 1968, it too was produced, and given to my nephew Paul and his wife, who had just had a baby girl, Caroline. Because of the world's increasing population, my attitude was that a marriage should ideally have one child of each sex but, if the first two children were of the same sex, it was not unreasonable to have one more attempt. Another reason for my view of no further offspring was that, aged 42, my reluctance to have further children was because their education might not be completed by the time of my retirement. The choice of our sons' names, Sebastian Zachary, Jolyon Meredith and Fabian Lucas was entirely Angela's, her reasoning being they all went well with our monosyllabic surname. We later heard of a dinner party where the discussion centred on the choice of babies' names and one couple said they knew a family whose children were called Sebastian, Jolyon and Fabian, whereupon the other couple responded "we didn't know you knew the Roses".

It was in 1969 we had the first of three annual family holidays in the Algarve in Portugal, staying at villas near Faro. The Portuguese cleaning women spoke no English but Angela picked up some of the language, which she later tried out on an educated Portuguese man, who commented that she spoke with an Algarve accent

Our skiing holiday in 1970 was in Lermoos, Austria when we took the opportunity to visit Neuschwanstein. Reading the story of Ludwig II, King of Austria and his drowning with his psychiatrist, which were understandably described as a mystery, from my professional point of view, there was little doubt that he killed his psychiatrist and then committed suicide,

In April 1971, we went to Cornwall to stay in a bed-and-breakfast farmhouse near Launceston, which was not successful, being very basic, with Jolyon and Sebastian sharing a double bed which one of them wetted during the night. During this trip we visited Angela's old nanny who had looked after her at the beginning of the Second World War before retiring to her family home. On our return journey we stayed at Holgate House, a hotel near Wincanton owned by the father of one of Angela's old school friends, with whom she had maintained contact. This friend was married to a local farmer, although she has since divorced and remarried.

That same year we decided to have a family holiday in Corsica, where we had never been before, and booked a hotel in Propriano. Unfortunately, in the week preceding our departure, an abscess developed in one of my teeth which was extremely painful and necessitated immediate and daily drainage. Dental problems were not new to me and were partly genetic, since my father had problems with his teeth and my mother and both sisters ended up with dentures. An event that aggravated my dental problems was when keeping wicket at medical school; with a fast bowler, the wicket keeper should stand either just behind the wicket or, better, at a longer distance; the untrained person such as me, would stand in between these two spots and, in my ignorance, a fast ball went straight to my mouth with a resultant dead upper incisor. My dentist, who was also a personal friend, began to drain the abscess but emphasised that daily drainage would be required for a week, which would mean cancelling our holiday. Telling him this, he asked where we were going and on hearing Corsica, he asked which place; on my replying Propriano, he asked which hotel; by sheer coincidence it transpired that he and his family were going to exactly the same hotel at precisely the same period as us. He took his dental draining equipment with him and treated me daily at our hotel, resulting in a successful holiday; this most remarkable coincidence must be unique.

Later that year, we won a long weekend break to the Mediterranean island of Malta, unfortunately I do not remember how. At that time there was only one neurologist serving the whole island but, being determined not to be distracted by professional work, I travelled as Mr Rose. The holiday was a success but, to my astonishment, just before we left our hotel, I received a telephone call from Dr Louis Vassalo, the only neurologist in the island's capital, Valetta, asking me to see two patients, siblings with a rare congenital disorder and give my opinion as to whether they should be transferred to London for marrow transplants. We went to his home and met his family, with the nine children each represented by a china piglet displayed on a shelf. Although intrigued by his patients, it had to be asked how he knew of my presence on the island, to which he replied that having discovered from my registrar of my holiday trip to

Malta, he had telephoned every hotel for Dr Clifford Rose but getting only negative responses, he contacted his friend, the Home Minister, who had access to every entry form filled in by tourists on arrival in Malta. Dr Vassalo, on finding my surname, Rose, wondered whether there was some illegal scam to explain the absence of my title and was relieved to hear the real reason.

Angela went every year to a piano summer school in the third week of August, initially in York, but for more than the past twenty years at the Royal National College of the Blind in Hereford. Accompanying her as an observer on several occasions, my visits included Hereford Cathedral to see the Mappa Mundi, an ancient and rare map, as well as other nearby places of interest, such as Elgar's statue and also a house where he lived, now a museum. However, most years I went on group walking tours of Italy; these were excellent holidays, in spite of the summer heat, and the daily distance walked of about sixteen miles. The first of these trips was to Tuscany where we stayed at a different place each night, giving us the opportunity to see each Tuscan town as we passed. Our luggage was transported by mini-van so we were unencumbered by a back-pack; also, if tired after walking in the morning, one could be driven to the next hotel after lunch; the lunches were picnics with delicious local food, presented and explained with a great deal of enthusiasm. My second trip ended in Siena with the Palio horse race. Tony Blair, then Prime Minister of the UK, happened to be watching the race from a balcony; he proved to be extremely popular with the Italian crowd. The third walking trip in August 2000 was to Umbria visiting Assisi; on this occasion, an American fellow-walker developed a septic foot which needed my daily attention. For this reason my usual habit on holiday was not to reveal my occupation until the last day otherwise the conversation always tended to turn to medicine; on the whole, fellow-travellers did not appreciate this reticence. On one holiday, the wife of the actor who played the priest in MASH, the long running American TV series, was unhappy that I delayed revealing my occupation until the final evening; but sure enough, on the following morning, she knocked on my door to request a prescription for her husband, rather shamefacedly admitting she might be my worst nightmare. Such events led me to write and ask the head office of the travel company that their computer records should not state my profession.

Another piano summer school that we attended several times was held in a private house in France, near a small market town called Prayssac in the Department of the Lot; the course being run by an English woman who is a keen amateur pianist and by profession an orthopaedic surgeon from Manchester. Originally by invitation with about nine participants, most with accompanying spouses, I am remembered by some for waking them during the night by noisily emptying the dishwasher, a task that is my regular chore at home. Master classes were held in the mornings and the afternoons spent practising or relaxing; the whole group went together to a different restaurant each evening. On one of these holidays another accompanying husband drove with me to the Bordeaux area as we were both interested in wine. After an excellent lunch, we visited wine shops in Pomerol and St Emilion, where we bought local wine more cheaply than could be found at home; I did succumb to a bottle of Petrus, but this was no bargain. On the way we stopped at a small town called Sainte-Foy-la-Grande, the unusual name of Foy being named after a 13 year-old girl born in 290 AD who preferred to be tortured and killed rather than give up her Christian faith; it was only in the nineteenth century that the town achieved its present fame, because it was the birth-place in 1824 of Paul Broca who, although a surgeon, is known in France as the founder of anthropology; to the medical world he is known for the localisation of speech to Broca's area in the brain, which he showed in 1860; he died in 1880 but the statue erected to him in Place Broca in 1887, was removed in 1942 during the German occupation.

In 1970, we took our family to Brittany where we rented a house; a memorable occasion since we learned about the local wines and the children practised after-dinner speeches; our ex-au-pair, Béatrice, joined us to help as we no longer had an au pair and she would take the children to buy croissants for breakfast and then go to the beach with them. One day we went down to the beach to find her in tears because she had lost

Sebastian. Angela went up and down asking if anyone had seen him, and then we discovered him playing happily just a few yards away.

Being the Principal Medical Officer of the Abbey Life Insurance Company, we were invited in 1972 to Abbey Life's annual "treat" for their more successful insurance agents, held that year in Glyfada, Greece. At one dinner table for five couples, Angela and I were the only couple who had not had previous marriages; although surprising at that time, divorce has increasingly become the norm, with more than fifty percent of couples being either unmarried or divorced. On this trip, one of the insurance agents persuaded, or rather goaded, me to go water skiing; although then 46 years of age and not having done it for many years, my attempt was apparently successful but no-one saw my bruising from the ski ropes.

In 1973, our skiing holiday was again in France, where we met Béatrice, our ex-au pair girl, who had had a baby since accompanying us on our previous holiday in Brittany. At the time we had not realised she was pregnant, although perhaps we should have guessed, as she slept every afternoon; she never married nor told us who her daughter's father was. The 1974 family holiday was also in France, this time in Cavalière in the South. Seeking a perfect hotel, we chose one on the Corniche but our bedroom overlooked a bend on the road, and the traffic was so noisy that we moved the next day to a hotel near the beach; there the mosquitoes forced us to leave once more and we drove inland to Valberg in the Alpes Maritimes, where we had gone previously on a skiing holiday.

In 1975 Angela and I returned to Tresco in the Scillies, the group of islands in the English Channel south of Cornwall, where we had previously gone with the children and stayed at a little hotel called the New Inn. When we went again without the children, we stayed at the Island Hotel, where a fellow guest was the "Radio Doctor" who later became secretary of the British Medical Association. In 1947 he chaired a meeting at BMA House on the NHS, which was to begin in the following year. During the debate, he claimed "Wild horses would not drag from me my politics", but this was revealed when he eventually became a Conservative Peer of the Realm. An embarrassing experience on this holiday was bumping into the

Professor of Psychiatry from my hospital, with a woman who was not his wife; understandably he did not want to know us. In April that year, the Association of British Neurologists met in Bangor, a university town in the north of Wales; following this Angela and the children drove up to meet me for a short holiday in Portmerion which, with its Italianate architecture was a unique experience for us all.

Another family holiday that year was to Corfu where, by chance, we were staying in the same hotel as Tom Stoppard and his wife, Miriam, and their young son. Miriam was a dermatologist (skin specialist) in Newcastle, but we first met when she worked in the pharmaceutical industry and, together, announced the new Glaxo drug for migraine (Sumatriptan) in 1991 at the Queen Elizabeth II Centre opposite the Houses of Parliament. The Stoppards were later divorced; Miriam became a TV "celebrity" and her husband, Tom, continued as a very successful playwright, being awarded the Order of Merit. In Corfu, we visited a patient of mine who was a local hotelier and treated the whole family to an excellent lunch sending us on our way with a magnificent fruit basket.

In January 1976 our skiing holiday was in Wengen, Switzerland where I had first skied in 1950. Later that year, we rented a holiday cottage in Norfolk, an old hunting-ground of mine, having been evacuated there for five years during the War, and the children were intrigued to visit places remembered from my long-ago school days.

When Sebastian started at Marlborough College in 1977, we bought a cottage nearby because over the next nine years all three sons would be boarding at the same school and we could bring them "home" at weekends rather than go to hotels. The cottage (originally two, or possibly three, small "tied" cottages) had been unoccupied for five years and was derelict with only a couple of electric lights and no mains water so we needed an architect to upgrade and modernise it. Fortunately, one of our London friends knew an architect who had a weekend cottage in Wiltshire, and this amazingly turned out to be in the neighbouring village. It took over a year for the work to be completed, since when the architect and his wife have become our best friends, so much so, that before his retirement from his London job, we would meet for coffee every Saturday morning at the Polly Tearooms in Marlborough before doing our weekly shopping. In 1980 we went with these friends, Martin and Carol Bailey, to Paris where he had opened an office.

In November 1977 Angela and I went on an Art Treasures Tour of Indonesia organised by the travel company, Swan Hellenic, which included Java, Sulawesi, Bali, Sumatra and also Singapore. We visited the Bantimurang butterfly forest and in Gowa, near Ujung Pandang, saw houses built on stilts. Nearby there was a Chinese graveyard as there was an influential, albeit small, Chinese population; in Rapala the Bugis people had a weaving centre, and in Toraja we saw a funeral at Bori, near Pangli, and also went to the Toraja Rock Graves built into small caves in the rock face at Lemo. We also participated in a wedding in Kalosi, Sulawesi.

In Bali there was a cemetery where menstruating women were forbidden to enter. Following a Balinese funeral procession which was accompanied by much music and beating of drums, at each cross road the "coffin bearers" would turn in circles to confuse any evil spirits who might be following. We were surprised to see a flock of ducks trained to follow a flag; this was achieved by the ducks seeing the flag as they hatched out of the egg and was called "imprinting". Our hotel, the Bali Hyatt, was a lovely place where we were entertained by local Barong dancers accompanied by gamelan music. In Eastern Java, near Surabaya, we saw a Bajang Ratu temple and later visited Jogjakarta, in central Java, the site of the famous Prambanan Temple, and Borobudur with its ninth century Buddhist monument featuring 504 statues of Buddha. In Medan, Sumatra, we visited the Sultan's palace and watched rubber trees being tapped.

In 1978, when travelling with the family from a meeting in Italy, we visited Florence, Sienna and Venice. We were due to go to Gibraltar, and I was then to speak in Spain, but found that we could not go direct from Gibraltar because the border was blocked for political reasons so we had to go to Tangiers first, which gave us an excellent opportunity of seeing this fascinating town. Later that year, having treated the manager of a Barbados hotel as a patient, we went to stay there for a very enjoyable holiday without the children. Whilst there we took the opportunity to visit the Sandy Lane Hotel, which was very famous, but we were not impressed. The same year, we went on holiday to Captiva Island, off the west coast of Florida, which had a reputation for causing the "Captiva" stoop, due to the popularity of collecting sea-shells from the beach. It was also famous for its mangrove swamps and sea birds, including pelicans and there were manatees in the small harbour.

In 1979, on a *Friends of the Royal Academy* visit to Moscow at the height of the cold war, there was a problem with Russian customs at the airport. Having taken "Moby Dick", the American novel by Herman Melville, published initially in 1851, to read on the flight which, the Russian customs officers examined the book very carefully and, in spite of my protestations that it was an old novel, they confiscated it, presumably because it was by an American writer, or possibly because it was in English, which they could not understand. Their vigilance was rewarded when another traveller, not one of our group, was found to have a suitcase full of jeans, which apparently could have sold in the Soviet Union at a great profit. The visits to museums and opera were splendid, but it was disappointing to learn that tourists had to pay more for their entrance fees than local citizens. Another disappointment was the enormous, faceless, prison-like Hotel Rossiya where we were staying; a woman warder, usually middle-aged and stout, sat at a desk on every floor to check our keys; the corridors smelt of disinfectant and there were no bath plugs. One incident when a member of our group was taking a snapshot of the Kremlin, by sheer chance, a soldier happened to walk past and was included in the shot; the result was that the camera was taken by a nearby policeman and the film exposed. We never visited Russia again until the Communist government was removed, and my dislike of dictatorship remains to this day.

In December 1979 we visited Australia, going first to Heron Island on the Great Barrier Reef, flying by helicopter from Brisbane. This tiny island took just twenty minutes to walk around and was mostly owned by Queensland University with just one small corner being a tourist resort. We spent only two days there, but went out in a mock-submarine, sitting in the hull of a boat surrounded by windows so underwater life could be viewed. We then went to Ayers Rock before the place became a fully developed tourist centre, flying in a small plane from Alice Springs and spending the night in very basic accommodation rather like stables. Woken at dawn for a tour round the Rock at sunrise, we then flew back to Alice before going to Sydney. We spent a few days in the Hunter Valley with Bob Johnston, a Sydney neurologist, and his wife; this trip was an annual wine buying expedition for them and an interesting experience for us, as we visited wineries and tasted wines from breakfast time onwards. Hiring a car in Sydney, we drove through the Blue Mountains and ski areas via Canberra to Melbourne; at one of our night stops the only hotel was actually closed as it was out of season, but the owners nevertheless gave us a room, sending us to a nearby pub to eat. Our Melbourne visit was primarily to visit Angela's uncle and family; her uncle Rolf wanted to take me to his Masonic Lodge but instead I returned to England early and Angela stayed behind to catch up with her uncle and cousins.

The family Christmas skiing holiday was to Davos in 1980, and in 1982 to Châtel in France; the latter was for me a shameful trip as I sustained a fracture, not of a leg, but my arm, and not whilst skiing, nor après-ski. Having attended ski- school that morning, the teacher told me to go to a more advanced class; feeling pleased with this good news, my initial intention was to return to the hotel but just nearby there was an icy patch which tempted me to skate down in my ski boots, the inevitable result being a fall with my upper arm across a very stiff spectacle case, resulting in a fracture. Not able to move my arm, , I was accompanied by Angela up the road by ambulance to the doctor's surgery, where first aid was given and my jacket cut off my arm, during which time she fainted. She then accompanied me to a hospital on the French side of Lake Geneva, where a huge plaster was applied, almost from my shoulder to the wrist. Explaining to the French orthopaedic surgeon that, as a doctor, my preference was to be in my own hospital, it was arranged for me to fly home the following day. On arrival at Heathrow Airport, the cigarette dropped from my driver's mouth when he saw me being pushed in a wheelchair, thinking perhaps that his job had come to an end (he actually worked for me for ten more years) and on arrival at Charing Cross Hospital, the huge plaster was replaced by a much smaller one, enabling me to return to work more or less immediately.

In 1982, the family went on holiday to the Club Mediterranée in Corfu, where the boys started to learn surfing, although not much French, as there were so many other British holidaymakers. Having forgotten to bring some essential tablets and fearful of cutting our holiday short, my visit to a local pharmacist was successful and being so relieved, I bought Angela a present of a gold chain, which she wore continuously until it fell apart some years later. Also in 1982, Angela and I went for a "pure" holiday to New Zealand where we hired a car to drive around the North and South Islands. Angela had spent six months there before we met, working for a short time in Wellington at the British High Commission; she was thrilled to see those places she had visited over twenty-five years before, particularly Coronet Peak near Queenstown, where she had looked after some young New Zealand cousins on a skiing holiday. At the time of her visit in 1962, for security reasons the British High Commission had required UK referees, but their request for these references took nearly a year to arrive in England, by which time Angela had already arrived back home. During a walking tour of Dunedin, our guide was impressed that my wife's maiden name was Halsted, which was well-known in New Zealand as was the original Hallenstein, because of a chain of men's shops with that name; there was also a Hallenstein Street in Queenstown. Dr Esmond de Beer, whose father was a director of Hallenstein Brothers and whose grandfather Bendix Hallenstein was the founder of the company, wrote six volumes on the diarist John Evelyn; he was also closely associated with Dunedin's art gallery as a benefactor. Although the Hallensteins retained this surname in Australia, the New Zealand and British branches changed the name to Halsted.

One of Angela's distant NZ cousins (whom she had taken skiing in Queenstown all those years ago) had married a farmer and they lived on the Marlborough Sounds at the north of the south island; we took a very small plane from Wellington to cross Cook Strait and land on a field of their farm from which they had to clear their sheep. We had a lovely walk in their nearby woods, being followed the whole way by a small bird, as we disturbed insects which provided the bird's food. At the end of our stay we went to lunch at a restaurant on the water's edge; the plan was for a water-plane taxi to pick us up and fly us to Nelson. As the weather became too windy, we had to get to Nelson by other means: this involved first being driven to an agreed spot where we were taken by motor boat across a strip of water to another waiting car, this in turn took us across another spit of land to another jetty, where we were left to wait for a final boat to take us to Nelson. We waited for about ten minutes, and wondered what we would do if the boat failed to materialise (it was before the days of mobile phones), but the boat finally appeared on the horizon, and all was well.

In June of 1984, after giving a talk in Palm Springs, California we went to see some old friends in San Francisco. Later that year we had a family holiday in Kenya but as Sebastian had already left school and had his own plans, only Jolyon and Fabian came with us. One of the highlights was a balloon safari which started at 5 am; we went in one balloon gondola (sadly Jolyon had been sick in the night so stayed at the hotel) whilst another carried a group of American grocers. It was wonderful to see the wild animals from the air as they were undisturbed by our floating over them, except for the elephants, perhaps because of their comparable size. On landing, a champagne breakfast was waiting; we were amused by the Americans who, hands on their hearts, toasted the President of the United States in the middle of Africa and Africans. In February 1985 we went to Cornwall for a short break to stay at the Hotel Tresanton, which belongs to Lord Forte's daughter, and to see some of the Cornish houses and gardens open to the public. Later that year we went on a short walking holiday in Dartmoor with our friends the Baileys, who were keen walkers, but Angela found it hard going although she enjoyed the Michelin-starred hotel, Gidleigh Park, where we were staying.

As 1988 was the year of our silver wedding, we celebrated with a driving holiday in Andalucia, which Angela had never visited, staying at various Paradors, the Spanish national hotels, in Ronda, Seville, Cordoba and Granada as well as a night in Marbella on arrival.

In June 1989, we went to see our middle son, Jolyon, graduate from the University of Bradford with a BSc degree in Environmental Science; he then took a job in Norfolk, working for the Health Education Department in the NHS, from where he was sent to London to study for a MSc degree in Health Education at the University of the South Bank; following this, he moved back to Norwich, where he bought a flat which he now rents out. Jolyon used his second degree to good effect when he decided to leave his job in Norwich and took a three-year appointment with VSO (Voluntary Service Overseas) helping the locals to teach health education in Vanuatu, an island country in the South Pacific which had gained independence in 1960, having been an Anglo-French Condominium then called the New Hebrides. While Angela went to see him every year for three years, I went only once. During the Second World War, Vanuatu had the largest Pacific base for American servicemen (as filmed in *South Pacific*). At the end of the war, when the Americans left suddenly following the atom bomb on Hiroshima, they offered the locals all the equipment, including new jeeps etc, for ten cents in the dollar. The locals, thinking that the Americans would anyway have to leave it all behind, refused the offer, whereupon, it is said, the Americans built a jetty into the Pacific and dumped all their valuable material in the ocean; this area is now an important protected heritage site much visited by divers and from which tourists are forbidden to take so much as a broken Coca-Cola bottle.

Towards the end of 1989, following an ALS (Motor Neurone Disease) meeting in Arizona, we went to Tanque Verde, a dude ranch. Horse-riding in a group through the desert, my saddle began slowly to slide sideways with the result that I fell off my horse although landing very gently; our wrangler (guide) was very concerned and asked several times if I was all right. Apparently the girth had not been properly tightened and the guide was concerned we might sue. Later, Angela competed in the "Rodeo", where it soon became evident that the horses were pre-programmed and knew exactly their way round the course, so all she had to do was to hang on and the horse did the rest and what is more she came first. At this ranch we had a ground floor bedroom with a panoramic window looking out onto the desert and all the passing wild life.

In 1989 we visited Berlin and went to operas both in the East and West of the City, celebrating the fact that the Berlin Wall was no more. Then in the following month, with the encouragement of neighbours who owned time-shares in Madeira, we went there for a week's "inspection" visit, staying in one of the flats at the Savoy Hotel above Funchal; at the end of the week the local representative was very surprised when we decided against going ahead with a purchase. Walking in Funchal, I recalled the time when a Portuguese doctor in Madeira used to send his patients with neurological problems to me and, just at that moment, we passed a house with a brass plate and that doctor's name on it. After telephoning him, he invited us for a drink where we met his wife, who was English; he had a very successful practice and was always called by Reid's Hotel for any guests who were sick.

In 1990 we went to Glyndebourne to see "The Magic Flute" as our young nephew, Ben Halsted, was singing the part of one of the three spirits. His singing teacher had entered him to audition as, at the time, she was coaching him for a scholarship to University College School in London and she had contacts at the opera house. He did not win a scholarship, but had the wonderful experience of singing at Glyndebourne.

Later same year there was a joint meeting of the Norwegian and British neurologists in Oslo. With these reciprocal visits, it was usual for members of the host country to invite visitors to dinner at their own homes. Because we were had our three sons with us, we made it clear that we would not expect such an invitation, since it would have meant the host entertaining five of us, to include three young children. Arriving in Oslo, we were therefore surprised to receive a dinner invitation; quickly pointing out this mistake to the President of the Norwegian neurologists, he checked and told me this host, a senior neurosurgeon, knew he would be entertaining the whole Rose family; it transpired that he knew me personally, having attended the Gordon Holmes Centennial Symposium that I had organised fourteen years previously in London. At dinner in his home, we learned some Norwegian traditions - the guest of honour sits on the right of the hostess, makes a speech and then, while toasting her, must look her directly in the eye; this occasion proved to be a great learning experience for the whole family.

August 1996 was my seventieth birthday and Angela "secretly" booked a room at Claridge's for the night, telling them not to confirm the booking, as she was doing my secretarial locum in Harley Street at the time, and did not want them to telephone or write there, as it would no longer be a surprise for me! Unfortunately they did telephone the office, but I did not tell her that I had discovered her plans. It was all very complicated, and on "the day" we met for tea at Claridge's I pretended to be surprised when told that we would be staying there for the night. In fact there had been a small drama when Angela checked into the hotel: having been taken up to the room and shown the various facilities, it was discovered that the fridge had old sandwiches left in it, and while the porter was looking for someone to clean it out, water started pouring through the ceiling of the bedroom. The result was we were moved to a very large and exotic suite and everything worked out very well, as Sebastian and Claire came down from Scotland for the occasion, and they stayed in our flat.

In March 2000 we went on a natural history tour in Morocco. We agreed beforehand that I would travel as Mr, rather than Dr, since revealing a medical background invariably provoked work-related discussions and questions. At the airport we met two women going on the same tour, one of whom was the widow of a close medical colleague; she knew me well and it was clear that my plan for anonymity would not work. We toured the foothills of the Atlas Mountains in a minibus with quite a lot of our time looking at birds, the main interest of our guide, Martin Jacobi, who was a retired school teacher. One of the rare sights was a collection of bald ibis, birds found uniquely in this area. Martin had already taken several groups on this tour over a period of seven years but could not guarantee that we would see them; on this occasion we were lucky, not only to encounter a flock but, whilst Martin was outside setting up his telescope, from the minibus I saw a mating pair of bald ibis. One of the group insisted we tell the guide, so I slid open the minibus door but unfortunately the noise frightened away the mating birds, much to Martin's disappointment. As these birds were under threat of extinction, my guilt at having disturbed the mating pair was relieved in the following year on reading that their numbers had increased. At the end of the tour we left the group to spend a few days in extreme luxury at the Mamounia Hotel, Churchill's favourite where his paintings still hang.

Ever since hearing the first talks on evolution as a sixth-former over fifty years previously, it had been a lifelong ambition of mine to visit the Galapagos Islands and this was finally realised in 2001. Two brothers with the surname of Darwin, who were descendants of Charles and belonged to the Savile Club and its wine-lovers circle, had told me about these remote islands 600 miles from the coast of Ecuador. One of the brothers was called Erasmus (named after Charles Darwin's grandfather, who was a doctor) so I invited him as my guest to an Osler Club meeting when the speaker was to talk on "Erasmus Darwin"; on introducing my guest to the President of the Club, he said, "No, the speaker is talking on Erasmus Darwin – what is the name of your guest?" This was exactly the confusion I had hoped for! Our cruise was with an American company called Lindblad and we flew independently to Miami and then on to Quito in Ecuador, where we spent a couple of nights. Although taken on some sightseeing trips, most of the group suffered from altitude sickness and did not really enjoy the city sights. Flying down to Guayaquil on the coast, we joined our ship, the *Polaris*, which accommodated a maximum of eighty passengers and was able to visit small islands inaccessible to larger ships, often using Zodiac inflatable landing craft to reach the smaller islands. It was fascinating to see the wild animals and birds, whether sea lions, frigate birds or marine iguanas, showing no fear of humans. On one island hike, when becoming more breathless than Angela, I became very worried; having been a heavy smoker (of cigars), my immediate thought was cancer of the lung. On returning to London my chest X-ray was normal, but a cardiologist diagnosed angina without pain; confirming the diagnosis, an urgent heart bypass operation was performed which proved highly successful.

In April 2002 we went on holiday to see the wetlands of Donana in South-west Spain, again with a group led by Martin Jacobi. This was the period of migration of African birds to fly to Europe and Donana is the perfect place to see this phenomenon. On this occasion, it was not necessary to remain anonymous as, out of the four couples in the group, all husbands and one wife were doctors! The following month we went on a tour of the art galleries in Holland, staying in a hotel in Utrecht and travelling by coach to different galleries each day, such as Rijksmuseum and van Gogh Museum in Amsterdam, Mauritzhaus in The Hague and the Krolle-Müller Museum.

As 2003 was the year of our fortieth wedding anniversary, we gave a party at the Savile Club: half the guests had been at our wedding, and only one couple had been divorced. My best man, Charlie Westbury, gave a complimentary speech to Angela and me and my reply was as follows: "Thank you very much indeed for your splendid toast, which lived up to its witty and delightful expectations; now you all know why I chose him as my best man. We would like to thank all of you for coming to celebrate our fortieth wedding anniversary – I am carefully avoiding calling it a ruby wedding for obvious reasons, as someone here has a particular weakness for gems of that type. The truth of why a marriage is successful must be largely luck, and the luckiest thing that ever happened to me was that event forty years ago today when I achieved a prize beyond rubies. We met at a party given by Angie's cousin, Veronica, whom we are delighted to have here tonight. We were engaged within two weeks and married within four months although I don't remember proposing." When asking Angie's parents about our proposed marriage, there was a condition from her mother and a warning from her father: her mother's condition was that I should also take the piano – at the time I thought it was a joke, but I soon discovered that a grand piano takes up a lot of space, let alone two grand pianos! When we moved permanently to Little Bedwyn, an extension was added to our cottage to house my books and her pianos; I optimistically called this new room a library, but this soon became the music room. Her father's warning, again not taken too seriously, was that she needed a lot of sleep; this changed my life from being a "nightingale", going to bed after midnight, to a "lark", going to bed before 10.00 p.m. This produced consequences to my sleep pattern which became rather peculiar with a great deal of reading and writing took place in the middle of the night. Both parent-in-laws gave me advice regarding their accountants – Erik's one was "chartered" whereas Win's was "turf"; I lost money with both recommendations."

We went on a short holiday to Tenerife in 2004 where Angela enjoyed her usual watercolour painting and drawing and this was followed by a trip to New York in April for the American Academy of Neurology meeting. In July we went once again to the Lot in France for Angela's piano week, where I again went on a wine buying expedition. That year's travels ended with an Indian Ocean cruise which, although very expensive, was not a huge success, possibly because it was a "first" voyage for the cruise company who had not yet ironed out the various problems that occurred. The cruise visited Madagascar, where we saw the famous lemurs and visited a private forest. The visit Aldabra, a research station on a coral atoll, was not a success for us. In the morning we were told to wait in our cabins for instructions about going ashore. After a very long wait we went up to find out what was going on, only to find all the passengers had left and we were put on a small boat with the crew and no guide. Apparently the rest of the passengers had not waited in their cabins...

In March 2005 we rented two adjacent self-catering "cottages", part of a converted farmyard, near St Austell in Cornwall. Angela and I occupied one cottage and Sebastian and family the other next door. Each had two bedrooms and having two separate houses worked very well. Our grandchildren, Megan and Angus loved the farm animals, and also the small indoor swimming pool. We visited the Eden Project and the Lost Gardens of Heligan and went to various beaches, which the children probably enjoyed more than the gardens.

In 2005 we went on another Lindblad cruise, this time to Costa Rica and Panama; the cruise ended with a trip through the Canal which Angela had done before in 1962 on her round the world trip to the Antipodes; we cruised through the Canal from west to east, and were then transported back to Panama City by coach. Our youngest son, Fabian, had been teaching English in Mexico and drove down in his car to spend a few days with us; our hotel was at the water's edge looking over the western entrance to the Canal so we could watch the ships coming and going all day long. On returning home, we found the latest brochure from Lindblad waiting; one particular cruise was very tempting as it crossed Scotland via the Caledonian Canal. As Sebastian, Claire and the grandchildren live in the Borders, we go to Scotland regularly, but tend not travel further afield, so we decided this canal cruise would be an ideal way to see more of Scotland. Telephoning the New York office of Lindblad the day after our return from their Costa Rica cruise to book this next holiday, surprised the booking clerk (two *Brits* booking a Scottish trip from an American company). The cruise started in Inverness on a boat accommodating 48 passengers, and visited Culloden, Loch Ness, Fort Augustus, Ben Nevis, Glencoe, Oban, Iona, Isle of Mull and Tobermory – we also went past the entrance of Fingal's Cave, immortalised by Mendelssohn's Overture..

August 29 2006 was my eightieth birthday, and having been ill quite recently, it was a low key affair with a family lunch party at home; a local caterer prepared the food, all the children and grandchildren came as well as our closest friends and it was a very happy occasion. We had another party in February 2007 for Angela's seventieth birthday, except we called it a 150th anniversary (80 + 70); this party was at the Harrow Inn in Little Bedwyn, which had been our village pub. When it was threatened with closure, a hundred or so villagers got together to buy it and ran it successfully for a number of years; it was subsequently sold and is now a Michelin starred restaurant. Christmas 2006 was spent at home; Jolyon came back from Germany, where he teaches English and runs a school of modern jive in Munich; he brought a Canadian/Indian friend called Bashir who had nowhere to go over the holidays, Fabian brought his girlfriend, Louise, and Lucie, the daughter of Angie's cousin Hal, was with us from Melbourne. They all left Bedwyn on 28 December and we drove up to Scotland for the New Year, where we rented a cottage for a week, and Megan and Angus stayed with us for New Year's Eve while their parents went partying for Hogmanay. On the way home we stopped in Leeds to visit my sister-in-law Terry who was 95 years old. She was nearly blind and lived alone since her husband, my older brother Sid, died fifteen years previously; they had no children and had originally gone to Leeds to avoid the London Blitz but, when Sid died, she decided to stay where she was. When we were with her she told us a horrific story of how she had decided to have a bath rather than her usual shower, but had then been unable to get out, in spite of draining the water; she covered herself with a towel and waited for two days until her niece in London raised the alarm after unsuccessfully trying to reach her by telephone. She finally decided it would be better to move into a care home, where she lived happily with many friends around her, until she sadly died just weeks before her hundredth birthday. I worked in Leeds between school and university, as a temporary civil servant helping on the change-over to the PAYE (Pay As You Earn) system; one of the other clerks asked me not to work so quickly, to which I readily agreed as my wage for a 39 hour week (in 1944) was only thirty-seven shillings. During this "gap" period I also dug onions and potatoes for one shilling an hour.

In the summer of 2007 we went on a Garden Cruise around Italy, also visiting the Italian islands. Although it was a very nice holiday, the gardens proved to be a disappointment, except for the magical gardens of Susannah, the widow of William Walton, the English composer. We met her again many years later when she presented her husband's work "Façade" at the Savile Club.

Chapter 17

HOBBIES

When first appointed a consultant at Charing Cross Hospital in 1965, it seemed natural to join the Royal Automobile Club (RAC) as it was a stone's throw away from the original site opposite Charing Cross Station in the Strand. The Club had several restaurants where one could have a snack or a full-blown meal, and in winter, in the main room, there was a large open fire and comfortable armchairs and sofas where members could enjoy a post-prandial snooze. There were squash courts and an Olympic size swimming pool; one of my regular squash partners was an entrepreneur, met when working as Principal Medical Officer of an insurance company in the City.   It was he who obtained for me a fixed rate mortgage of 8% when interest rates went up to twice that amount; he actively played the stock-market, eventually making his fortune. We lost contact for many years until he brought his daughter, who lived in Australia, to see me; she had a brain tumour which was successfully removed in the UK. Seven years after joining the RAC, the new Charing Cross Hospital opened in Hammersmith with its own Olympic size swimming pool and squash courts; since it was easier to use these facilities than the RAC I gave up my membership of the club. There were several good restaurants near the new hospital, one of which was the River Café, serving Italian food, and becoming one of the best in London – we returned there in 2007 and, telling them of my original visits there 25 years previously when it first opened, they responded by presenting me with a special commemorative lapel badge.

Working in Harley Street from 1991 until 2005, lunches were mainly at local restaurants until I joined the Savile Club, not far from Harley Street, going there three times a week to play bridge, on Monday evenings with dinner, and after lunch on Wednesdays and Thursdays, when I would return to my consulting rooms before

5 p.m .to sign my letters. I was also introduced to the Wine-lovers Circle at the Savile by another member, Fred Kendall, a great personality who had been a refugee from Hitler's Germany; he told me that when the Nazis won the German General Election in 1933, he bought Hitler's book, "Mein Kampf", which had been written in prison after the first attempt of the Nazis to gain power in 1928. Then a lad of 19 years, Kendall immediately decided to emigrate to England; starting with a job in a button factory in Darlington, he eventually became a successful publisher in London (spending some time with André Deutsch). I attended Christie's wine course of six two hour lectures and later invited Fred to come with me to a Master Class there, after which we dined in a restaurant in South Kensington. Before he died at the age of over 90, the Wine-lovers had a portrait done of him by Paul Merton which now hangs in the Club. Another story of Fred's was that on returning to Germany after his emigration to the UK, he met a friend, who had remained in Germany, was driving a smart car similar to the vehicles the Nazis used and was mistakenly told to follow the cavalcade to the applause of the assembled Nazi supporters. The Savile Club librarian, Colin Merton, who was the brother of Paul Merton, was always delighted to receive books written or edited by members and, having published over sixty books, all on neurological subjects, I gave him a few. The Club often held lunches with a Club member or invited expert giving a talk; on one occasion I gave a talk entitled "The Brain and Art", which was neither well-attended nor well received.

In 1969 we bought a house in Kingston-upon-Thames on a new estate before it was actually built, having seen the show house; it was round the corner from where were currently living, and we watched it grow day by day. It also meant we could make alterations to the basic plan before building started, so we added two extra rooms, and a wine cellar with advice on this from David Gummer, the Managing Director of the wine merchant Dolamore's, who was one of my squash partners.

When the Wellington private hospital opened in 1972 in St John's Wood, London, its menu included a very good wine-list, which persuaded me to take out private medical insurance. Although expensive, this decision has never been regretted, not least because longevity means increased disorders with age, necessitating extra medical care. Near the Wellington Hospital there was an excellent restaurant, also with a great wine list, where my neurosurgical colleague, Leslie Oliver, and I often met to discuss problems and exchange stories; it was there that I took the view there is no such thing as a good restaurant, but only restaurants where you are known. Angela, having heard me praise this establishment, went there one day with two of her friends for a birthday celebration. Not aware of her plans, imagine our surprise when these three ladies wandered in and at the end of the meal, to add "insult to injury", they sent their bill over to us – which we promptly returned.

In January 1976 I received a simple card that read:

> "St Andrews Hospital, Northampton: Brenda and Michael a'Brook regret to have to inform you that they are separated but send their best wishes, jointly and severally".

I met Mike a'Brook when we both worked at the Atkinson Morley's Hospital in Wimbledon, which was then part of St George's Hospital, and housed its departments of neurology, neurosurgery and psychiatry. He was there as part of his training to become a psychiatrist; a very good looking and charming chap, he told me that he had already been engaged to *seven* different girls serially and had given an engagement ring to each,. Receiving this unusual card eleven years later therefore came as no surprise. He eventfully became a psychiatrist and worked at St Andrew's Hospital, a private mental asylum in Northampton, where he would invite me to see patients with neurological disorders. One such person was the wine correspondent of a national daily newspaper, whose wine column I read regularly for many years. As it was thought that he might have Alzheimer's disease, it occurred to me to test his memory by asking him about wine, rather than the usual standard tests. It transpired that he knew very little about wine, and when asked about champagne, he surprisingly agreed his wine knowledge was scanty admitting his knowledgeable writings were obtained by abstracting them from his collection of wine books. On asking how he had obtained his prestigious appointment as wine correspondent, he told me that he applied to the editor of this national daily for a job as they were old school friends; the editor told him there were only two columns available on the newspaper at that time: "One was polo, which I didn't play, whilst the other was wine". He knew a bit about champagne because this was the only wine he enjoyed. My assessment was that he did not have an organic dementia.

The WFN Research Group on Headache and Migraine decided to meet in Bordeaux at the time of the vendange in 1976 and we took the opportunity to visit three chateaux with George Bruyn, a colleague and friend from Holland, and his wife Rosemary. The first vineyard we went to was Chateau Mouton-Rothschild which besides producing a famous First Growth claret, also welcomed visitors. "First Growth" refers to the 1855 classification of the best 60 (then 61) Bordeaux wines, which was based solely on their prices at that time. Over more than a century and a half later, some of these wines have improved, whilst others are less in demand; these variations are known to the cognoscenti and the division of First Growth clarets (*grands crus*) has been maintained; in fact there were originally four, but Mouton-Rothschild was added more recently. The next wine tasted was from Chateau Beychevalle which had improved since the label of Third Growth was awarded in 1855, and is now considered to belong to a higher rated growth. Obviously the year in which the grapes are harvested (the vintage) will also have a significant effect; we learned that the name of this wine was derived from "lower the sails", said to occur when the ships carrying the wine passed the residence of the local military commander, although this fact is still debatable. Our final visit was to Chateau Yquem, which is not in the 1855 classification because it is a white dessert wine, but considered by many to be the best dessert wine, particularly for a post-prandial sip. Even as a young man, when eating out, my tendency was to order the best affordable wine, which gradually increased my practical knowledge and later allowed me to attend Christie's wine courses and to acquire further understanding.

The Savile Club had an excellent wine list and the best wines were much cheaper than in a restaurant; for example, entertaining my senior registrar with a bottle of Chateau Yquem cost only three pounds and we drank a whole bottle between us, after which he went to sleep in my consulting rooms and did no further work that day. Within a year of my joining the Club, the prices of the best wines became more realistic and less affordable. The Savile had a "Wine-Lovers' Circle" with membership limited to about twenty, and by invitation only. One criterion for membership was to own a personal cellar so that whoever was chairing a dinner could choose his own wine; a maximum of twelve diners could attend each meeting as they were held in the Elgar Room which had limited seating (Sir Edward Elgar had been a member of the Savile). The chairman for the evening could invite a guest free of charge, but this was more than covered by the wine provided, which usually consisted of two bottles each of: champagne, white wine, two different clarets and post-prandial drinks, e.g. port, brandy or dessert wines.

As Angela did not play bridge, this meant that my last game was in 1963 before our marriage, but I took it up again in 1991 after my retirement from the NHS. In order to catch up with the changes in conventions over twenty-six years, I attended the bridge courses at Marlborough College Summer School every year; there were seven different bridge classes of varying standards which meant I could move up a level each year. When finally retiring from medicine, and living full-time in the country, I gave up bridge so that only the wine-lovers' circle drew me to the club. Getting older, my alcohol tolerance also became less, and I finally retired from the Club and its Wine-lovers' Circle in 2011, when, chairing my final dinner, I presented a selection of fantastic wines that none of the members had ever tasted before.

American wine-lovers pay a lot of attention to Robert Parker who was a former lawyer (attorney) in Maryland but became prominent in 1982, which was a year of superb claret. He used a 100-point scoring system and sampled more than 150 wines each year; his point scoring considerably influenced his readers and promoted over-oaked grapes which had been left longer on the vine than usual. Taking Angela on a tour of the champagne district in France, we met a man who told us he helped Parker with the wine tasting. As my wife does not drink any sort of alcohol, my excuse for this tour of the champagne chateaux was that having been to a Christie's study-evening comparing seven different years of Krug with seven of Bollinger, it was thought at this serial comparative tasting, that the former invariably seemed better than the latter. It was because the lecturer on that evening had no explanation for this difference that I wanted to go on this tour; it transpired that Krug still used oak vats whereas the other grand marques had adopted the modern steel ones. Angela enjoyed the tour for the social side and the sight-seeing and we dining at several different chateaux.

In June 1996, there was a meeting of AASH (American Association for the Study of Headache) in San Diego and I was asked to chair a session on "Wine and Headache", presumably because my group at the Princess Margaret Migraine Clinic at Charing Cross Hospital were the only researchers in this particular area. There were three main speakers, the first of whom was an Assistant Professor in the Department of Viticulture and Enology from the University of California's Davis campus; she spoke brilliantly on the Chemistry of Wine, not surprising as her centre is probably one of the best of its kind in the world, perhaps second only to Bordeaux. The following speaker was a neurologist from Holland who was critical of our research, his first slide being a statement that "Red wine migraine was a British disease", presumably because we were the only workers in this field; his next slide was again a simple statement "The British cannot tell the difference between red wine and vodka". This was because we had compared these two drinks, with the taste heavily disguised (darkened, frozen bottles, heavily altered taste so that an expert could not tell the difference). To my surprise, this comparison confirmed that those who drank the red wine mixture developed migraine whereas those who took the vodka control did not, suggesting that it was not alcohol itself that caused the headache but probably the congeners of the wine. The final speaker was the Head Wine-maker of Mondavi from the Napa Valley. When it came to the discussion (and wine-tasting) the audience assumed that, as Chairman, I would attack the Dutch neurologist; to their surprise, all the questions and discussions were directed at the two wine expert speakers. My only question, directed to the Napa Valley wine-maker was: "Why is it that Professor 'so-and-so' (the neurologist from Holland) thinks that French wine is always better than Californian wine?" Amid the laughter and the answer, the audience reckoned that justice had been done.

In July 1999, we organised a visit of the "Wine-lovers circle" to lunch at our village pub. Years previously, my three young sons came with me for a drink there (not strictly allowed because they were under age) but it was owned by an old lady and we had to walk through her kitchen to the bar and, as she was nearly blind, help ourselves to drinks. This old dear died a year or two later and it continued as a pub for a few more years, run very successfully by a couple who eventually split up and decided to sell the pub as a private house, which meant that the village would lose its last amenity besides the church. The residents were so upset at the thought of losing their pub that a meeting was called, when it was agreed they would club together to buy and run it. There was a small board of directors, with Angela as the token female, ostensibly to advise on décor. The pub thus continued, initially very well because a local couple, trained as chefs, were employed. Having built a successful business with a very good reputation, after a few years they decided to leave and start their own establishment beyond Marlborough; subsequent managers were less successful and the pub started to lose money. It was eventually sold to a couple who changed it into one of the most successful restaurants in Wessex with a Guide Michelin Star, but locals and Kennet and Avon Canal users could no longer drop in for a beer and a bag of crisps. Our 1999 lunch meeting was highly successful, not least because of the list of 200 different wines, and we repeated this visit of the "Wine-lovers' circle" ten years later.

After my marriage, we usually went for Sunday lunch to my parents-in-law. After the meal, my father-in-law would offer me a cigar, which was greatly appreciated. Although my father had been a cigarette smoker, ending with a "smoker's cough", I was never a cigarette smoker but did enjoy Havana cigars to the extent of always buying duty-free boxes of cigars when passing through foreign airports. One country where this was not possible was the United States because of its prohibition of buying

Cuban goods. The story told to me at the Savile Club by one of President J F Kennedy's Aids (the American Embassy is very near the Savile) was that, one day, JFK asked him to buy a large quantity of Havana cigars; the next day being asked whether this mission had been successful and getting a positive response, JFK opened a his desk drawer, removed a sheet of paper and signed the law once again forbidding the import of Cuban goods to the USA.

Only too well aware of the dangers of smoking cigarettes, similar statistics were not available for cigars, possibly because that habit was not nearly as widespread. As my income increased, there was no reason for me not to smoke two large Havanas every day, arguing that cigars were pure tobacco, without paper and therefore harmless but, looking back, it was probably self-denial. On a holiday visit to the Galapagos Islands everyone, including Angela, could walk further and faster than me without breathlessness and my thinking turned to the possibility of cancer of the lung. Immediately on returning to the UK, an X-ray of the chest proved negative and the explanation of my shortness of breath was found to be cardiac necessitating an immediate by-pass operation. In spite of giving up smoking completely, the damage was irreversible, leaving me with the dreaded "smoker's cough".

Angela had studied at the Royal College of Music for three years but realised that she was not good enough to be a concert pianist and did not want to become a full-time piano teacher, so had gone on to do a secretarial course. When we first met, she had a baby grand piano in her parents' Hurlingham flat and, when asking her mother's permission to marry her daughter (a tradition in those far-off days), she replied with evident relief: "As long as you take the piano". At the time, I thought this was funny, but housing a grand piano, even a baby grand, is no joke since it takes up a lot of room; indeed when we retired to our cottage in the country, we had to have an extension built to house the piano. Initially, I called this extension "My library", since my hundreds of books were housed there, but it is now inevitably called the music room. Certainly it was more used by her since she practises most days. An active committee member of the Bedwyn Music Society, for sixteen years she organised the annual Members Concert of that Society. Every year she went to a summer school for pianists, initially at York but, for more than a decade held in Hereford at the Royal National College of the Blind, now called the Royal National College. On three occasions, while she was at this piano course, I went on walking tours in Italy, either in Tuscany or Umbria. On three other years, I accompanied her to Hereford and had a delightful time exploring the surrounding countryside, including Elgar's museum, and attending the Course concerts every evening.

When we were first married, Angela's hairdresser was Vidal Sassoon in Sloane Street; one day in 1971, coming out of the hairdresser, she noticed an interesting exhibition of modern paintings in The New Art Centre next door. She had been left some money in her grandmother's Will and spent £300 of this on a painting by Brian Pearce, who belonged to the St Ives School. Her father was upset because this was a naïve painting that he thought any child could have done. Although my view was the same, I kept quiet because the money had been left to her to spend as she wished. To my surprise, we were later contacted by Brian Pearce's agent in St Ives telling us a retrospective exhibition of his paintings to celebrate his seventieth birthday was being organised at the Truro Museum and they would like borrow ours. We realised that the value of the painting had increased and we went to the exhibition where we bought another; over the ensuing years we bought several more because Angela loves them and, at a recent auction house in London, one of his paintings (larger in size than any of ours) sold for twenty eight thousand pounds.

Another hobby that changed my life was, surprisingly, politics. My first introduction was in 1936 when aged ten years, at the time of the Spanish Civil War (1936-1939) won by Generalissimo Franco. A member of the International Brigade told me of the cruelties of the Moorish soldiers and the interventions of the German and Italian bombers so it was inevitable that my sympathies became an anti-fascist, a view that became more intense during World War II. When the Labour Party won the 1945 general election, a rabid left-wing neighbour gloated that this was the greatest victory since the 1917 Russian Revolution. Fifteen years later, during the World War II, we were all impressed with the Russian Armies steadily pushing back the Nazis from Stalingrad and realised that Hitler had not learned about snow having defeated another conqueror in the previous century. I lost my enthusiasm for the Soviets when their armies invaded such countries as Czechoslovakia and Hungary and news came of the Katyn murders when 5,000 Polish officers perished, said by the Soviets to be due to German Nazis but now generally believed to be due to the Russians. When RMO at the National Hospital, Queen Square and nominally in charge of the junior residents, one of them, from a well-known banking family, approached me in 1959 saying: "There's going to be a general election this year. If the Conservatives win, the stock market prices will rise. Do you not think it would be a good idea for the juniors on the staff to form a syndicate and use the money accrued for investment in the markets?" In spite of my previous views, I readily agreed. There was an election, the Conservatives won and the market prices went up, and we all made a profit. As a consequence, my interest in the financial markets increased and over the next three decades I bought shares, using stockbrokers to advise me. I tried five different companies but received no good advice. On retirement from the NHS in 1991, we sold our house outside London, where we had lived for twenty-five years, making a large profit and I decided I would do my own investing. Reading several of the relevant books and attending meetings on the subject proved helpful. On one occasion going to the Business Centre in Islington, I came across a stall designated SIGnet, the initial three letters meaning Serious Investors Group ("net" being short for network). It was explained that these were not investment clubs but simply groups of investors meeting to discuss the various problems and techniques involved in investment. Never having heard of this before and admitting my ignorance, I asked "where were they based?" John Lander, the organiser, told me they hoped to have a centre in every county before too long. Within a week of our meeting he wrote asking me to start a local Wiltshire group which I did, acting as Chairman-Secretary for the first five years. Under new leadership, the group continues to flourish and expand, with several experts in different fields attending the meetings.

Chapter 18

WRITING

It is axiomatic that one of the best ways to learn about any topic is to write about it. This is partly because it necessitates wider reading of what is already known, but another explanation for my lifetime predilection for editing, co-editing and authoring and co-authoring was accepting the demands these activities necessitate. One further explanation for my out-pouring of publications in the 1960s and later was a reflection of massive medical research meriting the need to keep up with advances, as well as the willingness of publishers to produce these works. In the late 1970s it occurred to me that a new journal was needed for neuroepidemiology, a word that does not have its old meaning of the knowledge of epidemics, but is the study of groups. Apart from the different frequencies of illnesses in various countries, its importance includes finding the best treatments by comparing different drugs for patients. Although these clinical studies have many problems, they are still the "gold standard" for the most advantageous therapies, particularly important in disorders of the nervous system. In 1980, Thomas Karger, the owner of a Swiss publishing house, agreed to bring out such a journal to be entitled *Neuroepidemiology,* with myself as Chief Editor and Dr Bruce Schoenberg, senior academic epidemiologist at the National Institutes of Health in Washington DC, as my deputy. Before the first issue was published, Dr Osuntokun, a neurologist from Nigeria, was asked by Schoenberg to advise me to become deputy Editor with Schoenberg as Editor-in-Chief; this was not a problem for me, but unfortunately, within three years of the first issue, Schoenberg and Thomas Karger had such a strong disagreement that Karger informed me that he intended to stop its publication. The only alternative was for me to take on the task of Editor-in-Chief, which I accepted and performed until 1990, when that responsibility was taken by another American, Professor Milton Alter, Chairman of the WFN Research Group in Neuroepidemiology, but with my continuing as Senior Editor until he was well esconced. During this time, it was accepted that general journals should publish the more interesting papers in this field, with *Neuroepidemiology* printing the recondite offerings, a policy that allowed the new journal to catch up with its backlog and publish clinical trials on dementia, motor neurone disease and parkinsonism, a Congress of the latter to be held in Israel in 1988. After my five years' service, the journal became the official organ of the WFN Research Group in Neuroepidemiology. From 8-22 May 1981, I attended the Advanced Course on Neuroepidemiology, on principles and clinical applications, held in San Miniato, Italy, under the auspices of the WFN; my later editing of a book entitled "Clinical Neuroepidemiology" was published by Pitman Books, and may have been the first of its kind.

From 1980 until 1984, the job of editing the Transactions of the Medical Society of London fell to me. In spite of being on the Editorial Board of *Cephalalgia*, a global journal for headache and the official organ of the International Society of Headache, this work went well with *Core Journals in Clinical Neurology* published in Amsterdam from 1982-1987, and *Migraine Matters* (1982-1985) published in London.

By 1979 there had been few books on the neurology of children and Blackwells of Oxford persuaded me to take on the responsibility of editing one. The Chairman of the Research Group of Paediatric Neurology of the WFN, Ivan Lesny, wrote the preface: "As one of the first paediatric neurologists in Europe, if not the world, it is a great honour to write the foreword to the first multi-author book on paediatric neurology produced in the United Kingdom. As an independent branch of medicine, paediatric neurology began only a few years after World War II …" In my introduction it was pointed out that whereas 20% of medical admissions to hospital concerned the nervous system, in childhood it was 30%; this book included my own chapter on speech disorders in childhood. 1979 was also the year that we published a book on the third commonest cause of death, namely stroke, heart disease being the first and cancer the second,; this included work on when stroke occurred, how to manage its disablement, preparing a data-bank and social aspects.

Because there was a need for patients to understand their own illness, Oxford University Press asked me to prepare a small paperback on migraine for lay readership; this was published as a volume called "Migraine, the Facts", written with my registrar, Marek Gawel, and a second edition was issued twenty years later in 1981 but with another publisher, namely Class Publishing. Having co-authored another book for the lay on multiple sclerosis, the Director of Class Publishing wrote to me on 26 November 2001as follows:

> "Dear Frank
>
> **British Medical Association Book Awards**
>
> I enclose a citation, in the form of a scroll or frameable poster, for your brilliant book, which has been commended at the British Medical Association Book Awards. The award ceremony took place last week. I very much hope that you feel as proud as we do of your award, which is an accolade for your genius at empowering and communicating positive messages to people with multiple sclerosis. We are basking in your reflected glory. Yours sincerely, Dick"

This latter book was based on a Mansell Bequest Symposium held at the Medical Society of London where, for over thirty years, I had organised these Symposia every two or three years, inviting the best specialists from all over the world to attend and submit a chapter for the resulting books, all of which I edited. After each Mansell Bequest Symposium, we would usually invite some of the speakers to dinner at my home; one such party included Professor Carleton Gajdusek, an energetic American neuroscientist who kept diaries in yearly volumes which he circulated to people he knew. After qualifying in biophysics at Rochester University, New York State, in 1943, he studied medicine at Harvard. More than ten years later he went to Port Moresby, New Guinea to set up a study on a disease called Kuru which occurred in the Fore tribe of the Eastern Highlands. Within a year, he returned to the United States where he began inoculating extracts from Fore brains into primates, who became ill several years later, proving the relationship to the same disease as occurred in humans in Fore. He won a Nobel Prize in 1976 for "discovering a completely new infectious agent, what he called slow viruses but are now known as prions". At our dinner party, he spoke of his many adopted New Guinea "sons" whose American education was paid by him and who were encouraged to "please older women". My wife was very upset with Gajdusek's conversation and, after he left, told me in no uncertain terms: "Never invite this man again"; my reply that he was a Nobel Prize winner was met with the response: "So what?" The last time I saw him was on television in handcuffs, as one of his adopted sons had testified against him; convicted of paedophilia, he was sentenced to 19 months of which he served six in prison, dying at the age of seventy-four ten years later.

Because of an increasing demand for my editorial services, I joined the European Association of Science Editors from 1978-1984; from 1986 I was on the editorial board of the *British Journal of Clinical Practice*; from 1989, on the "*Review in Contemporary Pharmacotherapy*" contributing to its issue on drugs for facial pain (Trigeminal Neuralgia), but ending in 2004. From 1990 I was on the board of "*Megrim*", a booklet magazine that used the old name for migraine as its title. In the following year, Dr Seymour Diamond of Chicago asked me to be his co-editor of *Headache Quarterly*, a journal in America which was already associated with the journal "*Headache*" produced by AASH. Later there was a more scientific journal concerning pain in the head published by the organ of the International Headache Society (IHS) and named "*Cephalalgia*", the Greek word for headache. All three journals were sent to me but my co-editorship of "*Headache Quarterly*" ended in 2000; one unfriendly person had implied my acceptance of this latter position was because it was a paid appointment, which was not true

In 1990, I became consulting editor of the Journal of Tropical and Geographical Neurology, presumably because of my publication of a book with a similar name based on a "Mansell Bequest Symposium", but this was only for one year. Having lectured annually for three years in Budapest, in January 1993 I was elected a member of the International Advisory Board of "*Clinical Neuroscience*", a Hungarian Journal, only partly published in English. Even at the age of 85, my name is still appears on the editorial boards of two journals: the *Journal of the History of Neurosciences'* (having been its founder in 1992), and *The International Journal of Neurological Science,* the official organ of the WFN. In 2008, Dr Robert Brackenridge died. He had been a great supporter of Life Assurance Medicine and edited its standard work entitled *Medical Selection of Life Risks*, which went to five editions; he had asked me to co-author his chapter on *Disorders of the Nervous System.*

Chapter 19

PUBLICATIONS

This final chapter ends with lists of books, chapters and papers I have published, but should be ignored by the general reader, and are recorded for those few who may wish to pursue a particular topic.

BOOKS

1.   Marks V and Rose F.C (1965). Hypoglycaemia. Blackwell Scientific, Oxford.1a: Hypoglycaemia (1967) Spanish edition

1b: Hypoglycaemia (1981) 2nd edition

1c: Hypoglycaemia (1985) 2nd edition Japanese

2.   Espir M.L.E and Rose F.C (1970). The Basic Neurology of Speech. Blackwell Scientific, Oxford.

2a: Second edition (1976)

2b: Dutch edition (1980)

2c: Third edition (1983). The Basic Neurology of Speech and Language.

3.   Perkin G.D and Rose F.C (1979). Optic Neuritis and its differential diagnosis. Oxford University Press, Oxford, UK.

4.   Rose F.C and Gawel M (1979). Stroke: The Facts. Oxford University Press, Oxford, UK.

4a.   1981a: Paperback reprint

4b.   1981b: Jaqueca (Spanish edition, printed in Bogota, Columbia)

5.   Rose F.C and Capildeo R (1981). Stroke: The Facts. Oxford University Press, Oxford,

5a: (1982) Paperback

5b: (1982) Die Feiten Over Een Beroerte. Dutch edition.

6.   Rose F.C and Davies P (1987). Answers to Migraine. Macdonald Optima, London.

7.   Rose F.C and Gawel M (2004). Migraine: second edition. Class Publishing, London.

8.   Rose F.C (2012). The History of British Neurology. Imperial College Press, London.

BOOKS EDITED

1.   (1976) Medical Ophthalmology. Chapman and Hall, London.

1a: (1976). Moseby, USA

2.   (1977) Motor Neurone Disease. Pitman Medical, London.

3.   (1977) Physiological Aspects of Clinical Neurology. Blackwell Scientific, Oxford, UK.

4.   (1978) Clinical Neuroimmunology. Blackwell Scientific, Oxford, UK.

5.   (1979) Paediatric Neurology. Blackwell Scientific, Oxford, UK.

6.   (1979) Progress in Stroke Research 1. Pitman Medical, Tunbridge Wells, UK.

7.   (1979) Progress in Neurological Research, with particular reference to motor neurone disease. Pitman Medical, Tunbridge Wells, UK.

8.   (1980) Animal Models of Neurological Disease. Pitman Medical, Tunbridge Wells, UK.

9.   (1980) Clinical Neuroepidemiology. Pitman Medical, Tunbridge Wells, UK.

10.   (1981) Research Progress in Parkinson's Disease. Pitman Books, London.

11.   (1981) Metabolic Diseases of the Nervous System. Pitman Books, London.

12.   (1981) Progress in Migraine Research I. Pitman Books, London.

13.   (1982) Cerebral Hypoxia in the Pathogenesis of Migraine Attacks. Pitman Books, London.

14.   (1982) Advances in Stroke Therapy. Raven Press, New York.

15.   (1982) Historical Aspects of the Neurosciences. Raven Press, New York.

16.   (1982) Advances in Migraine Research and Therapy. Raven Press, New York.

17.   (1982) Research Progress in Epilepsy. Pitman Medical, London

18.   (1983) Immunology of Nervous System Infections. Elsevier, Amsterdam.

19.   (1983) The Eye in General Medicine. Chapman and Hall, London.

20.   (1983) Progress in Stroke Research 2. Pitman Books, London.

21.   (1983) Research Progress in Motor Neurone Disease. Pitman Books, London.

22.   (1983) Slide Atlas of Neurology. Gower Medical, London.
22a.   Japanese edition

23.   (1984) Progress in Migraine Research 2. Pitman Books, London.

24.   (1984) Progress in Aphasiology. Raven Press, New York.

25.   (1985) Neuro-Oncology. Karger, Basel, Switzerland.

26.   (1985) Modern Approaches to the Aphasias, Part 1: Etiology and Pathophysiology. Karger, Basel, Switzerland.
26a.   (1985) Modern Approaches to the Aphasias, Part 2: Clinical and Therapeutic Aspects. Karger, Basel, Switzerland.

27.   (1985) Migraine: Clinical and Research Advances). Karger, Basel, Switzerland.

28.   (1986) Handbook of Clinical Neurology, Vol 4 (48): Headache. Elsevier Science, Amsterdam.

29.   (1986) Stroke: epidemiological, therapeutic and socio-economic aspects (Ed). RSM Services, London.

30.   (1986) Atlas of Clinical Neurology. Gower Medical, London

30a: (1988) Japanese edition

31.   (1987) Multiple Sclerosis: Immunological, diagnostic and
       therapeutic aspects. John Libbey, London.

32.   (1987) Advances in Headache Research. John Libbey, London.

33.   (1987) Parkinson's disease: Clinical and experimental advances.
       John Libbey, London

34.   (1988) Physiological Aspects of Clinical Neuro-ophthalmology.
       Chapman and Hall, London.

35.   (1988) Aphasia. Whurr Publishers, London.

36.   (1988) The Management of Headache. Raven Press, New York.

36a: Paperback edition

37.   (1989) Clinical Trial Methodology in Stroke. Ballière Tindall,
       London.

38.   (1989) The Control of the Hypothalamo-Pituitary-Adrenocortical
       Axis. International Universities Press, Madison, USA.

39.   (1989) Neuroscience across the centuries. Smith-Gordon, London

40.   (1989) James Parkinson: His Life and Times. Birkhäuser, Boston.

41.   (1989) New Advances in Headache Research . Smith-Gordon, London.

42.   (1989) Neuromuscular Stimulation: Basic Concepts and Clinical Implications. Demos Publications, New York.

43.   (1990) New Drug Strategies in the Prevention and Treatment of Stroke. Smith-Gordon, London.

44.   (1990) Progress in Clinical Neurologic Trials, Vol.1: Amyotrophic Lateral Sclerosis. Demos Publications, New York.

45.   (1990)   Progress in Clinical Neurologic Trials, Vol.2: Parkinsons Disease. Demos Publications, New York.

46.   (1991) New Advances in Headache Research 2. Smith-Gordon, London.

47.   (1992) Parkinson's disease and the problems of clinical trials. Smith-Gordon, London.

48. (1992) Molecular Genetics and Neurology. Smith-Gordon, London.

49. (1993) Advances in Neuropharmacology. Smith-Gordon, London.

50. (1994) ALS – from Charcot to the present and into the future. Smith-Gordon, London.

51. (1994) New Advances in Headache Research 3. Smith-Gordon, London.

52. (1995) Recent Advances in Tropical Neurology. Elsevier, Amsterdam.

53. (1996) Towards Migraine 2000. Elsevier, Amsterdam.

54. (1999) A Short History of Neurology: The British Contribution 1660-1910. Butterworth-Heinemann, Oxford.

55. (2000) Multiple Sclerosis at your fingertips. Class Publishing, London.

56. (2001) Twentieth Century Neurology: The British Contribution. Imperial College Press, London.

57.   (2003) Motor Neurone Disease at your fingertips. Class Publishing, London.

58.   (2004) Managing your Multiple Sclerosis. Class Publishing, London.

59.   (2004) Neurology of the Arts: painting, music, literature. Imperial College Press, London.

60.   (2006) The Neurobiology of Painting. Elsevier, Amserdam.

61.   (2010) Neurology of Music. Imperial College Press, London.

BOOK CHAPTERS

(1963) Cyclophophamide Therapy in Intracerebral Tumour. In: G H Stanley and J M Simister (eds), Cyclophosphamide (Endoxana). John Wright and Sons, Bristol; pp: 120-121.

(1972) With A I Friedmann, P M A Bowden and D Perkin. In: D Macalpine, CJ E Lumsden and E D Acheson (eds), Multiple Sclerosis, a Reappraisal. 2nd edition, Churchill Livingston, London, p.151.

(1972) The Aetiology of Optic Neuritis. In: J S Cant (ed.), The Optic Nerve. Henry Kimpton Publishers, London, pp 217-219.

5) Neurological manifestations of systemic cancer. In: K D Bagshawe (ed.), Medical Oncology. Blackwell Scientific, Oxford, pp 143-158.

(1976) Ocular Palsies. In: F C Rose (ed.), Medical Ophthalmology. Chapman & Hall, London, pp 95-102.

(1976) Chiasmal Lesions. In: F C Rose (ed.). Medical Ophthalmology. Chapman & Hall, London, pp 184-195.

(1976) Developmental Dysphaisa. In: J Krauss (ed.), Encyclopaedia Handbook of Medical Psychology. Butterworth, London.

(1976) Stammering. In: S Krauss L (ed.), Encyclopaedia Handbook of Medical Psychology. Butterworth, London.

(1976) Retrospective Survey of Speech Disorders Following Stroke, with Particular Reference to the Value of Speech Therapy. In: Y Lebrun and R Hoops (eds.). Recovery In Aphasias. Swets and Zeitlinger BV, Amsterdam, pp: 189-197.

(1977) With Butler R C, Gawel M and Sloper J. Muscle biopsy in Motor Neurone Disease In: F C Rose (ed.), Motor Neurone Disease. Pitman Medical, London; pp 79-93.

(1977) Clinical Aspects of Motor Neurone Disease. In: F C Rose (ed.), Motor Neurone Disease Pitman Medical, Tunbridge Wells, pp 1-13.

(1977) With Kennard C, Gawel M and de M Rudolf N. Visual Evoked Potentials in Migraine Subjects. In: A P Friedman, M E Granger and M Critchley (eds.), Headache Today – An Update by 21 Experts. S Karger, Basel, pp 73-80.

(1978) With M J Gawel. Cerebral Circulation. In: D Geraint James (ed.), Circulation of the Blood. Pitman Medical, Tunbridge Wells, UK, pp 111-131.

(1978) With R Capildeo. The Design of an Acute Stroke Trial. In: A M Jukes (ed.), Baclofen: Spasticity and Cerebral Pathology. Cambridge Medical, Northampton.

(1978) With Grant E C G, Albuquerqe M and Steiner T J. Oral Contraceptives, Smoking and Ergotamine in Migraine In: R Greene (ed.), Current Concepts in Migraine Research. Raven Press, New York, pp 97-100.

(1978) SMON Outside Japan. In: M Gent and Shizematsu (eds.), Epidemiological Issues, McMaster Press, Hamilton, Canada.

(1979) Foreword in Clinical Neuroimmunology. F C Rose (ed.). Blackwell Scientific, Oxford, xvii.

(1979) Speech Disorders. In: F C Rose (ed.), Paediatric Neurology. Blackwell Scientific, Oxford, pp 247-260.

(1979) With G Murrells. Disorders of Speech. In: Ballantyne and Groves (eds.), Scott-Browns Textbook of ENT Diseases. Fourth edition.

(1979. With Gawel M J, Butler R, Partridge T A and Sloper J. Muscle biopsy in motor neurone disease. In: P O Behan and F C Rose (eds.). Progress in Neurological Research. Pitman Medical, Tunbridge Wells, pp 158-168.

(1979. With Haberman S and Capildeo R. Epidemiological aspects of stroke. In: R M Greenhalgh and F C Rose (eds.), Progress in Stroke Research. Pitman Medical, Tunbridge Wells, pp 3-14.

(1979) With Capildeo R. The assessment of neurological disability In: R M Greenhalgh and F C Rose (eds.), Progress in Stroke Research 1. Pitman Medical, Tunbridge Wells; pp. 106-116.

(1979) With Capildeo R and Haberman S. Towards a computer-based data bank for stroke patients In: R M Greenhalgh and F C Rose (eds.), Progress in Stroke Research 1 .Pitman Medical, Tunbridge Wells, pp 153-158.

(1979) With Court C and Capildeo R. Medico-social aspects of stroke: a domiciliary follow-up study In: R M Greenhalgh and F C Rose (eds.), Progress in Stroke Research. Pitman Medical, Tunbridge Wells, pp 237-246.

(1979) With Capildeo R and Haberman S. The classification and coding of neurological disease. In: F C Rose (ed.), Clinical Neuroepidemiology. Pitman Medical, Tunbridge Wells, pp 28-36.

(1980) With Steiner T J and Rail D L H. An animal model of atheroembolic cerebral infarction. In: P O Behan and F C Rose (eds.). Animal Models of Neurological Disease.   Pitman Medical, Tunbridge Wells, pp 452-466.

(1980) Stroke – The Third Killer: Prevention, Treatment and Cure. Transactions of the Medical Society of London.

(1980) The Aetiology of Optic Neuritis. Transactions of the Medical Society of London.

(1981) With Capildeo R and Haberman S. The classification of Parkinsonism. In: F C Rose and R Capildeo (eds.), Research Progress in Parkinson's Disease. Pitman Books, London, pp 17-24.

(1981) With Capildeo R and Flewitt B. Physiotherapy and assessment in Parkinson's disease using the polarised light goniometer In: F C Rose and R Capildeo (eds.), Research Progress in Parkinson's disease. Pitman Books, London, pp 404-414.

(1981) With Capildeo R. Metabolic aspects of coma following stroke. In: F C Rose (ed.), Metabolic Disorders of the Nervous System. Pitman Books, London, pp 334-342.

(1981) With Steiner T J and Smith F R. Vasomotor reactivity in migraine. In: F C Rose and K J Zilkha (eds.), Progress in Migraine Research I. Pitman Books, London, pp 33-40.

(1981) Clinical evaluation of Flunarizine in migraine. In: Cerebral Hypoxia in the Genesis of Migraine. Pitman Books, London.

(1981) Amine inactivity enzymes in headache patients. In: F C Rose and K J Zilkha (eds.), Progress in Migraine Research I. Pitman Books, London, pp 95-99.

(1981) The role of prostacyclin in the pathogenesis of migraine. In: F C Rose and K J Zilkha (eds.), Progress in Migraine Research 1 . Pitman Books, London, pp 124-132.

(1981) A Diagnostic Test for Multiple Sclerosis with glutaraldehyde fixed Erythrocytes and Laser Cytopherometry. In: A W Preece and P A Light (eds.), Cell electrophoresis in Cancer... Elsevier, North Holland.

(1981) With Gawel M J, Glover V, Peatfield R and Sandler M. Platelet monoamine oxidase activity varies with platelet count during severe exercise and noradrenaline infusion In: F C Rose and K J Zilkha (eds.), Progress in Migraine Research I. Pitman Books, London;

(1981) Sex differences in stroke. In: R M Greenhalgh (ed.), Hormones and Vascular Disease. Pitman Books, London, pp 119-129.

(1981) Sex differences in platelet function in stroke patients. In: R M Greenhalgh (ed.), Hormones and Vascular Disease. Pitman Books, London, pp 130-138.

(1981) Diabetes in cerebrovascular disease. In: R M Greenhalgh (ed.), Hormones and Vascular Disease. Pitman Books, London, pp 152-168.

(1982) Macdonald Critchley. In: F C Rose and W F Bynum (eds.), Historical Aspects of the Neurosciences. Raven Press, New York,   pp ix and x.

(1982)The neurological tradition of Charing Cross Hospital. In: F C Rose and W F Bynum (eds.), Historical Aspects of the Neurosciences. Raven Press, New York, pp 347-356.

(1982) Tyramine Response and Platelet MAO Activity. In: F C Rose (ed.), Advances in Migraine Research and Therapy. Raven Press, New York.

(1982) Pizotifen in the prophylaxis of migraine. In: F C Rose (ed.), Advances in Migraine Research and Therapy. Raven Press, New York, pp 211-216.

(1982) The abnormal CT scan in migraine patients. In: F C Rose and W K Amery (eds.), Cerebral hypoxia in the pathogenesis of migraine. Pitman Books, London, pp 105-109.

(1982) Possible role for flunarazine in the prophylaxis of migraine. In: F C Rose and W K Amery (eds.), Cerebral Hypoxia in the pathogenesis of migraine. Pitman Books, London, pp 195-200.

(1982) With Capildeo R and Haberman S. Stroke Trials: the Facts In: F C Rose (ed.), Advances in Stroke Therapy. Raven Press, New York, pp 53-62.

(1982) Ways to facilitate Rehabilitation in Neurology. In: J S Chopra et al (eds.), Advances in Neurology. Elsevier Science Publishers BV, Amsterdam, pp 471-180.

(1982) Naftidrofuryl. In: F C Rose (ed.), Advances in Stroke Therapy. Raven Press, New York, pp 71-78.

(1982. Migraine patients exhibit abnormalities in the visual evoked potential. In: F C Rose (ed.), Advances in Migraine Research and Therapy. Raven Press, New York, pp 85-92.

(1982) Autonomic Function in Migraine. In: F C Rose (ed.), Advances in Migraine Research and Therapy. Raven Press, New York, pp 93-98.

(1982) Why is Platelet Monoamine Oxidase Activity Low in Some Headache Patients? In: F C Rose (ed.), Advances in Migraine Research and Therapy. Raven Press, New York, pp 127-132.

(1982) Clinical and Experimental Studies of a Prostaglandin Inhibitor in Migraine. In: F C Rose (ed.), Advances in Migraine Research and Therapy. Raven Press, New York, pp 165-172.

(1982) Towards a New Classification of Headache. In: F C Rose (ed.), Advances in Migraine Research and Therapy. Raven Press, New York, pp 1-6.

(1982) Risk Factors for Cerebrovascular Disease. In: F C Rose (ed.), Advances in Stroke Therapy. Raven Press, New York, pp 101-116.

(1982) European Stroke Prevention Study. In: F C Rose (ed.), Advances in Stroke Therapy. Raven Press, New York, pp 143-146.

(1982. The use of Sulphinpyrazone in the Prevention of Restroke and Stroke in Man. In: F C Rose (ed.), Advances in Stroke Therapy. Raven Press, New York, pp 155-160.

(1982) Gait Assessment after Stroke: The Polarised Light Goniometer. In: F C Rose (ed.), Advances in Stroke Therapy. Raven Press, New York, pp 213-222.

(1983) Ocular palsies. In: F C Rose (ed.), The Eye in General Medicine. Chapman & Hall, London. pp 172-180.

(1983) Monitoring changes in the blood of patients with multiple sclerosis. In: Immunology of Nervous System Infections. pp: 333-338.

(1983) Epidemiological aspects of stroke. In: R M Greenhalgh and F C Rose (eds.), Progress in Stroke Research 2. Pitman, London, pp 1-12.

(1983) Hydergine. In: R Greenhalgh and F C Rose (eds.), Progress in Stroke Research. Pitman, London.

(1983) CSF Markers in Stroke. In: R Greenhalgh and F C Rose (eds.), Progress in Stroke Research. Pitman, London.

(1983) Morbidity of arch and carotid angiography prospective study. In: R M Greenhalgh and F C Rose (eds.), Progress in Stroke Research 2. Pitman, London, pp 136-153.

(1983) Multicenter General Practitioner Trial of Hydergine in Dementia Using a Screening Program – A Pilot Study. In: Aging Brain and Ergot Alkaloids. Raven Press, New York, pp 339-346.

(1983) Nervous Diseases. In: C W H Harvard (ed.), Current Medical Treatment. Balliere Tindall, London, pp 265-275.

(1983) Two chlobazam studies. In: F Rose and R Capildeo (eds.), Research Progress in Epilepsy. Pitman, London.

(1983) Epilepsy, Religiosity and Mystical States. In: R J Porter and A H Ward (eds.), Advances in Epileptology, vol XV. Raven Press, New York.

(1983) The Biochemical Investigation of Coma and Stupor. In: D L Williams and V Marks (eds.), Biochemistry in Clinical Practice. Heinemann, London, pp 413-425.

(1984) Aspirin in Migraine. In: RSM Symposium Series no 71, pp 82-86.

(1984) Neurotransmitters and Amino Acids in MND. In: F C Rose (ed.), Research Progress in MND. Biochemical Analysis of the CSF of ALS patients wih special reference to abnormal levels of neurotransmitters.

(1984) Epidemiological problems in stroke. In: N Callaghan and R Galvin (eds.), Recent Research in Neurology. Pitman, London, pp 63-67.

(1984) Markers of the migraine terrain. In: W K Amery, J M Van Nueten and A Warquier (eds.), The Pharmacological Basis of Migraine Therapy. Pitman Publishing, London, pp 191-201.

(1984) A case control study of amyotrophic lateral sclerosis. In: F C Rose (ed), Research Progress in Motor Neurone Disease. Pitman, London, pp14-19.

(1984) Autonomic function in motor neurone disease. In: Research Progress in Motor Neurone Disease. Pitman, London, pp 180-188.

(1984) Neurotransmitters and aminoacids in motor neurone disease. In: Research Progress in Motor Neurone Disease. Pitman, London, pp 276-282.

(1984) Histocompatibility typing in amyotrophic lateral sclerosis. In: F C Rose (ed.), Research Progress in Motor Neurone Disease. Pitman, London, pp 384-387.

(1984) Immunological changes in motor neurone disease. In: F C Rose (ed.), Research Progress in Motor Neurone Disease. Pitman, London, pp 368-378.

(1984) Dietary migraine: looking beyond tyramine. In: Progress in Migraine Research 2. Pitman Books, London, pp 113-119.

(1984) Involvement of Head Movements in Speech Production and Its Implications for Language Pathology. In: F C Rose (ed.), Progress in Aphasiology. Raven Press, New York, pp 247-262.

(1984) A Psychomotor Approach to Improving Speech by Modulating Suprasegmental Control in Motor Dysphasia and Articulatory Ataxia. In: F C Rose (ed.), Progress in Aphasiology. Karger, Basel, pp 337-352.

(1984) Urgent carotid surgery for progressing stroke. Successful intervention based on a clinical classification. In: R Courbier (ed.), Basis for a classification of cerebral arterial diseases. Elsevier Science (Excerpta Medical), Amsterdam, pp 132-138.

(1984) The classification and coding of stroke. In: R Courbier (ed.), Basis for a classification of cerebral arterial diseases. Elsevier Science (Excerpta Medical), Amsterdam, pp 294-300.

(1985) Does the Mode of Action of β-receptor Blockers in Migraine Involve Alteration of Platelet Function? In: F C Rose (ed.), Migraine Research and Clinical Advances Karger, Basel, Switzerland, pp 115-120.

(1985) Cluster Headache: a New Approach Using Fluorescent Histochemistry of Nerves in Temple Skin. In: F C Rose (ed.), Migraine: Clinical and Research Advances. Karger, Basel, Switzerland, pp 162-165.

(1985) Membrane Tranducing Mechanisms in Cluster Headache. In: F C Rose (ed.), Migraine: Clinical and Research Advances Karger, Basel, Switzerland, pp 166-168.

(1985) The Prevalence and Inheritance of Dietary Migraine. In: F C Rose (ed.), Migraine: Clinical and Research Advances.   Karger, Basel, Switzerland, pp 218-224.

(1985) Discussions. In: J D Carroll, V Pfaffenrath and O Sjaastad (eds.), Migraine and Beta-blockade   A B Hässle, Mölundal, Sweden, pp 170, 183 and 221.

(1985) Beta-blockers in migraine prophylaxis elevate plasma thromboxane levels. In: J Olesen, P Tfelt-Hansen and K Jensen (Eds.), Headache, 1985. Copenhagen (Second International Headache Congress), pp 416-417.

(1985) Leukotriene B4 Synthesis and release from leukocytes of migraine patients. In: J Olesen, P Tfelt-Hansen and K Jensen (eds.), Headache, 1985. Copenhagen, Denmark, , pp 478-479.

(1985) Double-blind dose-ranging comparison of metoprolol with placebo in the prophylaxis of classical and common migraine. In: J Olesen, P Tfelt-Hansen and K Jensen (Eds.), Headache, 1985. Copenhagen, Denmark, pp 558-559.

(1985) Diseases of the Nervous System and Associated Disorders. In: R D C Brackenridge (ed.), Medical Selection of Life Risks. Macmillan Publishers, London, pp 595-651.

(1985) Unilaterality of Headache and Focal Symptoms. In: V Pfaffenrach, P O Lundberg and O Sjaastad (eds.), Update in Headache.

(1985) Migraine prophylaxis. In: V Pfaffenrath, P O Lundberg and O Sjaastad (eds.), Up-date in Headache. Springer, Berlin, pp 177-180.

(1986) Headache: Definitions and classification. In: F C Rose (ed), Handbook of Clinical Neurology, Vol.4 (48) Headache. Elsevier, Amsterdam, pp 1-11.

(1986) With Peatfield R.C and Fozard J.R. Drug Treatment of Migraine In: F C Rose (ed.), Handbook of Clinical Neurology. Vol.4 (48) Headache. Elsevier, Amsterdam, pp 173-216.

(1986) Randomised double-blind placebo-controlled clinical trial of naftidrofuryl. In: Stroke: Epidemiological, Therapeutic and Socio-economic aspects. Royal Society of Medicine Services, London; pp: 85-100.

(1986) The Importance of Age in the Treatment of Acute Cerebral Infarction. In: Maurer et al (eds.), What's New in Angiology? Trends and controversies. Pratorium Zuckschwerdt, Munich.

(1986) Migraine Equivalents. In: W K Amery and A Wauquier (eds.), The Prelude to the Migraine Attack. Ballière Tindall, pp: 112-116.

(1986) Clioquinol. In: W Kalow, H W Goedde and D P A Garwal (eds.), Ethnic Differences in reactions to Drugs and Xenobiotics. A R Liss, New York, pp: 323-330.

(1987) Headache. In: G Adelman (ed.), Encyclopedia of Neuroscience, Vol.1. Birkhäuser, Boston, pp 481-482.

(1987) Migraine. In: G Adelman (ed.), Encyclopedia of Neuroscience, Vol.2. Birkhäuser, Boston, pp 668-669.

(1987) Cerebral blood flow imaging in migraine patients with [99M]Te-HM-PAO and single-photon emission tomography; preliminary findings and a report on its efficacy. In: Advances in Headache Research. John Libbey, London, pp 75-80.

(1987) Red wine as a migraine trigger. In: Advances in Headache Research. John Libbey, London, pp 123-128.

(1987) Leukotriene B4 levels in migraine and cluster headache. In: Advances in Headache Research. John Libbey, London, pp 203-208.

(1987) Preface. In: F C Rose and R Jones (eds.). Multiple Sclerosis: Immunological, diagnostic and therapeutic aspects. John Libbey, London,

(1987). Platelet-basophil interactions in migraine. In: Advances in Headache Research. John Libbey, London; pp: 45-50.

(1987) Effects of 17-β-oestradial on aggregability of platelets from migraine sufferers and normals, and the possible relevance to menstrual migraine. In: Advances in Headache Research. John Libbey, London, pp 51-58.

(1987) The composition of parkinsonian tremor: a behavioural study. In: Parkinson's Disease (Ed: F C Rose). John Libbey, London, pp 59-70.

(1987) The Role of Physioltherapy in the Management of Motor Neurone Disease. In: International Conference of Amyotrophic Lateral Sclerosis. Simul International, Osaka City, Japan, p 215.

(1987) The Management of Motor Neurone Disease. In: V Case et al (eds.), Amyotrophic Lateral Sclerosis: Therapeutic, Psychological and Research Aspects. Plenum, New York, pp 167-174.

(1988) Problems Encountered in the Assessment of Treatment of Headache and Migraine. In: A Hopkins (ed.), Headache: Problems. W B Saunders, London, pp 305-348.

(1988) Pain and disorders of consciousness: overview. In: Currer Opinions in Neurology and Neurosurgery. Gower, Vol.1, No.2, 176.

(1988) Preface. In: C Kennard and F C Rose (eds.), Physiological Aspects of Clinical Neuro-ophthalmology. Chapman and Hall, London, p XIII.

(1988) With Espir M.L.E. The Clinical Neurology of Aphasia In: F C Rose, R Whurr and M A Wyke (eds.), Aphasia. Whurr Publishers, London, pp 250-255.

(1988) Speech Fluency in Aphasia. In: F C Rose, R Whurr and M A Wyke (eds.), Aphasia. Whurr Publishers, London , pp 302-326.

(1988) Clinical Characterisation of Migraine. In: J Olesen (ed.), Basic Mechanisms of Headache. Elsevier, Amsterdam, pp 3-8.

(1988) Prophylactic Therapy. In: F C Rose (ed.), The Management of Headache Raven Press, New York, pp 81-96.

(1988. CSF Patterns in Different Types. In: R Hoefer (ed.), Radioactive Isotopes. pp 250-

(1988) Preface. In: Clinical Trial Methodology in Stroke. Ballière Tindall, London; pp: v and vi.

(1989) Preface. In: F C Rose (ed.), The Control of the Hypothalamo-Pituitary-Adrenocortical Axis. International Universities Press, Madison, USA, pp xix.

(1989) Nimodapine: a Calcium Entry Blocker; Platelets and Migraine. In: A Hartman et al (eds.), Central Ischaemia and Calcium. Springer Verlag, Berlin, pp 398-402.

(1989) Foreword. In: F C Rose (ed,), Neuroscience across the centuries. Smith-Gordon, London; p.vii.

(1989) Preface. In: F C Rose (ed,), James Parkinson: His Life and Times. Birkhäuser, Boston, pp v-vi.

(1989) Parkinsonism since Parkinson. In: F C Rose (ed.), James Parkinson: His Life and Times. Birkhäuser, Boston, pp 151-175.

(1989) Preface. In: F C Rose (ed.), New Advances in Headache Research. Smith-Gordon, London, p v.

(1989) The International Headache Society classification of headache. In: New Advances in Headache Research. Smith-Gordon, London, pp 1-8.

(1989) Reduced Tyramine Sulphoconjugation in Migraine in Relation to Depression. In: F C Rose (ed.), New Advances in Headache. Smith-Gordon, London, pp 169-174.

(1989) Caution in Extrapolating from Regional Cerebral Blood Flow Studies of Migraine to Hypotheses of Pathogenesis. In: F C Rose (ed.), New Advances in Headache. Smith-Gordon, London, pp 169-174.

(1989) Platelet Fibrinogen-binding Sites in Patients with Classical Migraine and Cluster Headache. In: F C Rose (ed.), New Advances in Headache. Smith-Gordon, London, pp 213-220.

(1989) Preface. In: F C Rose, R Jones and G Vrbova (eds.), Neuromuscular Stimulation. Demos Publications, New York.

(1989) A Comparison of Hospital Based and Community Services for Epilepsy in an Inner City London District. In Advances in Epilepsy, vol.17. Raven Press, New York.

(1990) Clinical Diagnosis and Therapy of Stroke. In: W Meier-Ruge (ed.), Vascular Brain Disease in Old Age. Karger, Basel, pp 135-175.

(1990) Introduction, Differential Diagnosis and Summing up the Future. In: Modern Management of Headache. IBC Technical Serviers.

(1990) Foreword and Preface. In: F C Rose (Ed.), Amyotrophic Lateral Sclerosis. Demos, New York; pp: v, vii-viii.

(1990. The Current Status of Migraine Therapy. In: M Sandler and G Collins (eds.), A Spectrum of Ideas. Oxford University Press, Oxford, pp 278-293.

(1990) Beta-adrenoceptor Blockers in the Prophylactic Treatment of Migraine. In: M Gallagher (ed.), Drug Therapy of Headache. Marcel Dekker, New York.

(1990) With P T G Davies. Aspirin in Headache and Migraine. In: J Vane and R Botting (eds.), Aspirin and Other Salicylates. Chapman and Hall, London.

(1990) Aspirin in Cerebrovascular Disease. In: J Vane and R Botting (eds.), Aspirin and other Salicylates. Chapman and Hall, London.

(1991) With Peatfield R.C. A prospective study of unilateral classical migraine. In: F C Rose (ed), New Advances in Headache Research 2. Smith-Gordon, London, pp 35-38.

(1991) Urinary tribulin output during migraine attacks. In: F C Rose (ed,), New Advances in Headache Research 2. Smith-Gordon, London, pp 149-154.

(1991) Membrane transduction in migraine and cluster headache. In: F C Rose (ed.), New Advances in Headache Research 2. Smith-Gordon, London, pp 161-164.

(1991) Anticardiolipin antibodies in vascular headache. In: F C Rose (ed.), New Advances in Headache Research 2. Smith-Gordon, London, pp 165-168.

(1992) Diseases of the Nervous System and Associated Disorders In: R D C Brackenridge and W J Elder (eds.), Medical Selection of Life Risks. Macmillan Publishers, Basingstoke, pp 727-782.

(1992) With Fields W.S. Aspirin in ischaemic stroke. In: J R Vane and R M Botting (eds.), Aspirin and Other Salicylates. Chapman & Hall, London, pp 354-372.

(1992) The effect of aspirin in headaches and migraine. In: J R Vane and R M Botting (eds.), Aspirin and Other Salicylates. Chapman & Hall, London, pp 373-394.

(1992) Preface. In: F C Rose (ed.), Parkinson's disease and the problems of clinical trials. Smith-Gordon, London, pp v-vi.

(1992) Preface. In: F C Rose (ed.), Molecular Genetics and Neurology. Smith-Gordon, London; p.v.

(1992) Drug Therapy for Headache. In: M Gallagher (ed.), Treatment of Migraine Headache-Prophylaxis. MarcelDekker, New York.

(1993) The treatment of primary headache. In: S C Gandevia, D Burke and M Anthony (eds.), Science and Practice in Clinical Neurology. Cambridge University Press, Cambridge, pp 334-362.

(1993) Prophylaxis of Migraine. In: K Ekbom (ed.), Migraine in General Practice. Smith-Gordon, London, pp 75-82.

(1993. Headache Clinics. In: J Olesen, P Tfelt-Hansen and K M A Welsh (eds.), The Headaches. Raven Press, New York, pp 865-870.

(1994) Charcot and motor neurone disease. In: F C Rose (ed.), A.L.S – from Charcot to the present and into the future. Smith-Gordon, London, pp 337-340.

(1994) Preface. In: New Advances in Headache Research 3. Smith-Gordon, London; p:v.

(1994) Preface. In: F C Rose (ed.), Recent Advances in Tropical Neurology. Elsevier Science, Amsterdam, p: v.

(1996) The History of Cerebral Trauma. In: R W Evans (ed.), Neurology and Trauma. W B Saunders, Philadelphia, pp 18-27.

(1996) Preface. In: F C Rose (ed.), Towards Migraine 2000. Elsevier, Amsterdam.

(1997) History of the Methodology of Headache Trials. In: : J Olesen and P Tfelt-Hansen (eds.), Headache Treatment: Trial Methodology and New Drugs. Lippincott-Raven, New York, pp 3-14.

(1998) Diseases of the Nervous System (with Brackenridge R D C) In: R D C Brackenridge (ed.), Medical Selection of Life Risks Macmillan Reference, London, pp 749-788.

(1999) John Fothergill (1712-1780). In: A Short History of Neurology: The British Contribution 1660-1910. Butterworth-Heinemann, Oxford, pp 88-92.

(1999) James Parkinson (1755-1824). In: A Short History of Neurology: The British Contribution 1660-1910. Butterworth-Heinemann, Oxford, pp 108-116.

(1999) Three early nineteenth century British neurological texts. In: A Short History of Neurology: The British Contribution 1660-1910. Butterworth-Heinemann, Oxford, pp 117-131.

(2000) With Isler H. Historical Background. In: J Olesen, P Tfelt-Hansen and K M A Welch (eds.), The Headaches, Second Edition   Lippincott Williams and Wilkins, Philadelphia, USA, Chapter 1.

(2001) Preface. In: Twentieth Century Neurology: The British Contribution. Imperial College Press, London.

(2003) Preface. In: S Neilson and F C Rose (eds.), Motor Neurone Disease at Younr Fingertips. Class Publishing, London, pp xi-xii

(2003) Marshall Hall. In: M J Aminoff and R B Daroff (eds.), Vol.2. Academic Press, Amsterdam, pp 449-450

(2003) Charles Bell. In: M J Aminoff and R B Daroff (eds.), Vol.1. Academic Press, Amsterdam, pp 374

(2003) Macdonald Critchley. In: M J Aminoff and R B Daroff (eds.), Vol.1. Academic Press, Amsterdam, pp 802

(2003) Henry Head. In: M J Aminoff and R B Daroff (eds.), Vol.2. Academic Press, Amsterdam, pp 508

(2003) Gordon Holmes. In: M J Aminoff and R B Daroff (eds.), Encyclopedia of the Neurological Sciences.Vol.2. Academic Press, Amsterdam, pp 579-580

(2003) James Parkinson. In: M J Aminoff and R B Daroff (eds.),Encyclopedia of the Neurological Sciences. Vol.3 Academic Press, Amsterdam, pp: 816

(2003) S A Kinnier Wilson. In: M J Aminoff and R B Daroff (eds.), Encyclopedia of the Neurological Sciences Vol.4. Academic Press, Amersterdam, pp 758-759.

(2004) The Neurology of Art: An Overview. In: F C Rose (ed.), Neurology of the Arts. Imperial College Press, London, pp 43-76.

(2004) Silas Marner, George Eliot and Catalepsy. In: F C Rose (ed.), Neurology of the Arts. Imperial College Press, London, pp 421-432.

(2006) A Naïve Artist of St Ives. In: F C Rose (ed.), The Neurobiology of Painting. Elsevier, Amsterdam, pp 241-252.

(2006) Van Gogh's Madness. In: F C Rose (ed.), The Neurobiology of Painting. Elsevier, Amsterdam, pp 253-269.

(2006) The Deafness of Goya (1746-1828). In: F C Rose (ed.), The Neurobiology of Painting. Elsevier, Amsterdam, pp 301-315.

(2006) The History of Cerebral Trauma. In: R W Evans (ed.), Neurology and Trauma, 2nd Edition. Oxford University Press, Oxford, pp 19-29.

(2009).History of Neurology. In: S Finger, F Buller and K.L Tyler (eds.), Handbook of Clinical Neurology, vol. 95 (3rd Series). Elsevier, Amersterdam, Chapter 39.

PAPERS

1.   (1952) Congenital anterior angulation of the tibia (with Bound J.P, Finlay H.V). *Arch. Dis. Child*, Apr; 27 (132): 179-84

2.   (1954) The effect of periarticular procaine infiltration on joint temperature (with Fletcher E and Jacobs J.H). *Ann. Phys. Med.*, Oct; 2 (4): 123-7

3.   (1954) The familial occurrence of ankylosing spondylitis (with Jacobs J.H). *Br. Med. J.*, Nov. 13; 4897: 1139-40

4.   (1955) Pneumonia occurring during ACTH and cortisone therapy (with Jacobs J.H). *Tubercle.*, Apr; 36 (4): 113-8

5.   (1955) Psoriasis spondylitica (with Fletcher E). *Lancet*, Apr. 2; 268 (6866): 695-6

6.   (1958) Thoracic actinomycosis (with Jepson E.M and Tonkin R.D). *Br. Med. J.*, May 3; 14 (5078): 1025-7

7.   (1958) Robert Boyle's uncommon observations about vitiated sight (London, 1688) (with Hunter R.A). *Br. J. Ophthalmol.*, Dec; 42 (12): 726-31

8.   (1958) Torulosis of the central nervous system in Britain (with Grant H.C and Jeanes A.L). *Brain*, Dec; 81 (4): 542-55

9.   (1960) Neuropathies in rheumatic disease and steroid therapy. *Proc. R. Soc. Med.*, Jan; 53 (1): 51-53

10.   (1960) Persistent memory defect following encephalitis (with Symonds C.P). *Brain*, 83: 195-212

11.   (1960) Peripheral neuropathy in the "collagen diseases": a case of scleroderma neuropathy (with Kibler R.F). *Br. Med. J.*, Jun; 11 (5188): 1781-4

12.   (1960) A leucine-sensitive insulin-secreting tumour (with Marrack D and Marks V). *Lancet*, Dec; 17 (2): 1329-30

13.   (1961) Hyperinsulinism in the pathogenesis of neuroglycopenic syndromes (with Marks V and Marrack D). *Proc. R. Soc. Med.*, Sep; 54: 747-9

14.   (1961) Carcinomatous neuropathy with papilloedema. *Proc. R. Soc. Med.*, <u>55</u>: 236

15.   (1961) Glucagon and tolbutamide tests in the recognition of insulinomas (with Marrack D and Marks V). *Proc. R. Soc. Med.*, Sep; 54: 749-52

16.   (1962) The neuroglycopenic syndromes (with Williams D). *Electroenceph. Clin. Neurophysiol.*, 14: 790

17.   (1962) Chordome intracranien. *Rev. Neurol.*, Mai; 3/4: 501-502

18.   (1964) Zoster encephalomyelitis (with Brett E.M and Burston J). *Arch. Neurol.*, Aug; 11: 155-72

19.   (1964) Endoxana (Cyclophosphamide) in the treatment of intracerebral malignancy (with Bhagwati S.N and McKissock W). *J. Neurol. Neurosurg. Psychiatry*, Oct: 27: 470-2

20.   (1964) Optic Atrophy. *Postgrad. Med. J.*, Dec: 40: 692-5

21.   (1964) L'EEG dans l'anévrysme intracranien rompu. *Rev. Neurol.*, 111 (4): 383-385

22.   (1964) The Chromosomal pattern in Leber's disease (with Friedmann A.I). *J. Med. Genet.*, Dec; 38: 110-1

23.   (1965) Compressive visual failure (with Richardson A). *Trans. Ophthalmol. Soc. U.K.*, 85: 421-7

24.   (1965) The neuro-ophthalmological complications of diabetes. *Proc. R. Soc. Med.*, <u>58</u> (7): 537-538

25.   (1965) Epilepsy after ruptured intracranial aneurysm (with Sarner M). *Br. Med. J.*, Jan (2); 5426: 18-21

26.   (1965) Hyperinsulinism due to metastasizing insulinoma: treatment with diazoxide (with Marks V and Samols E). *Proc. R. Soc. Med.*, Aug; (58): 577-8

27.   Rose F.C, Fraser G.R, Friedmann A.I and Kohner E.M (1966). The association of juvenile diabetes mellitus and optic atrophy: clinical and genetical aspects. *Q. J. Med.*, Jul 35 (139): 385-405

28.   (1967) The diagnosis of pyogenic meningitis (with Condon J). *Postgrad. Med. J.*, May; 43 (499): 376-8

29.   (1967)   Clinical presentation of ruptured intracranial aneurysm (with Sarner M). *J. Neurol. Neurosurg. Psychiatry*, <u>30</u>: 67-70

30.   (1967) Papilloedema in sarcoidosis (with James D.G, Zatouroff M.A and Trowell J). *Br. J. Ophthalmol.*, Aug; 51 (8): 526-9

31.   (1967) Optic nerve glioma (with Condon J.R). *Br. J. Ophthalmol.*, Oct; 51 (10): 703-6

32.   (1967) Recent advances in neuro-ophthalmology (summary). *Proc. R. Soc. Med.*, <u>61</u> (2): 122-123

33. (1968) Werner's syndrome (with James D and Kohner E.M). *Ghana Medical Journal*, 7 (1): 41-49

34. (1969) Dysthyroid eye disease. A trial of guanethidine eye drops (with Bowden A.N). *Br. J. Ophthalmol.*, Apr; 53 (4): 246-51

35. (1969. Investigations of endocrine exophthalmos (with Bowden A.N). *Proc. R. Soc. Med.*, 62 (1): 13-15

36. (1969) The neurological manifestations of dissecting aneurysm of the aorta (with Condon J.R). *Postgrad. Med. J.*, Jul; 45 (525): 419-22

37. (1969) Receptive aphasia in childhood. *Proc. Soc. Brit. Neurological Surg.*

38. (1969. Transient blindness. *Br. Med. J.*, Sep 27; 3 (673): 763-4

39. (1970) Difficulties in optic nerve and chiasmic compression (with Friedmann A.I). *Trans. Ophthalmol. Soc. U.K.*, 90; 79-91

40. (1970) Problems associated with pallor of the disc of non-ocular aetiology. *Trans. Ophthalmol. Soc. U.K.*, xc: 211

41. (1970. The heart in Leber's optic atrophy (with Bowden A.N and Bowden P.M). *Br. J. Ophthalmol.*, Jun; 54 (6): 388-93

42. (1970) Speech disorders in children. *Lond. Clin. Med. J.*, Jul; 11 (2): 39-46

43. (1970. The aetiology of optic neuritis. *Clin. Sci.*, Dec; 39 (6): 17P

44. (1971) The radiological investigation and surgical treatment of sudden blindness due to extra-cranial vascular lesions (with Bliss B.P and Harington M). *Trans. Ophthalmol. Soc. U.K.*, 91: 261-6

45. (1972) Strabismus (with Arnott E.J). *Brit. J. Hosp. Med.*, Dec: 717-730

46.	(1972). The aetiology of optic neuritis. *Monogr. Hum. Genet.*, 6: 196

47.	(1972) Speech and language disorders in children. *Trans. Med. Soc. Lond.*, 88: 72-6

48.	(1972) Speech and language disorders in children. *Midwife Health Visit.*, Apr; 8 (4): 139-41

49.	(1973) Geriatric neuro-ophthalmology. *Proc. R. Soc. Med.*, Feb; 66 (2): 161-2

50.	(1973) Acquired ocular palsy. *Brit. Orthopt. J.*, 30: 17-22

51.	(1973) Disorders of memory. *Brit. J. Hosp. Med.*, Feb: 225-232

52.	(1974) Medical ophthalmology. *Trans. Med. Soc. Lond.*, 90: 87-96 Review

53.	(1974) Effect of cerebrovascular lesions on speech. *Health (special stroke issue)*: 19-22

54.	(1974) A trial of corticotrophin gelatine injection in acute optic neuritis (with Bowden A.N, Bowden P.M, Friedmann A.I and Perkin G.D). *J. Neurol. Neurosurg. Psychiatry*, Aug; 37 (8): 869-73

55.	(1974) Neuro-ophthalmology. *J. R. Coll. Physicians Lond.*, Oct; 9 (1): 79-86

56.	(1975-77) Motor neurone disease. *Trans. Med. Soc. Lond.*, 92-93: 121-6

57.	(1975) Smoking and optic neuritis (with Perkin G.D and Bowden P). *Postgrad. Med. J.*, Jun; 51 (596): 382-5

58.	(1975) Relapsing meningoencephalitis ? cerebral sarcoidosis. *Proc. R. Soc. Med.*, Sep; 68 (9): 594-6

59. (1976) Uhthoff's Syndrome (with Perkin G.D). *Brit. J. Ophthal.*, 60 (1); 60-63

60. (1976) The Migraine Clinic at Charing Cross Hospital. *Hemicrania.* Leading article; 2-5.

61. (1976) Social network diagram (with Capildeo R and Court C). *Br. Med. J.*, Jan 17; 1 (6002): 143-4

62. (1976) The metabolic and hormonal response to glucagons. Part 1. Normal subjects (with Goodwin P.M, Capildeo R, Harrop J S and Marks V). *J. Neurol. Sci.*, Mar; 27 (3): 373-80

63. (1976) The metabolic and hormonal response to glucagons. Part 2. In patients with migraine (with Goodwin P.M, Capildeo R, Harrop J S and Marks V). *J. Neurol. Sci.*, Mar; 27 (3): 381-8

64. (1976) Nomifensine in parkinsonism (with Teychenne P F, Park D M, Findley LJ, and Calne D B). *J. Neurol. Neurosurg. Psychiatry*, Dec; 39 (12): 1219-21

65. (1977) Transitory decrease in platelet monoamine-oxidase activity during migraine attacks (with Glover V, Sandler M, Grant E, Orton D, Wilkinson M and Stevens D). *Lancet*, Feb 19; 1 (8008): 391-3

66. (1977) Schistosomal myelopathy (with Cohen J, Capildeo R and Pallis C. *Br. Med. J.*, May 14; 1 (6071): 1258

67. (1977) New classification of stroke: preliminary communication (with Capildeo R and Haberman S). *Br. Med. J.*, Dec 17; 2 (6102): 1578-80

68. (1978) The changing mortality of cerebrovascular disease (with Haberman S and Capildeo R). *Q. J. Med.*, Jan; 47 (185): 71-88

69. (1978) Visual evoked potentials in migraine subjects (with Kennard C, Gawel M and Rudolph N M). *Res. Clin. Stud. Headache*, 6: 73-80

70. (1978) The definition and classification of stroke. A new approach (with Capildeo R and Haberman S). *Q. J. Med.*, Apr; 47 (186): 177-96

71. (1978). Speech disorders and neurological diagnosis. *Practitioner.* Jul; 221 (1321): 85-8

72. (1979-80). The aetiology of optic neuritis. *Trans. Med. Soc. Lond.*, 96: 41-3

73. (1979-80) Stroke: 1980. The third killer: prevention, treatment and cure. *Trans. Med. Soc. Lond.*, 96: 48-65

74. (1979) New approach to treatment of recent stroke (with Steiner T. and Capildeo R). *Br. Med. J.*, Feb 10; 1 (6160): 412

75. (1979) Exercise and hormonal secretion (with Gawel M.J, Park D.M and Alaghband-Zadeh J). *Postgrad. Med. J.*, Jun; 55 (644): 373-6

76. (1979) Disturbed liver function in migraine patients (with Williams D.C). *Headache*, Jul; 19 (5): 270-2

77. (1979) Extracranial to intracranial micro-revascularization for the treatment of completed ischaemic stroke (with Greenhalgh R.M, Illingworth R.D, McFie J, Mills S.P and Perkin G.D). *Br. Med. J.*, Jul 7; 2 (6181): 18-9

78. (1979) The platelet release reaction during migraine attacks (with Gawel M and Burkitt M). *Headache*, Sep; 19 (6): 323-7

79. (1979) Neurotoxicity of halogenated hydroxyquinolines: clinical analysis of cases reported outside Japan (with Baumgartner G, Gawel M.J, Kaeser H.E, Pallis C.A, Schaumburg H.H, Thomas P.K and Wadia N.H). *J. Neurol. Neurosurg. Psychiatry*, Dec; 42 (12): 1073-83

80. (1980) Cholesterol crystal embolization in rat brain: a model for atheroembolic cerebral infarction (with Steiner T.J and Rail D.L). *Stroke*, Mar-Apr; 11 (2): 184-9

81. (1980) Platelet activation following cerebral angiography (with Gawel M and Burkett M). *Acta. Neurol. Scand.*, Apr; 61 (4): 240-3

82. (1980) Posture and headache after lumbar puncture (with Smith F.R and Perkin G.D). *Lancet*, Jun 7; 1 (8180): 1245

83. (1980) The eye as a mirror of systemic disease (with Fasler J). *Br. J. Anaesth.*, Jul; 52 (7): 695-703

84. (1980) Migraine in patients attending a migraine clinic: an analysis by computer of age, sex and family history (with Steiner T.J, Guha P and Capildeo R). *Headache*, Jul; 20 (4): 190-5

85. (1980) West Indian amblyopia (with Fasler J). *Postgrad. Med. J.*, Jul; 56 (657): 494-500

86. (1980) Extracranial to intracranial micro-revascularization for the treatment of completed ischaemic stroke (with Greenhalgh R.M, Illingworth R.D, McFie J, Mills S.P and Perkin G.D). *Am. Heart J.*, Dec; 100 (6 Pt 1): 937-8

87. (1981-82) Failing memory. *Trans. Med. Soc. Lond.*, 98: 11-6

88. (1981) The specific activity of platelet monoamine oxidase varies with platelet count during severe exercise and noradrenaline infusion (with Gawel M.J, Glover V, Burkitt M and Sandler M). *Psychopharmacology (Berl.)*, 72 (3): 275-7

89. (1981) Visual and auditory evoked responses in patients with Parkinson's disease (with Gawel M.J, Das P and Vincent S). *J. Neurol. Neurosurg. Psychiatry*, Mar; 44 (3): 227-32

90. (1981) Sex differences in the incidence of cerebrovascular disease (with Haberman S and Capildeo R). *J. Epidemiol. Community Health*, Mar; 35 (1): 45-50

91. (1981) Communication aids in patients with motor neurone disease (with Perry A R and Gawel M). *Br. Med. J. (Clin. Res. Ed.)*, May 23; 282 (6277): 1690-2

92. (1981) Pentoxifylline for prevention of transient ischaemic attacks (with Gawel M J and Steiner T.J). *Lancet*, Jun 6; 1 (8232): 1266

93. (1981) Ranitidine in migraine (with Peatfield R C). *Ann. Neurol.*, Jul; 10 (1): 61

94. (1981) Migrainous visual symptoms in a woman without eyes (with Peatfield R C). *Arch. Neurol.*, Jul; 38 (7): 466

95. (1981) Exacerbation of migraine by treatment with lithium (with Peatfield R C). *Headache*, Jul; 21 (4): 140-2

96. (1981)Differential contributions of major lipid components of atheroma to outcome of cerebral atheroembolism. A study in an animal model (with Rail D L and Steiner T J). *Stroke*, Jul-Aug; 12 (4): 445-53

97. (1981) Reactive hyperaemia and migraine (with Peatfield R.C and Gawel M J). *Lancet*, Aug 8; 2 (8241): 305

98. (1981) The effect of infused prostacyclin in migraine and cluster headache (with Peatfield R C and Gawel M J). *Headache*, Sep; 21 (5): 190-5

99. (1981) Platelet monoamine oxidase activity and headache (with Glover V, Peatfield R, Zammit-Pace R, Littlewood J, Gawel M, and Sandler M). *J. Neurol. Neurosurg. Psychiatry*, Sep; 44 (9): 786-90

100. (1981) Asymmetry of the aura and pain in migraine (with Peatfield R C, and Gawel M J). *J. Neurol. Neurosurg. Psychiatry*, Sep; 44 (9): 846-8

101. (1981) Treatment of migraine and cluster headache (with Peatfield R C). *Practitioner*, Sep; 225 (1359): 1321-5

102. (1981) The seasonal variation in mortality from cerebrovascular disease (with Haberman S, and Capildeo R). *J. Neurol. Sci.*, Oct; 52 (1): 25-36

103. (1981) Effect of levodopa on thyroid function and prolactin release. A study in patients with Parkinson's disease (with Lavin P J, Gawel M J, Das P K, and Alaghband-Zadeh J). *Arch. Neurol.*, Dec; 38 (12): 759-60

104. (1982) Platelet function in migraineurs (with Gawel M.J). *Adv. Neurol.*, 33: 237-42. Review

105. (1982-84) Presidential address. The medicine of art. *Trans. Med. Soc. Lond.*, 99-100: 53-9

106. (1982) The Princess Margaret Migraine Clinic, Charing Cross Hospital, London. *Panminerva. Med.*, Jan-Mar; 24 (1): 29-31

107. (1982) Platelet aggregation, beta-blockers, and migraine (with Petty R G). *Lancet*, Feb 6; 1 (8267): 337

108. (1982) Dysarthria (with Espir M L). *Br. J. Hosp. Med.*, Mar; 27 (3): 269, 273-5

109. (1982) Treatment of migraine and cluster headache (with Peatfield R C). *Panminerva Med.*, Apr-Jun; 24 (2): 85-7

110. (1982) Platelet phenolsulphotransferase deficiency in dietary migraine (with Littlewood J, Glover V, Sandler M, Petty R, and Peatfield R). *Lancet*, May 1; 1 (8279): 983-6

111. (1982) Migraine patients exhibit abnormalities in the visual evoked potential (with Connolly J F, and Gawel M). *J. Neurol. Neurosurg. Psychiatry*, May; 45 (5): 464-7

112. (1982) Neuroepidemiology in the developing countries (with Capildeo R, and Haberman S). *J. R. Soc. Med.*, May; 75 (5): 305-6

113. (1982) Platelet monoamine oxidase: specific activity and turnover number in headache (with Summers K M, Brown G K, Craig I.W, Littlewood J, Peatfield R, Glover V, and Sandler M). *Clin. Chim. Acta.*, May 20; 121 (2): 139-46

114. (1982) Posture and lumbar puncture headache: a controlled trial in 50 patients (with Handler C E, Smith F R, and Perkin G D). *J. R. Soc. Med.*, Jun; 75 (6): 404-7

115. (1982) North West Thames registry of neurological disease (with Haberman S, Benjamin B, and Capildeo R). *J. R. Soc. Med.*, Jun; 75 (6): 443-9

116. (1982) Diverging trends in cerebrovascular disease and ischaemic heart disease (with Haberman S, and Capildeo R). *Stroke*, Sep-Oct; 13 (5): 582-9

117. (1982) Platelet size: no correlation with migraine or monoamine oxidase activity (with Peatfield R C, Gawel M J, Guthrie D L, Pearson T C, Glover V, Littlewood J, and Sandler M). *J. Neurol. Neurosurg.*, Sep; 45 (9): 826-9

118. (1982) Cluster headache in women (with Peatfield R C, and Petty R G). *Cephalalgia*, Sep; 2 (3): 171-2

119. (1982) Single-dose pizotifen, 1.5 mg nocte: a new approach in the prophylaxis of migraine (with Capildeo R). *Headache*, Nov; 22 (6): 272-5

120. (1982) A comparison of phenytoin and pheneturide in patients with epilepsy: a double-blind cross-over trial (with Gibberd F B, Park D , Scott G, Gawel M J, Fry D E, Page N G, Engler C, and English J R). *J. Neurol. Neurosurg. Psychiatry*, Dec; 45 (12): 1113-8

121. (1983) Why neuroepidemiology? (with Capildeo R. Haberman S, and Benjamin B). *Psychol. Med.*, Feb; 13 (1): 15-6

122. (1983) Chronic paroxysmal hemicrania: first reported British case (with Petty R.G). *Br. Med. J. (Clin. Res. Ed.)*, Feb 5; 286 (6363): 438

123. (1983) Biochemical predisposition to dietary migraine: the role of phenolsulphotransferase (with Glover V, Littlewood J, Sandler M, Peatfield R, and Petty R). *Headache*, Mar; 23 (2): 53-8

124. (1983) Migraine patients exhibit abnormalities in the visual evoked potential (with Gawel M, and Connolly J.F). *Headache*, Mar; 23 (2): 49-52

125. (1983) An emergency domiciliary stroke unit (with Steiner T.J). *Practitioner*, Mar; 227 (1377): 457-61

126. (1983) Head movement correlates of juncture and stress at sentence level (with Hadar U, Steiner T.J, and Grant E.C). *Lan. Speech*, Apr-Jun; 26 (Pt. 2): 117-29

127. (1983) CT changes associated with migraine (with De Boulay G.H, Ruiz J.S, Stevens J.M and Zilkha K.J). *AJNR Am. J. Neuroradiol.*, May-Jun; 4 (3): 472-3

128. (1983) Paroxysmal language disturbance in an epileptic treated with clobazam (with Wilson A, Petty R, and Perry A). *Neurology*, May; 33 (5): 652-4

129. (1983) Double blind comparison of mefenamic acid and acetaminophen (paracetamol) in migraine (with Peatfield R.C, and Petty R.G). *Cephalalgia*, Jun; 3 (2): 129-34

130. (1983) Food related antibodies in headache patients (with Merrett J, Peatfield R.C, and Merrett T.G). *J. Neurol. Neurosurg. Psychiatry*, Aug; 46 (8): 738-42

131. (1983) Pressor sensitivity to tyramine in patients with headache: relationship to platelet monoamine oxidase and to dietary provocation (with Peatfield R, Littlewood J T, Glover V, and Sandler M). *J. Neurol. Neurosurg. Psychiatry*, Sep; 46 (9): 827-31

132. (1983) Antecedent events in motor neuron disease (with Gawel M, and Zaiwalla Z). *J. Neurol. Neurosurg. Psychiatry*, Nov; 46 (11): 1041-3

133. (1983) Migraine: definition and classification (with Capildeo R). *Cephalalgia*, Dec; 3 (4): 225-9

134. (1983) Development of a neurological score for the clinical evaluation of sylvian infarctions (with Orgogozo J.M, Capildeo R, Anagnostou C.N, Juge O, Pere J.J, Dartigues J.F, Steiner T.J, and Yotis A). *Presse Med.*, Dec 29; 12 (48): 3039-44. French

135. (1983) Identification, evaluation and treatment of dementia patients in society (with Capildeo R, and Wallace M.G). *Presse Med.*, Dec 29; 12 (48): 3176-8. French

136. (1984). Progress in aphasiology. Introduction. *Adv. Neurol.*, 42: 1-

137. (1984) Clioquinol neurotoxicity: an overview (with Gawel M). *Acta. Neurol. Scand. Suppl.*, 100: 137-45. Review

138. (1984) Migraine and cluster headache: links between platelet monoamine oxidase activity, smoking and personality (with Littlewood J.T, Glover V, Sandler M, Petty R, and Peatfield R). *Headache*, Jan; 24 (1): 30-4

139. (1984) Erythrocyte choline concentrations and cluster headache (with de Belleroche J, Cook G E, Das I, Joseph R, Tresidder I, Rouse S, and Petty R). *Br. Med. J. (Clin. Res. Ed.)*, Jan 28; 288 (6413): 268-70

140. (1984) Leprosy masked by steroids (with Prendiville J.S, Cream J.J, Scott J.T, Woodrow D F and Water M F). *Br. Med. J. (Clin. Res. Ed.)*, Mar 10; 288 (6419): 770-1

141. (1984) Low platelet monoamine oxidase activity in headache: no correlation with phenolsulphotransferase, succinate dehydrogenase, platelet preparation method or smoking (with Littlewood J, Glover V, Sandler M, Peatfield R, and Petty R). *J. Neurol. Neurosurg. Psychiatry*, Apr; 47 (4): 338-43

142. (1984) The prevalence of diet-induced migraine (with Peatfield R.C, Glover V, Littlewood J.T, and Sandler M). *Cephalalgia*. Sep; 4 (3): 179-83

143. (1984) Metabolic abnormality in cluster headache (with de Belleroche J, Das I and Cook G.E). *Headache*, Nov; 24 (6): 310-2

144. (1984) Involvement of head movement in speech production and its implication for language pathology (with Hadar U, and Steiner T.J). *Adv. Neurol.*, 42: 247-61

145. (1984) Neurotoxicity of halogenated hydroxyquinolines (with Baumgartner G, Gilland O, Kaeser H.E, Pallis C.A, Schaumburg H.H, Thomas P.K and Wadia N.H). *J. Neurol. Neurosurg. Psychiatry*, Jan; 47 (1): 100

146. (1984) Elevated levels of amino acids in the CSF of motor neuron disease patients (with de Belleroche J, and Recordati A). *Neurochem. Pathol.*, Spring; 2 (1): 1-6

147. (1984) Platelet monoamine oxidase activity and headache: relationship to personality and smoking (with Glover V, Littlewood J T, Sandler M, Peatfield R, and Petty R). *Psychopharmacol. Bull.*, Summer; 20 (3): 536-8

148. (1984) A psychomotor approach to improving speech by modulating suprasegmental control in motor dysphasia and articulatory apraxia (with Hardar U, Twiston-Davies R, and Steiner T J). *Adv. Neurol.*, 42; 337-51

149. (1984) Platelet phenolsulfotransferase activity and the headache spectrum (with Sandler M, Littlewood J.T, Glover V, Peatfield R, and Petty R). *Psychopharmacol. Bull.*, Summer; 20 (3): 539-41

150. (1984) Central distal axonopathy syndromes: newly recognised models of natural occurring human degenerative disease (with Thomas P K, Schaumburg H H, Spencer P.S, Kaeser H E, Pallis C.A, and Wadia N H). *Ann. Neurol.*, Apr; 15 (4): 313-5

151. (1984) The relationship between head movements and speech dysfluencies (with Hadar U, and Steiner T.J). *Lang. Speech*, Oct-Dec; 27 (Pt. 4): 333-42

152. (1985) Beta-blockers used in migraine prophylaxis elevate plasma thromboxane levels (with Joseph R, Steiner T J, Das I and Schultz L.U.C). *Cephalalgia Suppl.3*: 416-7

153. (1985) The classification of headache. *Neuroepidemiology*, 4 (4): 193-203

154. (1985) Bilateral pontine gaze palsy. Nuclear magnetic resonance findings in presumed multiple sclerosis (with Joseph R, Pullicino P, and Goldberg C D). *Arch. Neurol.*, Jan; 42 (1): 93-4

155. (1985) The effects of exercise on platelet numbers and size Peatfield R C, Gawel M J, Guthrie D L and Pearson T.C. *Med. Lab. Sci.*, Jan; 42 (1): 40-3

156. (1985) Intracranial space-occupying lesions in patients attending a migraine clinic (with Joseph R, Cook G.E, and Steiner T.J). *Practitioner*, May; 229 (1403): 477-81

157. (1985 Aspects of stroke trials. *Br. J. Clin. Pract. Suppl.*, June; 39: 34-9

158. (1985) Cultured rat spinal cord neurons: interaction with motor neuron disease immunoglobulins (with Digby J. Harrison R, Jehanli A, and Lunt G.G). *Muscle Nerve*, Sep; 8 (7): 595-605

159. (1985) Serotoninergic immunofluorescent nerve fibres appear in human temple skin after lithium treatment (with Dhital K. Steiner T, Joseph R, Adams J, Appenzeller O and Burnstock G). *Lancet*, Oct 5; 2 (8458): 779

160. (1985) Problems in the management of stroke. *Ann. Acad. Med. Singapore*, Jan; 14 (1): 12-5

161. (1985) The role of platelets in migraine. *Cephalalgia*, May; 5 Suppl 2: 83-5

162. (1985) Thromboxane synthetase inhibition: potential therapy in migraine (with Joseph R, Steiner T.J, Poole C.J, and Littlewood J). *Headache*, June; 25 (4): 204-7

163. (1985) Cluster headache and herpes simplex: an association? (with Joseph R). *Br. Med. J. (Clin. Res. Ed.)*, Jun 2; 290 (6482): 1625-6

164. (1985) Migraine is not a platelet disorder (with Steiner T J, and Joseph R). *Headache*, Nov; 25 (8): 434-40

165. (1985) Is there a place for placebo controlled trials of antiepileptic drugs? (with Shorvon S D, Espir M L, Steiner T J, and Dellaportas C I). *Br. Med. J. (Clin. Res. Ed.)*, Nov 9; 291 (6505): 1328-9

166. (1986) Platelet release reaction in migraine may be beneficial (with Joseph R, Steiner T.J, Sitsapeson M, Das I and Hadar U). *Neurology*, Suppl. 36: 1100

167. (1986) Towards a model stroke trial. The single-centre naftidrofuryl study (with Steiner T J). *Neuroepidemiology*, 5 (3): 121-47

168. (1986) Ethnic differences in drugs and xenobiotics. Clioquinol. *Prog. Clin. Biol. Res.*, 214: 323-30

169. (1986) Determination of free choline in plasma and erythrocyte samples and choline derived from membrane phosphatidylcholinby a chemiluminescence method (with Das I, de Belleroche J, and Moore C J). *Annal. Biochem.*, Jan; 152 (1): 178-82

170. (1986) Headache clinics: their role in health care systems and science. *Headache*, Mar; 26 (3): 112-6

171. (1986) Abnormal membrane composition and membrane-dependent transduction mechanisms in cluster headache (with de Belleroche J, Kilfeather S, and Das I). *Cephalalgia*, Sep; 6 (3): 147-53

172. (1986) Multiple sclerosis: increased expression of interleukin-2 receptors on lymphocytes (with Selmaj K, Plater-Zyberk C, Rockett K.A, Maini R.N, Alam R, and Perkin G.D). *Neurology*, Oct; 36 (10): 1392-5

173. (1986) Leukotriene B4 generation by polymorphonuclear leukocytes: possible involvement in the pathogenesis of headache (with Selmaj K, de Belleroche J, and Das I). *Headache*, Oct; 26 (9): 460-4

174. (1986) Trigger factors and natural history of migraine. *Funct. Neurol.*, Oct-Dec; 1 (4): 379-84

175. (1986) Visual hallucinations and migraine (with Arnaud J.L, Diamond S and Arnaud P). *Funct. Neurol.*, Oct-Dec; 1 (4): 473-9

176. (1987) Headache – including migraine (with Davies P.T.G). *Hospital Update*, Oct: 763-777

177. (1987) Laterality of pain in migraine distinguished by interictal rates of habitual or electrodermal responses to visual and auditory stimuli (with Gruzelier J.H, Nicolaou T, Connolly J F, Peatfield R C, and Davies P T). *J. Neurol. Neurosurg. Psychiatry*, Apr; 50 (4): 416-22

178. (1987) Parkinson's disease: further steps forward (with Nashef L). *Gerontology*, 33 (6): 369-73

179. (1987) The management of motor neurone disease. *Adv. Exp. Med. Biol.*, 209: 167-74

180. (1987) Neurological morbidity of cerebral arteriography in cerebrovascular disease: the effect of contrast medium and radiologist (with McIvor J, Steiner T J, Perkin G D, and Greenhalgh R M). *Ann. Radiol. (Paris)*, 30 (2): 125-7

181. (1987) Neurological morbidity of arch and carotid arteriography in cerebrovascular disease. The influence of contrast medium and radiologist (with McIvor J, Steiner T J, Perkin G D, and Greenhalgh R M). *Br. J. Radiol.*, Feb; 60 (710): 117-22

182. (1987) Do migrainous headaches become more consistently lateralised? (with Peatfield R C, and Bond R A). *Cephalalgia*, Mar; 7 (1): 73-5

183. (1987) T lymphocyte-derived demyelinating activity in multiple sclerosis patients in relapse (with Selmaj K, Alam R, and Perkin G.D). *J. Neurol. Neurosurg. Psychiatry*, May; 50 (5): 532-7

184. (1987) Trials in acute stroke (with Steiner T.J). *Lancet*, May 2; 1 (8540): 1032

185. (1987) Migraine is not a platelet disorder (with Steiner T.J, and Joseph R). *Headache*, Jul; 27 (7): 400-2

186. (1987) Alcohol, seizures and epilepsy (with Espir M.L). *J. R. Soc. Med.*, Sep; 80 (9): 542-3

187. (1987) Study of the expression of the interleukin 2 receptor on the lympocytes of patients with multiple sclerosis using anti-Tac monoclonal antibodies (with Selmaj K, Plater-Zyberk C, Rockett K.A, Alam R, Maini R N, and Perkin G D). *Pol. Tyg. Lek.*, Nov 2; 42 (44): 1389-91. Polish

188. (1987) Zinc, glutamate receptors, and motor neurone disease (with de Belleroche J.S). *Lancet*, Nov 7; 2 (8562): 1082-3

189. (1987) Clinical characterisation of migraine. In: Basic mechanisms in headache (Eds: Olesen J and Edvinsson L). Amsterdam, Elsevier: 3-8

190. (1988) Classification and diagnostic criteria for Headache (with others). *Cephalalgia*, <u>8</u>, suppl. 7

191. (1988) A controlled study in migraine of selective beta-blockade and platelets: a case for preferring beta 1-adrenoceptor blockers for migraine prophylaxis (with Joseph R, Steiner T J and Schultz L U C). *Stroke*, <u>19</u>: 704-708

192. (1988). Problems encountered in the assessment of treatment of headache (with Steiner T.J). In: Headache: problems in management (Ed: A Hopkins). W.B Saunders, London: 305-348

193. (1988) Cryptococcal meningitis presenting as uveitis (with Stone S.P, Bendig J, Hakim J, Kinnear P E, and Azadian B S). *Br. J. Ophthalmol.*, Mar; 72 (3): 167-70

194. (1988) If I had an episode of grand mal. *Br. J. Clin. Pract.*, May; 42 (5): 210

195. (1988) Platelet activity and selective beta-blockade in migraine prophylaxis (with Joseph R, Steiner T.J, and Schultz L.U). *Stroke*, Jun; 19 (6): 704-8

196. (1988) Metoprolol in the prophylaxis of migraine: parallel-groups comparison placebo and dose-ranging follow-up (with Steiner T.J, Joseph R, and Hedman C). *Headache*, Feb; 28 (1): 15-23

197. (1988) Haemangiopericytic meningioma of the sacral canal: a case report (with Bridges L.R, Roche S, and Nashef L). *J. Neurol. Neurosurg. Psychiatry*, Feb; 51 (2): 288-90

198. (1988) Red wine as a cause of migraine (with Littlewood J.T, Gibb C, Glover V, Sandler M, and Davies P.T).*Lancet*, Mar 12; 1 (8585):558-9

199. (1988) Hepatic cytochrome P450-mediated oxidation function in migraine (with Amery W.K, Davies P.T, Caers L.I, Heykants J, Steiner T.J, and Woestenborghs R). *Cephalalgia*, Jun; 8 (2): 71-4

200. (1988) Differential changes in receptor-mediated transduction in migraine and cluster headache: studies on polymorphonuclear leucocytes (with de Belleroche J, Morris R, and Davies P T). *Headache*, Jul; 28 (6): 409-13

201. (1988) New mutations in Duchenne muscular dystrophy (with Lane R.J, and Partridge T). *Lancet*, Oct 22; 2 (8617): 971-2

202. (1989) Therapy of Migraine. *Maternal and Child Health*, Feb: 52-56

203. (1989) Tyramine sulfoconjugation in relation to depression in migraine. A pilot study (with Sandler M, Jarman J, Fernandez M, Glover V, Davies P T, and Thompson C). *Clin. J. Pain*, 5 (1): 19-21

204. (1989) Cerebral hemisphere function and migraine (with Crisp A H, Levett G, Davies P, and Coltheart M). *J. Psychiatr. Res.*, 23 (3-4): 201-12

205. (1989) Psychiatric morbidity, platelet monoamine oxidase and tribulin output in headache (with Littlewood J, Prasad A, Gibb C, Glover V, Sandler M, and Joseph R). *Psychiatry Res.*, Oct; 30 (1): 95-102

206. (1990) Neuropsychological assessment of cognitive change in dementia (with Hadar U). *Neuroepidemiology*, 9 (4): 189-92

207. (1990) High incidence of endogenous depression in migraine: confirmation by tyramine test (with Jarman J, Fernandez M, Davies P.T, Glover V, Steiner T.J, Thompson C, and Sandler M). *J. Neurol. Neurosurg. Psychiatry*, Jul; 53 (7): 573-5

208. (1991) Tension-type headache. *Headache Quarterly*, 4 (2): 151-7

209. (1991) Anticardiolipin antibodies in migraine (with Hering R, Couturier E.G, Steiner T.J and Asherson R). *Cephalalgia*, 11: 19-22

210. (1991) Platelet [3H] imipramine binding in migraine and tension headache in relation to depression (with Jarman J, Davies P.T, Fernandez M, Glover V, Steiner T.J, and Sandler M). *J. Psychiatry Res.*, 25 (4): 205-11

211. (1991) First clinical study of the selective 5-HT3 antagonist, granisetron (BRL 43694), in the acute treatment of migraine headache (with Couturier E.G, Hering R, Foster C.A, and Steiner T.J). *Headache*, May; 31 (5): 296-7

212. (1991) Chocolate is a migraine-provoking agent (with Gibb C.M, Davies P.T, Glover V, Steiner T.J, and Sandler M). *Cephalalgia*, May; 11 (2): 93-5

213. (1991) Kinetics of platelet 5-hydroxytryptamine uptake in headache patients (with Hannah P, Jarman J, Glover V, Sandler M, and Davies P.T). *Cephalalgia*, Jul; 11 (3): 141-5

214. (1991) Cutaneous aspects of Refsum's disease (with Ramsay B.C, Meeran K, Woodrow D, Judge M, Cream J.J, and Gibberd F.B). *J. R. Soc. Med.*, Sep; 84 (9): 559-60

215. (1991) The pathogenesis of migraine. *J. R. Soc. Med.*, Sep; 84 (9): 519-21

216. (1991) Some clinical comparisons between common and classical migraine: a questionnaire-based study (with Davies P.T, Peatfield R.C, Steiner T.J, and Bond R.A). *Cephalalgia*, Nov; 11 (5): 223-7

217. (1991) Urinary output of endogenous monoamine oxidase inhibitor and isatin during acute migraine attacks (with Jarman J, Przyborowska A, Glover V, Halket J, Davies P.T, and Sandler M). *J. Neural. Transm. Gen. Sect.*, 84 (1-2): 129-34

218. (1991) Ways to facilitate rehabilitation in neurotraumatology. *J. Neurol. Sci.*, Jul; 103 Suppl: S49-51

219. (1992) Migraine and heredity (with Catarci T). *Pathol. Biol. (Paris)*, Apr; 40 (4): 284-6

220. (1992) Sumatriptan arrests in migraine aura. *Headache*, Jul; 32 (7): 366

221. (1992) Lord Walton of Detchant. *Postgrad. Med. J.*, Jul; 68 (801): 497-9

222. (1992) Robert Boyle. *Neurology*, Oct; 42 (10): 2058-9

223. (1993) Sumatriptan: An overview. *Headache Quarterly*, 4; suppl. 2: 27-31

224. (1993) Rising mortality from motor neurone disease: an explanation (with Neilson S, Robinson I, and Hunter M). *Acta. Neurol. Scand.*, Mar; 87 (3): 184-91

225. (1993) Is parkinsonian arm tremor a resting tremor? (with Hadar U). *Eur. Neurol.*, 33 (3): 221-8

226. (1993) European neurology from its beginnings until the 15th century: an overview. *J. Hist. Neurosci.*, Jan; 2 (1): 21-44

227. (1993) Hypokalaemia in acute Refsum's disease (with Dick J.P, Meeran K, and Gibberd F.B). *J. R. Soc. Med.*, Mar; 86 (3): 171-2

228. (1993) Adverse reactions and sumatriptan. *Lancet*, Jun 26; 341 (8861): 1663-4

229. (1994) El Escorial WFN criteria for the diagnosis of ALS. *J. Neurol. Sci.*, 124, suppl: 96-107

230. (1994) Menstrual migraine. *Headache*, Jul-Aug; 34 (7): 446

231. (1994) Sumatriptan does not arrest migraine aura. *Headache*, Jul-Aug; 34 (7): 446

232. (1994) The neurology of ancient Greece: an overview. *J. Hist. Neurosci.*, Oct; 3 (4): 237-60

233. (1995) What did the Greeks mean? (with Patsioti J.G). *J. Hist. Neurosci.*, Mar; 4 (1): 67-76

234. (1995) The history of migraine from Mesopotamian to Medieval times. *Cephalalgia*, Oct; 15 Suppl 15: 1-3

235. (1995) Mortality from motor neurone disease in Japan, 1950-1990: association with radioactive fallout from atmospheric weapons testing (with Neilson S, and Robinson I). *J. Neurol. Sci.*, Dec; 134 (1-2): 61-6

236. (1996) Ecological correlates of motor neuron disease mortality: a hypothesis concerning an epidemiological association with radon gas and gamma exposure (with Neilson S, and Robinson I). *J. Neurol.*, Apr; 243 (4): 329-36

237. (1997) Chronic cluster headache. In: Treatment of the Difficult Headache. Teaching course, European Federation of Neurological Societies (EFNS). Teaching Course No.5, Prague, Czechoslovakia

238. (1997) Food and headache. *Headache Quarterly*, VIII (4): 319-329

239. (1997) Carbamazepine in the treatment of non-seizure disorders: Trigeminal Neuralgia (with Johnson N J). *Contemporary Pharmacotherapy (RICP)*

240. (1997) The history of head injuries: an overview. *J. Hist. Neurosci.*, Aug; 6 (2): 154-80

241. (1999) Trigeminal neuralgia. *Arch. Neurol.* Sep; 56 (9): 1163-4

242. (2002) Historiography: an introduction. *J. Hist. Neurosci.*, Mar; 11 (1): 35-7

243. (2003) An overview from Neolithic times to Broca. In: Trepanation, history, discovery, theory: (Eds: Arnott R, Finger S and Smith C U M) 347-364

244. (2005) An autobiographical sketch of a practitioner-neurohistorian. *J. Hist. Neurosci.*, <u>14</u> (2): 93-99

245. (2006) The history of the Migraine Trust. *The Journal of Headache and Pain*, 28.02.06 1D: JHP 2006-0015

Printed in Great Britain
by Amazon